DAVID KIRK

Black & Blue

Contents

For my boys

in the hope that the spirit of the game can still
do for them what it has done for me

Barefoot in the Park

I remember vividly my first ever game of rugby. I was six. It was wet. We were standing on the hundred-acres of Ongley Park with its ten pitches – too large for a six-year-old to see across. The game we were watching was played without positions, or any rules that I could make out. However, there were two teams and to that extent it resembled a competitive sport; the purpose seemed to be to get the ball and have everyone chase you.

I don't know if there was an injury or whether a boy had to go home early but at halftime there was a place on the field and I was asked if I wanted to run on. I was dying to, even in my jeans and white sandshoes, and I ran out without any clear idea of what I was to do, beyond getting the ball and running with it.

The match report from that first game is sketchy. The main news was that conditions were heavy and I did get hold of the ball; I fell over; my jeans got dirty . . . and that's it. That's all I can salvage from that day thirty years ago when my rugby playing career began.

Twenty years later I was playing for the best team in the world when it was playing the best rugby that had ever been played (I left in the middle of the second longest unbeaten run the All Blacks have ever had). I learned a lot of things through those years: about people, about winning and losing, about belonging and not belonging. I also learned that being part of so great a tradition is to be put in your place.

Having said that, that era was so peculiar it was hard to know where your place was. We were part of a great sea-change, one that was happening all over the world but most visibly in New Zealand. The spirit of the time, loosely known as the Eighties, was sweeping through business, management, politics, art, philosophy and, of course, sport. A great eruption of energy was released, the old structures were breaking down, the new wave was coming through.

As a result, the game of rugby was transformed. The style of play changed, the rules changed, the coaching, the attitude of the players, the role of the administrators, indeed, the whole experience of sport changed as dramatically as the country had.

The Fifties and Sixties were held to be the golden age of New Zealand, the end of the golden weather. But when you look at that flickering black and white rugby footage you are aware of a sense of trench warfare about golden-age play. It was a game dominated by position. Teams inched their way up the touchline (if you were forced into touch you got the throw-in). Many teams based their whole game plan on kicking up the touchline, from lineout to lineout. These teams held the ball in close, the first five-eighth frequently turned the ball back to the forwards. A Welsh story from those years was typical of the whole culture: "At Pontypool," they said, "if we pass the ball from the fly-half to the inside centre – that's a move. At Pontypool we don't believe in moves."

It was a very different game from the fast, free-ranging game of today. But then again, some things never change. I watch my son at the age of five play and his game is almost identical to the one I played at Ongley Park. It's the enduring cousin of a later playground game we called scrag: it consists of a ball and kids, and that's it. You get the ball and people get you.

Scrag is probably a remote relation of a much older game, perhaps the oldest football game of all, one that was played in England in medieval times with whole villages on each side and a pitch – or playing area – covering four or five ridings. This was a game that had an objective but no rules at all, except ordinary laws against murder. As far as I know there wasn't even a time limit.

That game endures forever in schoolyards all over the world. Boys run, with or without the ball, but never with any sense of teamwork. There is no co-operation in scrag, they tackle to put the man down and get the ball off him. At five, Hugo knew how to scrag but didn't know how to score a try. Brigit felt this was a lack in his education and she taught him what was involved. As Brigit is the person least interested in rugby that I've ever met ("How many runs do they need to win?") it's unlikely that Hugo's technique is classically correct, but we don't mind in Pencarrow Avenue.

I took to the game immediately, instinctively. Twelve months after my first touch of that large, fat ball I went along to my first full year of play and the selector asked the only question that could have got me into the bigger team: "Which of you boys played last year?"

I said, accurately, but not informatively, that I had indeed played last year and I was put on the wing (we had positions now). They gave me a tiny jersey with blue and white hoops. By an historical irony the first colours I wore were also the last: we little six-year-olds from Russell Street Primary School in Palmerston North were playing in the colours of the mighty Aucks.

So, today, the only rugby trophies in my house are two blue and white hooped jerseys hanging on my wall. One would fit a six-year-old and was given to me by the present pupils of Russell Street. The other is the Auckland representative shirt. I'm very proud of both.

At the age of seven, then, we were playing recognisable rugby. That one year's seniority made the difference between a Saturday runabout and a full approximation of the game: goal kicking, lineouts, penalties, scrummaging, mauls and – most excitingly – tries.

It is partly this early seriousness that makes New Zealand rugby what it is. Ultimately, the credit for our national success is probably due to the coaches. My first coach, Murray Walker, who played senior rugby for High School Old Boys, was a taxi driver. The credit must go to Murray and the hundreds of people like him who bring their own enthusiasm to every winter Saturday morning, and inspire children with their own enjoyment of, and passion for, the game. This is the practical effect of the amateur ethic and remains the driving force of New Zealand rugby.

Murray had a series of aphorisms, often from the taxi industry, to guide us through the game: "If someone gets the ball you've to get up his exhaust pipe," was his instruction for support play. This is quite a sophisticated idea for six-year-olds, getting up someone's exhaust pipe.

The beginning of co-operation, the fundamentals of teamwork – the foundations, in effect – are laid early, very early. The West Indies play great cricket because their infants pick up a stick in the dusty byways and practise forward defensive strokes with an imperfectly spherical ball. New Zealanders learn from the age of six and seven that you've got to get up your team mates' exhaust pipe if you want the team to score. The early years lay the basis for all future endeavour, so they are especially significant. What you learn then determines how you'll play later on. After a few games on the wing I went to halfback and stayed there all my career. And so I began to build the skills that would, over the years, turn into automatic behaviour.

I also confronted the need I had to win and the fear of failure that went with it. It happens early, all this, between the ages of six and eight. I first coped by developing a sense of safety in numbers – it's not just me losing, I reasoned, it's everyone on my side. I wasn't going down alone. Fear was dissipated by having others in the same boat with you. Numbers helped you hide in defeat. This was an understandable defence mechanism for a little boy. A safety in numbers psychology is intrinsic to team sports: "We lost", people say, not "I lost".

But if you are to succeed you have to abandon this defence. The higher the level of the sport you play, the lonelier the field becomes. I'll go further: it's only by embracing that loneliness, the intensely personal responsibility to do well, that you can go all the way in sport. This is the bargain with your personal Mephistopheles you have to feel is worth making before you start on the real path. These ideas start early and continue long. The child is indeed the father of the man.

Now, there are those who will find it psychologically unhelpful – or even unhealthy – that a six-year-old should feel the pressure of failure so keenly but there was nothing to be done about it. No-one else created the pressure but myself. And as soon as I became aware that a score was kept I wanted to be on the right side of the ledger.

I wanted to play in that older team among bigger, faster, stronger boys. And I also wanted to win. Now, I know that we have a culture inherited from Britain and that means we have a mixed view of winning. Our winners must stay part of the group; they mustn't allow success to elevate them out of the group culture – that has a certain sense of disloyalty about it (we don't like that in New Zealand).

A strong part of the sporting ethic has meant we are not to be seen to exult in triumph. We must do more than lose gracefully, we must win modestly.

We probably inherited this from the old English amateurs. There was one who trained for years, finally won a gold at the Olympics and when asked for a comment said, "Pure fluke." Oxford undergraduates still think it important to appear nonchalant about exams ("Haven't done a stroke.") The All Blacks in those flickering news clips of fifty years ago scored tries with apparent indifference – a hurried spin of the ball to someone, head held low in the long walk back to halfway.

But it's fake. It's an image. However cool they appear, all top sports people are like soccer players who hug and kiss each other in the penalty box. Some hide it more effectively. Inside, we're all Italians, inside we're exulting rudely in victory and grievous in defeat.

How do we know this? We are alone; we can speak frankly; the central point about sports people at this level is that they are first and foremost competitive people, they are competition junkies. Michael Jones is the nicest person you could ever want to meet. But when he plays he is a different man. After he scores he turns back and notices the carnage he has left in his wake. He'll go to help his victims up almost with surprise.

There is a profound selfishness at work in the great collective of team spirit. Winning is deeply important to sports people and they train ruthlessly and individually to fill their personal potential. And it's necessary, the game doesn't work without it. The difficult task is to harmonise the private drive with the collective effort towards the great conclusion.

And what is the objective? Scoring? No. Winning your match? Not so small a goal. Winning the season's championship? The World Cup? I don't think so.

I now know that winning isn't the point of playing. I also found out that winning is not the life and death matter that some say it is. It's necessary to win – that is, it is necessary to play in a way that results in winning – but there is a larger goal than the result. I was part of this discovery – which was made by our team in the first World Cup. It had a decisive effect on the way we played the game. In its way, it's the secret of rugby, perhaps even the meaning of sport itself. And it took a number of experiences to combine and evolve over time, and it took a mixture of failure and success to understand how it all worked.

I think it's probably luck that I've been associated with successful teams. The Manawatu under-10 reps won our little tournament. At prep school we beat Huntly, at Wanganui Collegiate we won the quadrangular tournament; Otago University won the club championship, Auckland University won the club championship. And in my last year of New Zealand rugby, the year we won the World Cup, I wasn't in a losing team at any level the whole year. Then, in the subsequent year, I went to Oxford and we hardly won anything at all.

Even back at the beginning there it was a competitive little team in a pool with five or six other schools whom we played on Thursdays. I remember dodging and scooting round the scrum, making tackles and cover defending. I also remember my first ever pair of boots. Each boot was a one-piece construction moulded out of plastic. We used to put them on the heater to soften them up but they still caused terrible blisters. They had to last all that season though (yes, we suffered in those days), and next time round I got a pair of leather-type boots with real sprigs – but the nail-in type, not the flash screw-ins.

Growing up in Palmerston North has changed less than growing up in Auckland. We walked to school then from the age of six, crossing one quiet side street. That's still possible, I believe. After school you'd disappear to friends' houses and ring home only if you wanted to stay out for dinner. We had a wide range of friends from all sorts of backgrounds. Some didn't have much money – we knew that because they didn't buy presents for birthday parties but brought back-copies of their comics instead. But there was no sense of better or worse; that's how it was in those days.

It's changed, of course, but early childhood doesn't change much wherever you live in New Zealand. The beach, the bush, the playing fields, the long summer holidays, the advent of autumn – and the rugby. You'd go back to school one day and the rugby posts would be up. My boys will remember their New Zealand childhood much as I remember mine. They will grow up in Auckland which for many New Zealanders is an increasingly remote culture. But in our quiet suburb with our back lawn and our local park it's strangely similar to growing up in Palmerston North. The big difference will be that Hugo won't be sent away to school, as I was.

It happened quite suddenly; my quiet, little-boy's life was over. This isn't said to sound pathetic, I was actively looking forward to this next step, but I was sent away from home to make my way in a wider world. Ten is young to be sent away but there were boys aged seven at St George's (seven-year-olds are awfully small, even when you're ten). There we were.

I went to prep school and put childish things behind me. I started learning Latin, poetry and boxing on Saturday morning. This was a very different experience from my barefoot days in Palmerston North. The school had a uniform, it was built on an imposing scale and it was run on the English tradition.

It was a world of forbidding corridors and older boys. You had to conform to a new code of behaviour, and you might be beaten without notice with anything that came to hand – roman sandals, cricket bats, canes, a piece of waste wood.

To say we were beaten is maybe to give the wrong impression. If a master hit you with a roman sandal, a cricket bat or a piece of waste wood it would usually just be one blow across the seat of the pants. Only the headmaster caned boys and that only for serious offences like breaking bounds or fighting in the dormitories. Breaking bounds was the biggest crime in the calendar. Runaways were not deemed to be unhappy creatures who needed kindness and support – they were criminals, traitors even. One unhappy boy made it home where his parents found him up a tree – he wouldn't come down (and he was right not to, in the event). When they got him down they sent him back to school and he was beaten with one of the three or four specialist canes that were kept in the headmaster's study.

In one way, the regime was fair – the rules were well-known and indifferently applied. But there was little sensitivity to boys' individual needs, or a recognition that people developed differently. This was what it was to be socialised in New Zealand in those days.

We had a double period of Latin every morning except Friday (it was a single period on Friday). The first period was always Roman history which we learned from an edited version of Livy. Our partially deaf, war-wounded teacher read the story, wrote it on the board and we copied it down. As a result, I now know that Hannibal came from Carthage and he crossed the Alps on elephants; that the Roman republic had tribunes as well as consuls, and that Scipio was a great Roman general who went to Africa. It doesn't seem very much, now I look at it.

We also had four periods of languages, all rote lessons and mostly all grammar, but beyond amo, amas, amat the only Latin I know now isn't Latin at all (only the words are):

Caesar adsum jam forte,
Pompei aderat;
Caesar sic in omnibus,
Pompei in is at.

The English poetry we learned by rote stayed with me longer; three in particular: *Horatius at the Gate* ("Then out spake brave Horatius, captain of the Gate . . . Oh Tiber, Father Tiber, to whom the Romans pray, Dum de dum de dum de dum, Take my soul today . . .") .

Second, Ozymandias, a sonnet by Shelley which I can remember in its entirety – a haunting description of a ruined statue discovered in the desert ends with the marvellously tragic inscription "My name is Ozymandias, King of Kings: Look on my works ye mighty and despair!"

And thirdly, *The Highwayman* – a sensual, morbid poem quite inappropriate for boys on the brink of puberty (I remember it as well as the day I learnt it). Bess the black-eyed daughter of the innkeeper curls a ribbon into her hair as she waits for her outlaw lover coming down a road which is "like a ribbon of moonlight over the purple moor". He has frequently come before, riding, riding, riding, up to the old inn door. But this time, because the authorities are waiting to ambush him, she fires off a warning musket (but she is bound tight, and the musket is pointing directly at her, and she "shattered her breast in the moonlight and warned him with her death". So she dies. And when her lover hears about it he dies too. "And he lay in his blood on the highway, with a bunch of lace at his throat". It was what ten and twelve-year-olds had in the Sixties instead of *Pulp Fiction.*

A boarding prep school has its own culture, and it's very different from the free and easy democracy of life at a public primary. St George's was strictly hierarchical. You slotted in at a particular place – often a very particular place – in the scale of seniority. There were tests every day and at the end of three weeks the form master would read out the form order and we had to arrange our desks according to the list. The twenty-fifth in the class would have his desk right under the teacher's nose and the top pupils were given the privilege of lurking at the back of the room.

Because I always had the benefit of an elder brother going ahead of me I never suffered homesickness like some boys; neither this school nor the one I went up to later were as strange to me as they might have been. In fact, they were stranger to look back on than they were at the time.

It was an education that was preparing us for a world that's gone now, but had largely gone then as well.

We slept in dormitories; the headmaster would stride through in the morning and we'd jump out of bed and follow like goslings. In the summer he'd lead a procession of boys in dressing gowns down the fire escapes to the swimming pool where we would swim naked. The practice has been discontinued; people are so suspicious these days.

The rugby, however, was a quantum leap from Russell Street. I can measure out my career in these leaps; as you move from one level to another you are thrown into a whole new game, with higher standards, bigger players, faster runners, harder tackles – and more severe penalties. The first person I ever saw sent off was about this time – for kneeing. I was as shocked by the kneeing as by the sending off. It was a whole new dimension to the game. The shame we felt falling on the head of the offender was very powerful. Some years later at Collegiate I was equally shocked when a boy punched one of our props in the face. Punched him, as in a fight! We'd never seen such a thing before. Our prop cried out, "You ruddy sod!" (he meant it to sting). In all the games, and of all the names I've heard props call their opposite numbers, I've never heard the words "You ruddy sod!" again.

Our prep school coach was a hard-bitten character for our age-group. His broken nose formed an impressive saddle. He trained us intensely, we were properly coached – scrums, lineouts, moves – we went over our stuff again and again, we were drilled – that's what caused the leap in quality. I visited prep schools in England and they took their rugby seriously too, but I venture to say we were a league ahead of prep schools in the northern hemisphere – not because we practised obsessively or even for longer – but because the atmosphere was intense, the expectations of our coaches was high and we rose to meet their expectations. That's how it is with children.

My own game developed in another way too, as two qualities which marked my play came through – the ability to run with the ball and the pleasure I took in tackling. To progress as a halfback you have to make that crucial first leap of faith – throwing yourself into a tackle and believing the heels flying up behind your target won't smash you in the face. I was lucky: that didn't happen until later.

I was also aware of the higher dimensions of the game. We had contraband transistors with earplugs; on one such transistor, later than I'd ever been awake, I listened to the All Blacks losing to Llanelli in 1972 – a converted try and a penalty goal to a penalty goal. It was a cold, wet, miserable match (and played in Wales) and the invincible All Blacks had lost.

Going from the comfort and security of my kids' school at Russell Street was like leaving home in the village to go to the market town. The move to Wanganui Collegiate was like landing in a metropolis. If you exclude the prisons, it was the biggest boarding establishment in New Zealand.

Your parents drive you through the gates and you're immediately aware the scale is enormous. Suddenly you're a small fish again.

You'd been at the top of your previous school – like that character in the Molesworth books, "captain of everything and winner of the Mrs Joyful prize for raffia work" – and quite abruptly you're way out of your depth. The prefects look like masters, the buildings look forbidding, the corridors are longer and stranger and the timetable is intricate and difficult.

You were immediately reduced by the size of the place. Maybe you'd been captain of your prep school team (not that I had been – in fact my only prize had been a cup for perseverance) but it was of no account, you had to start proving yourself all over again to a whole new group of sceptics. The lesson's a valuable one. You have to prove yourself to everyone you play with or play against. Whether it's a new rugby team, a new city or a new job, you start from scratch every time. This treadmill comes from a very meritocratic tradition. It leads to continuous insecurity but also stimulates a growing self-confidence.

In the first two weeks Collegiate inducted new boys into the school mystery. You were taught the school song, learned the names of the house masters, tutors, house matrons. There were a series of mottos – Mr Empsom's mottos they were called (after an early headmaster) and they went along the lines of "Don't squeal: sweat and be saved."

After two weeks new boys were called into a prefect's study where questions were fired at you and you were punished for ignorance.

Prefects weren't allowed to cane boys any more (that had been stopped two or three years earlier), but masters were allowed to lay about themselves, and did so as a matter of course, right up to the sixth form. Fagging was going strong; you fagged for a prefect, for matron or for your house master or tutor. But duties were not heavy or humiliating. The film If (about a mythical but characteristic English boarding school) had come out some years before with the immortal line, "Fag! Warm a lavatory seat. I'll be ready in two minutes." We were run on English lines, but not that English.

Rugby was compulsory in the third and fourth form. And, as a matter of interest, so was butter. You could only get out of playing rugby or eating margarine if you had a doctor's certificate. Hockey and soccer were only permitted after it had been well-established that a boy wouldn't, or couldn't, play rugby.

In some sense, school rugby was uneventful until you got to the first XV. There are no real test matches as you move up through the school. But when you get to *the* XV it all starts again, the sense of joining a tradition, of joining a phantom community of players who have gone before, whose exploits were recorded in the school's annals. The coach tells you about players and previous matches – this one who was a legendary tackler, that one who caught a spilled ball and scored in the last second. Suddenly you have examples to live up to, and you are taught – though no-one says so in so many words – that it is important to sustain this tradition, to do right by the team. Your loyalty is fortified by your current team mates, but actually inspired by the ones who've gone before. The team is composed of the living and the dead, the current players and all their predecessors. Individuals come and go – and the fact is, we are rarely missed. The team has a vitality of its own, stronger than its members.

In the same way, badly wounded soldiers drop out of the close relationship they have with their regiment. At the Falklands memorial service in Britain, I understand the soldiers in wheelchairs were placed in an alcove off to the side of the back of the cathedral where they couldn't see or be seen. In the same way, as a team member, you give everything – but you only get a return while you are fit and able. You have to be able to play in order to belong. Without that, you are remote, excluded, out of it. You're a spectator, you're ancillary, you're an official, an observer. It's cruel, actually, but nothing else inspires that sense of comradeship that hangs around a team like the steam from the communal baths, the almost animal sense of family.

I don't think I'd find an argument with the school when I say I was a difficult 16-year-old. Far from being Head of House, I wasn't even a prefect, at least not at first. There were successes in the measurable sense – I'd won the hundred metres, a half academic scholarship, was captain of cricket, a player in the XV, but at the same time I was (how shall I say it?) unforgiving and generally difficult with teachers whom I didn't respect. And that wasn't what prefects were like, in a strongly Christian school with a strongly religious headmaster – nor captains of the Collegiate XV.

It was at school here that began the uneasy tension between wanting to retain my individual purpose and still to be part of a team. How do you keep your own integrity when you have surrendered part of yourself – a deep, important part of yourself – to the group? This is a vital question at a boarding school – because if you don't fit in you're nowhere. I found the question remained after school, wherever team games were played.

It was a tension that would continue when I was an All Black and be most starkly illustrated by the rebel tour to South Africa. All the All Blacks (bar John Kirwan and myself) wanted to go. I felt I had to go as a matter of loyalty to the team; I didn't want to go because I felt it was wrong. It was one of the biggest dilemmas I ever faced.

But what would the summary of my time at Collegiate be? On the whole, undoubtedly good. Collegiate was, and is, a distinguished school. Its standards were, and are, high – not then as high academically as in sport, but well set. You can't hide. The masters pursue you and seek you out. They demand you perform. If you have a talent they require you to work at it.

But not everything about Collegiate was entirely admirable. The culture of the school was determined by the majority of the pupils – farmers' sons. Collegiate had a far more agricultural tone to it than Christ's or King's. And in those days of government subsidy for farmers even quite small holdings were disproportionately wealthy. It was a sort of unearned wealth that created complacency. The boys knew they needn't excel – or even achieve – academically because their inheritance would provide for themselves and their own sons (just as long as the government kept up with the subsidies, and how could it not?) There was as a result a rather taciturn acceptance that the boys in their thousand-acre jackets were born to rule. An error, as it turned out.

As always, the rugby took its tone from the All Blacks. Forwards in those days were the centre of the team's gravity; they were the heavyweights, and the culture of the time required a laconic, almost sullen attitude. As Greg McGee put it in his famous play *Foreskin's Lament*, "Good forwards should be like pit-ponies – blind from lack of light."

School rugby was more free-spirited but much of our play was still based on a big forward pack, a powerful scrum and strong-running centres.

The combined effect of the school culture and the boarding ethos had a long-lasting effect on most of us who went through it. This sort of schooling has the strongest effect on males – perhaps the strongest effect on our character other than our parents at one end and marriage at the other.

To board at this sort of school you become part of a guild, a mystery as they called it in medieval times. Boarders were at the heart of it; no-one else knew what went on in boarding houses when the day boys had gone home to their families and their own bedrooms. There might be horror stories to tell, it might have all been harmless – the point was it was just between ourselves. It was an experience of team; the collective spirit is strong at school but probably never stronger than at boarding school. You feel the power of public opinion very directly, very personally; you can run but not hide.

So you learn how to become self-sufficient. That can be helpful in today's world but it has its downside too; you can become emotionally closed down. Because you had to be under control all the time (revealing vulnerabilities was a form of suicide) you were bound to end up less emotionally capable. You just hadn't had the practice at living an emotional life. Even now I suffer from this at times . . .

I don't think girls fall for it. Boys feel a peculiar need to conform. Boys try to control what's happening to them and this creates a whole mental habit, a whole psychological apparatus for dealing with an overpowering situation. We need a plan; we buy into the plan and adapt ourselves to it.

Girls don't buy into it like boys do. They don't get deformed by it. If Brigit is any example, girls tend not to take it all so seriously. They see the limitations of their stern spinster role models. They rebel, but not against a weight of peer pressure, male expectations and traditions. They smoke under the trees and get suspended, simply because they want to.

I remember a fight breaking out with a Maori boy on the wing after he made a head-high, flying tackle; and when he was abused for it he came storming back to punch the boy he'd crippled. Then he refused to be sent off. "You toffee noses!" his father shouted at us.

We'd never been aware of class, as such, in New Zealand – to be toffee noses; it was obviously something to do with being stuck-up. And while we weren't stuck-up, it obviously looked as though we were. We have been told subsequently about the egalitarian nature of New Zealand, but it wasn't something everyone felt equally.

New Zealand was a country where people took pains to conceal their differences from each other. Holiday baches were deliberately plain. The kitchens of people's houses were, to modern eyes, all equally primitive. The plumbing was all done by the same plumber. There was only one make of toilet bowl available in the whole country. There were two refrigerators but both were made by the same manufacturer to the same specifications.

One of our provincial towns, Dannevirke I think, was founded back in the nineteenth century by the New Zealand Company – they allowed only one farrier, one plumber, one cobbler, "in order to minimise the destructive effects of competition".

One effect of pioneer egalitarianism was that cleverness was distrusted; “smart” wasn’t a good thing. Flair was flash. This was the ethos that prevailed in New Zealand through my generation – and by all accounts through my father’s generation too. But it was all about to change. In those days there was still a sense of team in the whole country, an inarticulate sense of the collective. It was expressed in everything we did – the way we decorated our houses, the way we dressed and spoke. There were no fences between our suburban houses in those days – why would you want to cut yourself off from your neighbours?

But there was also a sense of cultural inferiority we suffered from, too (that’s almost gone now). Maybe we huddled together to keep that at bay, we kept close to each other for protection – maybe we were hiding in numbers so that we weren’t seen to fail individually.

But however it was, that strong culture of egalitarianism was, by the time I was growing up, starting to conceal increasingly important differences.

I'm at Otago – I must be nearly grown-up

Most committed players remember the moment when it dawns on them they won't be All Blacks (I had more than one moment like that, even when I was an All Black). Players fight this moment because the possibility seems to be tantalisingly there – we come out of the school top team and can't see any reason why we shouldn't make the top grade. But then there comes a time when players realise that, although they may be playing for their club's A team, their two-year window has passed. They haven't been selected for their province, there is an incumbent playing well in that position already, their chance is slipping away, they can never achieve their childhood ambition.

Every serious rugby player wants to play for the All Blacks, whether or not they admit it, just as every politician wants to be Prime Minister. But in my first year at Otago University I wasn't a backbencher – I wasn't even a candidate for high office. I was the number two halfback for the number two team.

The following year I thought I'd ease off on my studies (I was over-achieving somewhat in my medical training), to give rugby one good go and see if I had it in me to make the grade. A lot of what it takes to succeed (in anything, but particularly in rugby) is wanting to succeed. Why did I want to? Some people have this hunger for competition, a reckless sense, almost, of playing out of your depth, just to see whether you can survive. Then of course if it turns out that you can, there is the fame and fortune and party invitations. But more essentially the drive to do well comes from a deep curiosity to find out what you're made of. So I got back on the treadmill.

It was a help that a number of people didn't turn up for trials that year. As a university team there was an element of enjoyable chaos about the administrative lines. Team arrangements go up on noticeboards and some people see them and others – who are in the library, the pub, in bed – don't.

I turned up. So it was I who got the place in a trial team because someone else hadn't seen it. Throughout my career – and it's the same for most of us – I remember most vividly the formative moments when the direction of my life changed forever. One such moment was in that trial at Kettle Park, out by the beach in Dunedin in 1980. I charged a kick down, chased it, got a good bounce and scored. And as this made an impression on the watching authorities it started a season in which I went from the decent obscurity of the under-21 B-team reserve to displacing the senior A team halfback who was also the current provincial halfback. While it made a great *Boy's Own* story I was mistaken in thinking that I was on the way.

Two years on I was precisely where I had been. I was still the club halfback, my window of opportunity had almost passed and Otago province still hadn't selected me. You might be good enough for the All Blacks, you might want it more than anyone, but if you don't get selected for your province you won't be considered.

Why wasn't I being selected? I certainly wanted it enough. I was ambitious enough, I was playing enough, I was training enough – the only answer I could come up with was that I wasn't good enough. That's a conclusion you avoid for as long as you can. But if you succeed in avoiding it completely you never get any better. So I finally came to it and asked the next important question: why wasn't I good enough? That was too hard for me to see from where I was standing, so I rang up my old school coach, Jim Wallace, in Wanganui to ask him if he thought it worth giving me some one-on-one coaching. It was the best call I ever made.

I went up to Wanganui for the day and went back again to my basic technique. We concentrated on passing, as we always did because that's what halfbacks are for. Running is all very well, and exhibiting flair is a happy bonus if you have it, but top halfbacks pass the ball accurately all the time without mistakes. There are three qualities to a pass: speed, accuracy and length – and the greatest of these is speed.

Running speed is something you've got or you haven't. There aren't many training techniques useful to develop the ability to run fast, but passing is different. A fast halfback's pass is about technique. When the ball comes out of the scrum your inside foot has to be as close to the ball as possible and your other foot needs to go as far away as you can put it in the direction of the pass; then you sweep the ball away as fast as you can. The key is to get into position early, to be balanced on the balls of your feet. When the old trainer had Rocky Balboa chase the chicken to develop his footwork I knew exactly what he meant. Good halfbacks have to be good at catching chickens.

Anyway, it's those extra millimetres in the stance that make the difference between a club halfback and a provincial representative.

As it happens, my passing fell off in latter years but during my University days I worked very hard at it, and it showed: speed, accuracy and length; speed, accuracy and length.

When I'd been a schoolboy Jim had bailed me up one morning. He'd seen me practising kicking for position. "Why are you using your right foot?" he demanded.

I didn't know the right answer to that and said, "Because I can kick further with it?"

"Why practise the things you're good at? You should be kicking with your left foot."

There was no debate. In this coach's mind you should be able to kick equally well with either foot – and of course he was right. He was always right. He thought it was vital to run holding the ball in both hands (this made it easier to develop elusiveness), he taught me how to do stabbing grubber kicks and why you had to be in the gap when kicking. But most of all he bore into me with lessons of mental toughness.

He was hard on me, he'd always been hard on me. I was itching for praise which was never forthcoming. "Why do you need me to tell you what you're good at?" he said once.

"Because I want praise. Because it's tough out there where you've got all your capabilities up for public inspection and everyone's so chary with their compliments, and I want to know from someone I respect that I'm any good. I'm a boy. I want admiration." This was what I didn't say to him.

He told me, "I only criticise you because you've got potential. I don't give the others a hard time because they're playing to their limit." It was his only attempt to make me feel better, and then only so I would take the lesson better. He was exactly the coach I needed in these formative years. This was a crucible, and from it came self-belief, ambition and resilience. For these qualities I would swap all the easy talent in the world. It's like that humorous sheet you sometimes see on office walls about talent and determination. It says something to the effect of, 'The world is full of talented failures, of clever people who never made it, of educated people who never fulfilled their potential. It's only determination and persistence that bring success.'

I never got this personal intensity of coaching again. It was such a great time to learn these things. That's why I went back to see Jim, and it was that which changed my life.

Up to that point I'd been a university player. I'd come out of a structured, disciplined school and walked through the enormous gates of Otago University with its ambitious, neo-Gothic architecture, its cloisters and towers. It's the only university in New Zealand that dominates its city, it has a strong sense of community and Otago graduates hang together the rest of their lives.

The buildings are arguably the best university buildings in the country; they were built in a wealthy province in a wealthy time. It remains a traditional university producing professionals and highly educated graduates. However, the undergraduates of Selwyn College c. 1979 were different. If you looked into the dining rooms on a Friday night, underneath the ceiling vaults you would be aware of one of the old traditions, its origins hidden in the mists of time, of the Selwyn College food fight. "Food fight!" someone would shout, and the hall would fill with food. Male students lived this simple, traditional life: drinking, vomiting, trying to find women to go out with on Saturday nights, and throwing each other into baths of slime. The women had their own quite separate way of life which was considerably more adult.

After Selwyn, I oscillated between mixed flats and single sex flats. The men were more relaxed and invariably more filthy, the women expected more of their flatmates. At that age I could only take a year of each.

In our first flat ($6.75 a week each) we spent the whole time in the kitchen because that had the only source of heating (the gas stove). The sitting room was uninhabitable owing to the lack of floorboards ("Floorboards? *Loox*ury!") There was an agitator washing machine.

Later, my flatmates were called "Donk" (short for Donkey, but we won't go into that), "Truck", "Fool" and "Ironman". I was called "Kirky", the only one without a proper nickname. Why didn't I have a proper nickname? Short Stuff, or Mouth, or Bounce or something. Maybe I was on another team and was therefore outside the deep camaraderie of that hardcore foursome. It was rugby that put me apart. Had ambition distracted me from friendship? Did hunger for success drive a wedge between me and my mates? It may have, but to get on in that world of rugby you had to train, and serious training interfered with bonding practices back at the flat. I'd come back from a morning's Teutonic training to find them playing Scullopoly (players buy properties and develop them by drinking beer) – and they'd been playing this since getting out of bed. You couldn't play a winning game of Scullopoly and also throw spiral passes through to the second five-eighth; they were mutually exclusive activities. And for all the talk of rugby being a New Zealand religion, Scullopoly champions were very highly regarded in those circles, and more highly regarded than captains of the University rugby team. (As a matter of record, Truck, Fool, Ironman and Donk are now a lawyer, a surgeon, a banker and a university professor.)

Mike Brewer moved in after me – I later fell out with him. We had a philosophical difference over Laurie Mains. Laurie kept picking people other than myself, and I couldn't see the sense of it. I wanted a coach who would pick me.

My rugby career wasn't taking off, and there was a good chance it never would. I was three years into my university career and my window of opportunity had virtually passed. Dean Kenny had come to town and he'd been picked ahead of me. He was a very good halfback who'd established himself in the Otago team. He had played against the Springboks on their controversial 1981 tour. As a result, I was unlikely to be selected for the province and I worried I would never catch a selector's eye. There were many promising players who'd never progressed to the next level, and but for Dean's injury I might easily have been one of them.

However, Dean had a recurring shoulder injury which invalided him out of the 1982 season. It wasn't chronic, or even long-term. But owing to his being unavailable I moved into position as the leading contender for the province. In May I read the news in the paper. I had been picked for my first game of rugby at provincial level.

Playing for the province is again a quantum leap up the scale. It's a new game again. The level of violence is increased, the players are bigger, faster and more ferocious. I experienced the recurring shock of playing at a new level. These levels are all precisely defined and go up in stages from the under-21 club to senior club, from senior club to province, from province to the South Island, from inter-island to mid-week internationals and on to test matches. Each level has its own quite separate level of difficulty and skill. It is the ability to adapt and grow that marks out the players destined to be stuck at one level or progress to the next.

Even among the international teams a hierarchy exists. South Africa are the toughest, usually, followed by Australia, France, and sometimes even England – and all of them are on an altogether different level in physical and mental intensity than the others.

I played my first-ever, first-class match against Southland, a typically ferocious local derby which we won by having a little more flair in the backs; then against North Otago (a walkover in Oamaru in which I scored three tries), and then, crucially, in the annual South Island-North Island match – my third-ever first-class game.

We were a team of nobodies. The North Island had fourteen All Blacks in their team and they were captained by Graham Mourie, with Andy Haden, Gary Whetton, Andy Dalton, Greg Burgess, Gary Knight, Geoff Old and Glenn Rich in their pack. Their backs included Mark Donaldson, Bernie Fraser, Stu Wilson, Allan Hewson, and 1996 New Zealand First MP Tu Wyllie. They were my boyhood idols, as large as life (not quite as large as they were on television but still enormous). Mark Donaldson, I remember, had been one of my idols and role models as he steered Manawatu during its Ranfurly Shield era of the late 1970s.

I still vividly remember the door to the changing room opening at Spriggens Park and coming face-to-face with all those famous faces; the glamour of the All Blacks hung around them personally and as a team.

I was the most nervous I had ever been before a match – for days before – it was the most important match of my limited career and against the most prominent and distinguished opposition. Our team consisted of "good old boys from the South" as the paper called us. We had one or two All Blacks, one or two up-and-comers and the rest were obscure provincial players. We were expected to be hammered. We expected to be hammered. We were playing the core of the current generation of test All Blacks. Stu Wilson scored a magnificent try and gave me to realise the difference between aspiring provincial players and an All Black. I thought I had him covered; actually I did have him covered. I was moving in and was about to take him out and he casually stood me up and glided past me – much faster and more elusive than I'd ever seen a player on a pitch. You'd look at the game today and find it scrappy and slow but at the time it was fast, hard and demanding.

We were down at halftime but in the break we started to believe we could win. Our forwards may have been unknowns but they were saying, "They're soft, they're soft. They've got four Auckland guys in their forward pack. Soft Aucklanders, that's what we like!"

In later life when I was playing for Auckland this conversation came back as an insight into how much the rest of New Zealand resents Auckland. It's not just that Auckland is the best team in the country and not just that people resent the wealth, opportunity and energy of the place – particularly the sense of assurance (or arrogance) that goes with that. In a deeper sense I think people worry that Auckland is decoupling from the rest of the country and establishing its own culture, identity and financial structure separate from the rest of the country (the English have the same feelings about London, and for the same reason, but it's been going on since the Industrial Revolution).

But anyway, not to put too fine a point on it, we beat them. We were far from the better team that day but we played with more cohesion and commitment. And we badly wanted to beat them. And it's a funny thing about sport – you start well, you're mentally prepared and you perform, your aggression has a momentum that builds on itself. But it also works the other way. When some things go wrong other things start to go wrong. It's like farmers talking about water on the farm; they always say to fix a leak at once, no matter how trivial. When one thing goes wrong with water it starts a chain reaction and a leak can end up in a landslip.

With rugby it's not so easy to fix but the same chain reaction can happen. The North Island made some mistakes and a sense of frustration came into their play, mistakes started a disjointed rhythm and allowed us to get on top of them. Steve Pokere ran the blindside and just made the line with a big stretch, Robbie Deans kicked goals well, and I also was well reviewed. It turned out to be a significant match for me.

The rest of the season I played for the province. We were losers. In fact, we lost every game in the national championship bar two (we scrambled into the play-off for relegation). We were captained by an ex-All Black whose captaincy skills had come to exceed his playing ability. He also had an awesome appetite for alcohol and I remember seeing him polish off a bottle of whisky by himself after a long night's beer drinking. Good captains and tight forwards are hard to come by – so despite the fact that ours was slow and overweight he was still on the team.

The tour we went on that year – my first – was also an eye-opener. We played North Auckland, Auckland, Hawke's Bay and Wairarapa Bush (losing them all). North Auckland was first. At the time, the northlanders were one of the most physically aggressive teams in New Zealand – muscular and tough, and while they lacked something in speed and finesse they made up for these deficiencies by directness and brutality. I remember being taken out with my back to the ball; someone hit me with their whole body in the middle of the spine – I can still feel the whiplash.

It was then that I realised there is a dimension of physical survival that has to be mastered if you want to continue playing at the top of rugby. I have been favoured by injury, quite often gaining places where others were injured. If that sounds like I slipped into teams at others' expense it is worth saying that keeping fit – surviving – is a crucial part of the sport. It's the unseen recoveries between the matches that make the difference between playing for better teams and not playing at all.

Anyway, after North Auckland we went on down to Auckland to be thrashed at Eden Park. I remember Bryan Williams – the old man – playing fullback and taking a pass flat on the blind side and bursting through our forwards to score and feeling that we were boys against men.

Age and experience are said to beat youth and enthusiasm – and this is often true. But there also comes a time when it's suddenly age and experience playing youth and experience and the winners usually will be the younger.

Rugby generations go, roughly, in five-year spans. The early 1970s were dominated by Ian Kirkpatrick and later by Andy Leslie and their teams. This generation was a new wave which finally overtook the Brian Lochore/Colin Meads generation which had probably gone on for too long. Sid Going was one who ran through to 1977 when Graham Mourie emerged with a new team. Now the leading players were Loveridge, Haden, Knight, Dalton, Wilson, Shaw, Fraser, Mexted. This group dominated and went on getting stronger through to the end of the decade and into the Eighties. This was the group I began with.

It was a group that was still playing in 1985, however, and that was probably one or two seasons too many. During this transition period the selectors were choosing the older players and failing to bring younger players through.

Eventually the next new wave came through in 1986-87 – Grant Fox, Michael Jones, Sean Fitzpatrick, Wayne Shelford, Steve McDowell, John Drake, Gary and Alan Whetton, John Kirwan, Craig Green, John Gallagher and myself. This wave brought the new style of rugby into the All Blacks. It retained the power and formidable strength and muscularity of the traditional All Blacks but added to it with speed, elusiveness and a chess-like ability to create movements, to play fifteen-man rugby – it was an open, running style with a strong, rational underpinning. Essentially it was the style that John Hart had created over the years in Auckland grafted onto the world's top team. It made the All Blacks unbeatable.

I first came across the John Hart style in that match against Auckland on our 1982 North Island tour. It was a further revelation. I'd come from that part of the country where the only acceptable statement was understatement. The verbal intensifier they all used was "a wee bit". Mussolini would have been a wee bit full of himself. These Auckland players were a wee bit different. They weren't just chatty, they were garrulous. Next to the Southland granite they sounded like a Tupperware party. I couldn't believe the lip the referee got, nor how team members spoke to each other. Greg Burgess took the ball into a ruck and it didn't emerge and Andy Haden said to him in derisive tones, "Might be good enough at club level but it's not good enough here, Burge!"

Auckland were just beginning to establish themselves. They had never won a national championship when John Hart took over. In the fifteen subsequent championships Auckland has won eleven times.

The Otago-Auckland match of September 1982 was my first experience of the new wave which was building in New Zealand rugby. I didn't understand what it was all about. In fact, as an opponent of Auckland I didn't like what I saw.

Hart's strategy was to remove the random element from the game. This was an amazing ambition – some said it was an insane ambition. His purpose was to instill a whole new level of accuracy, of eliminating mistakes. It was a clinical sense that was new to us all. Laurie Mains later took up that ambition with us in Otago, but like many coaches he seemed not to realise it was just stage one. Doing the basics well was like building a big vocabulary – but knowing a lot of words doesn't make you a great orator. Catching the ball is important – but then what do you do with it? That's stage two.

As their opposition, Otago was overpowered by the cohesiveness of Auckland's play. Every one of them knew the sequence of moves that was obtaining. In the scrum there was such clear communication about where the ball was going and how it was going to get there – and a clear knowledge that the scrum was only part of the sequence.

I became aware they were thinking all the time, they were playing a vigorous mental game. They were all calculating the lines they were running off the ball – it was bewildering to see a fullback running right across the line of play, I couldn't see what he was doing or why – but one cross and two passes later, things would become clear. There were times when the ball didn't come – but two of our players had been diverted to cover the phantom line the fullback was running.

Everything they did they did for a larger reason – that's very disconcerting for an opposition player to realise. I could see they were all thinking two or three steps/links/moves ahead. The ball would go from the scrum to the halfback to the fullback to the wing who'd go into a tackle and set the ball up for the loose forwards to take possession again.

The concept of continuity is commonplace now but multi-phase football of this detail was all new for New Zealand rugby then – they were playing the game at a new level, one that required a collective and individual thought process. They were calculated. And they weren't as physical as North Auckland. Their purpose wasn't to run at you as hard as they could to knock you over. They'd run to you and then turn and look for the support. They kicked less, they passed more, they kept the ball, possession was nine tenths of their law.

And to keep in touch with each other there was all this talking. Our discipline was to have only the captain and the halfback talking. That was a rule. Auckland were always making calls: a bewildering array of numbers, names and codes. *Deli One! Trees! Branches! Sixty nine!* There was also another level of conversation where they reviewed what had gone wrong: "When you get tackled turn to your left because that's where I'll be coming from."

By contrast, we in the south were still very monosyllabic. The whole experience was alien to us, these connected moves, these lines and phantom lines, the contact between the players – it was all a new culture. The skills prized in our province were how far you could run with a man on your back.

Hitherto the values of New Zealand rugby were recognisably the same in the country as a whole. The one was an expression of the other. This routinely happens in rugby all round the world – the style countries play in reflects the national character. In New Zealand's case, some differences existed between north and south, urban and rural, but as in the rest of the country, the conformity was greater than the diversity.

New Zealand's values were still informed by an older generation who valued security above everything. And that wasn't surprising; they'd been brought up in hard times, they'd survived the Depression and World War Two, they knew how uncertain life could be. Prudence is a central virtue if you've had your life systematically threatened, if you've had friends and neighbours killed in a world war. Security, solidarity, neighbourliness – these were important elements for lives that had been lived in times of such turmoil. The values of what's been called the "khaki generation" were in political terms the values of "Rob's Mob", those followers of Prime Minister Muldoon.

Rugby rather mirrored this. But the new style which was just emerging had a strong parallel with what was going on in the wider community. The political changes brought in by Roger Douglas under the David Lange government had caused a great upheaval in the country. A new individualism was undermining all the big old power blocks, the secure state monopolies, and the jobs-for-life culture that made public service departments a branch of social welfare. The Post Office, the telephone system, the Railways, were all in the process of being restructured and were showing enormously improved financial results – and an enormous increase in unemployment. But suddenly, in a loss of nerve, David Lange called for "a cup of tea", signalling a halt to the progress that had been made.

The same thing happened in rugby. The big, slow, immensely powerful, inexorable forwards were being superseded by faster, passing players. Trench warfare was giving way to desert rat-style rugby – fast, elusive, powerful Commandos.

The "cup of tea" in rugby arrived three years later than for the political establishment. In 1991, the administrators effectively called for a halt to progress along the lines Lochore, Wyllie, Hart and others had put in place. We lost the semi-final of the 1991 World Cup, something was wrong, change wasn't working, the national administration reinstated the old guard. They didn't really do it to bring back the older style of playing – that would have been like bringing back Rob Muldoon to run the country – they just reached for the security of what they grew up with. The results speak for themselves.

Today, we are back on track. The 1995 team started a new cycle and it is as positive and strong as the 1987-89 period.

The rule changes and the advent of professionalism have moved the game and the players onto a new level again. Play has become less confrontational in the forwards as it has become more confrontational between individual runners. The ball is in play more, lineouts and scrums are fewer, defending is more difficult and tries flow more freely. Flair is valued and rewarded by the structure of the game.

But back then when it was all beginning, we may have had the reputation of being the best rugby team in the world but the conventional wisdom was slightly patronising. The English were particularly skilful at saying the secret of All Black success was because we did the basics well. If you read between the lines you could hear them implying that the basics were all we could do well. "Anyone can do the basics," I could hear them saying, "particularly if they're basic people. But without wanting to sound *de haut en bas* about it, we're probably fractionally more ambitious so we are trying to do something a little more sophisticated than the basics. That's why we lose all the time, but we don't care." In their nonchalance about losing there was a germ of truth. Winning wasn't the meaning of rugby; but it was extraordinarily important nonetheless.

Change was in the air, but at that time we in Otago had no idea how it was to be effected. We had no idea that there was a new wave or who would be a part of it. We were a physical team without mental resources. We'd been beaten by Hawke's Bay, for instance – we had no answer to their forwards even though they had no observable intelligence or finesse. And we had no answer to the questions of why we were losing all the time, why we couldn't get commitment. We were trapped in a vicious circle of defeat.

Perhaps it was a coaching mistake to fire us up with the need to win all our matches. Perhaps the coach had overestimated the quality of the team. We might have identified the teams we really could beat and focused on beating them. We could have tried to play those teams early in the tour, for instance. If you set out with the objective of winning all your matches then your morale is blown at your first loss.

We were going to beat North Auckland (got thrashed). We were going to beat Auckland (got crushed). We were going to beat Hawke's Bay (got beaten). So when we got to Wairarapa Bush we had little grounds for believing we were going to beat even them. So we didn't.

We were playing physical rugby without physical resources. If

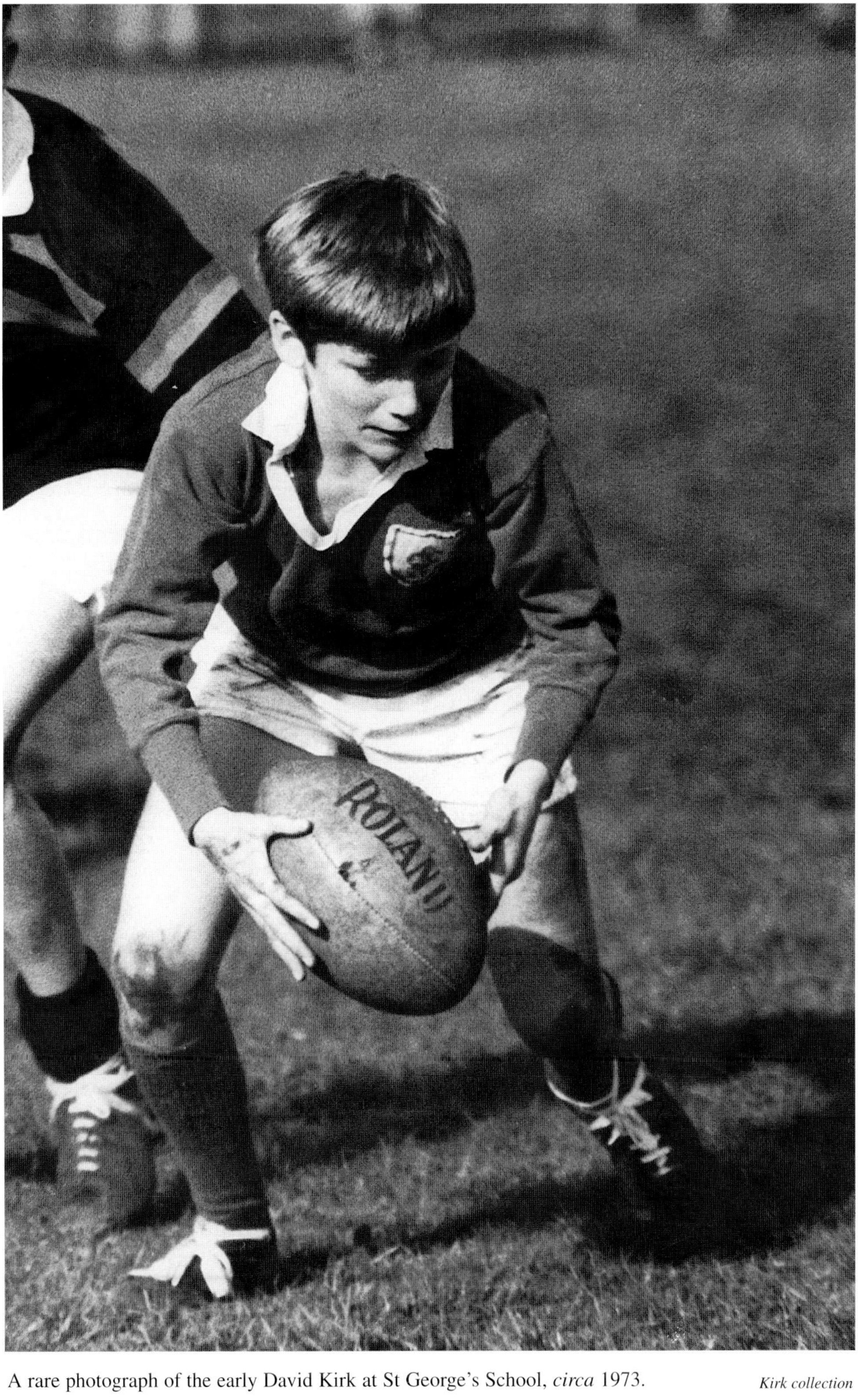

A rare photograph of the early David Kirk at St George's School, *circa* 1973. *Kirk collection*

Playing for Collegiate against Nelson College in the annual quadrangular tournament, this time at Wanganui.

Wanganui Newspapers

Try time for Varsity A in the final of the Dunedin senior club championship, 1983. I'm jubilant (with arms raised high) while Dean Kenny, my rival for the Otago halfback spot, is less than impressed.

Otago Daily Times

Breaking past French centre Eric Bonneval during Otago's match with the tourists in 1984. Other identifiable Otago players are, from left, prop Steve Hotton and flanker Andy Hollander. We lost 10-20.

Rugby News

The All Black trial of 1985. I was captaining the Probables, with Dave Loveridge captaining the Possibles. Loveridge was undoubtedly the halfback of our time – despite this, my team got home 17-10, and I was to be rewarded my first test cap. *Rugby News*

In action for Auckland University. Above: 'Foxy' offering characteristic advice ("Give me the ball!"). Below: An extraordinarily youthful Sean Fitzpatrick with myself, Grant Dickson and a partially obscured John McDermott. *Rugby News*

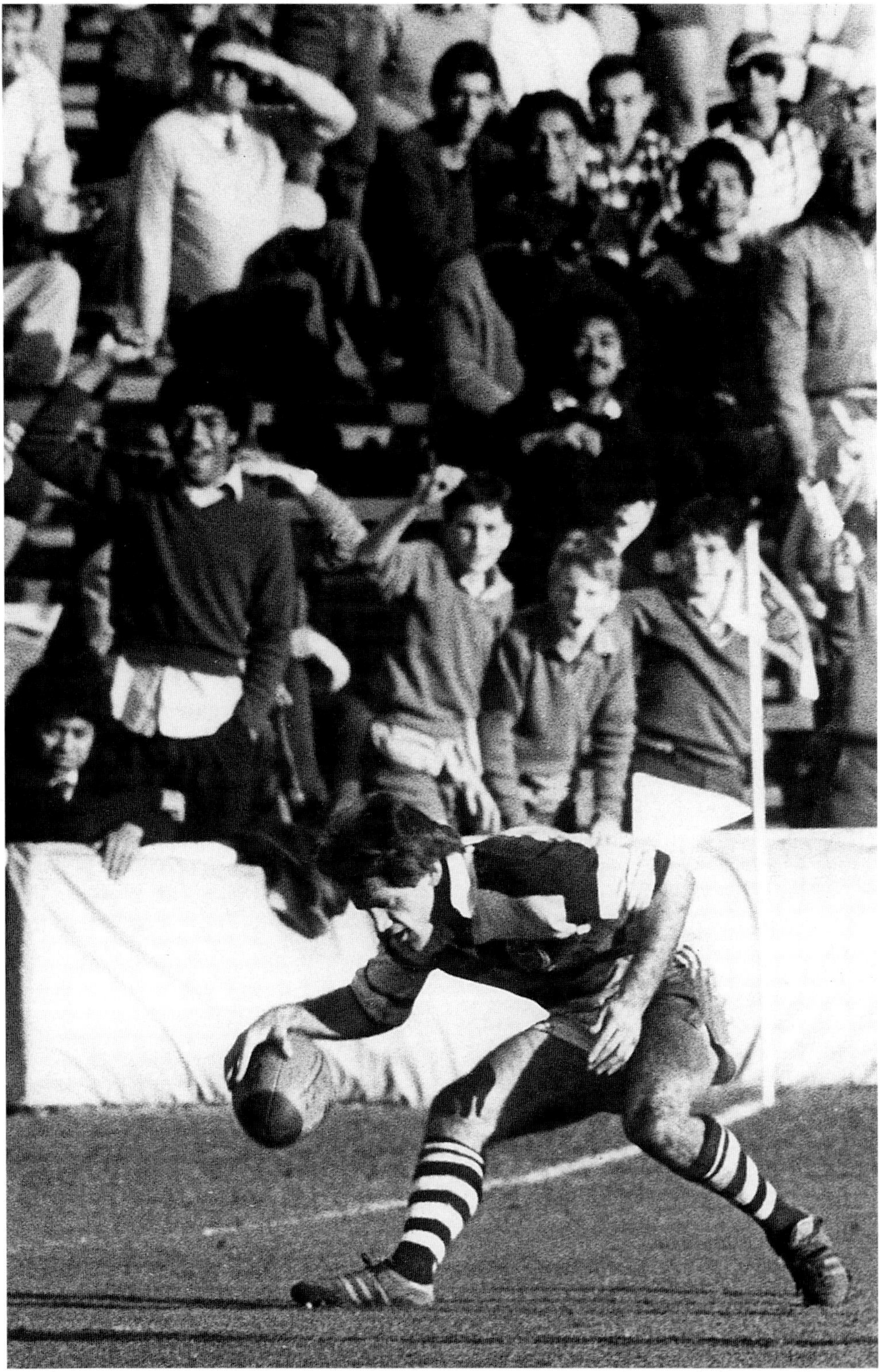

One of the bright memories: Scoring a try for Auckland in their successful Ranfurly Shield defence against North Harbour in 1986. It was Harbour's second year of life, and we won 18-6. *Rugby News*

Auckland versus England 1985. It was unusual in those days for a provincial team to be so confident of beating a national touring side. Above: Preparing to kick with Glenn Rich and Andy Haden watching on. Below: Taking a pass from Glenn Rich, who is being tackled by Stuart Barnes, now a celebrated rugby writer. *Rugby News*

The best of sport is the sense of life being taken on the wing . . . *Rugby News*

we'd had a mental dimension we would have means of improvement – but all we could do was try and run further with more men on our backs. Other teams were able to run further with bigger loads. If that's your competitive difference then you've got a simple competition on your hands.

So that's how we got to second to bottom place in the first division, playing Bay of Plenty for our place in the first division. On our previous form we would have fumbled the kick-off, lost the resulting scrum and started losing immediately. In the event there were tries galore, running backs, driving forwards, a classic exhibition match which we easily won on a hot, sunny day that suggested an early summer.

We had gone through the season relentlessly unsuccessful but I felt quite good about the world. It was this season that suggested to me something about individuality and the selfishness of rugby. If the team wins and you have played badly the victory is not particularly sweet. Conversely, if the team loses and you play well the pain is diminished. So, because I had quite a good playing season, one loss after another was not enough to cast me down. I had hopes for the following season. I had thought my window of opportunity was passing, but there was still a chink for me. Otago had had a rotten year, but there had been some personal solace for me. I had played for the South Island, had an All Black trial, represented Otago all year and the All Black selectors knew who I was.

But the next year, Laurie Mains was appointed coach of Otago. Laurie had had a strange All Black career. He'd had three tests in 1971 as a slow fullback in the Don Clark tradition; he'd had a comeback five years later when he toured as the only specialist goal kicking fullback to South Africa but he didn't play any of the tests. His strengths were in kicking, not in running with the ball or eluding the opposition, and as most of us are biased in favour of the things we can do well, it was these strengths he preferred in his overall game plan as a player and subsequently as a coach.

I also realised that Dean Kenny was fit now and playing for Laurie's club so it was unlikely that I'd be chosen. And picking up the paper one day I read that it was so. My provincial career was effectively on hold. I thought I was a halfback through and through. I was temperamentally and by experience that gatekeeper between the two spheres of influence in the team; I was the opportunist on the edge of two worlds, a creature of peripheral vision, always busy. That's not what wingers are like, not at all. They have very different qualities – look at John Kirwan, Jonah Lomu and Jeff Wilson.

The next two years in Dunedin were more difficult for me. I was on the reserves bench at least as often as I played. I also had a difficult relationship with Laurie Mains. My honest assessment is that I don't come out of that period with particular credit. Good team men don't show disappointment when they're not picked (I showed).

I also made things difficult for him when he tried to get me on the field – on the wing. I was never a winger and felt the position would be a graveyard for me. I did play a couple of games in that position but I didn't want to play in that position and made those feelings known.

And while the media were divided about the merits of Kirk or Kenny at halfback, I understood Dean was a perfectly good, rational choice for halfback. He was bigger and stronger than I was, he made longer passes and was a bigger kicker. I was quicker and bossier, perhaps. And as we are all biased in favour of things we do well, I took it on myself to be the sort of halfback who determines when the team should kick and when to run it. Some coaches like halfbacks who can control the flow of a game, others look for the player who will implement the coach's instructions to the letter.

However, while I wasn't picked for Otago, the South Island selectors (Spud Tait and Neville Goodwin) never failed to pick me for the inter-island matches. Consequently I have the highest regard for Spud and Neville's ability and vision as selectors. They helped keep me busy, and there were also the occasional inter-university games which cast me on a larger stage.

It wasn't unheard of for All Black selectors to pick provincial reserves – but it wasn't all that common either. This was also when I realised that things happen in the season early on. Essentially you play for your position at the end of the season before – that's why you have to finish well. This ensures early exposure next season and the chance to establish yourself for the next season. And so it goes on. But other very good players were playing every Saturday. Selectors were always watching. I was a weekly absence and that was a clear disadvantage.

The All Black team to tour England and Scotland was to be announced the Saturday night Otago played Counties in Pukekohe. Both Dean and I were in the frame to be picked. I played the first game of the three-match tour against Bay of Plenty (which we won), and Dean played against Waikato (a narrow loss) and Counties (a heavy loss). I'd been reserve for that match and was standing there in the Counties Hotel having a beer at the after-match function trying to act as nonchalantly as I could with my stomach churning when a woman I'd never seen before ran up to me and said, "You're in!"

I said, "I don't believe you!" but it was true. I was in the All Blacks. I'd been chosen. The number nine jersey had been a focus of longing since I'd first started to play, and now I was to be part of that special company, the world's greatest team.

Twelve months previously I wouldn't have believed it: there were too many people ahead of me and beside me – David Loveridge (the greatest halfback of his generation) and Andrew Donald were settled – Bruce Deans, Neil Sorensen, Tim Burcher and others too. After the North-South match and All Black trial the previous year I had jumped up the list. Still, the odds against me a year earlier were so high as not to be worth calculating.

You never believe it's possible until it happens; you daren't let yourself believe, the let down would be too great. And then it happens, and suddenly you can allow yourself to take in fully how much this means to you. You remember yourself as a kid under the blankets at prep school in the impossibly early hours of the morning listening to heroes on the other side of the world who carry your hopes and those of everyone you know, young and old. And while you have imagined it in the moments before sleep, running out on the pitch in their company, you have never truly dared imagine yourself in the shirt, not actually in the black shirt with the silver fern on it, one of history's five hundred.

It was on the radio. I heard it through the news before any official contacted me. The selectors in those days had the remote and powerful authority of a college of cardinals. They rarely spoke to players directly. You only found out what they meant when you saw the puff of smoke coming out of the papal chimney. It was the same as when I was eventually captain of the All Blacks and was dumped – I heard it on the radio first.

My team mates were very supportive and genuinely pleased for me. For Dean it was disappointing but his turn was coming.

The team assembled in Auckland at the Poenamo Hotel, as we were to do all through my All Black career. Things were suddenly different; I was in a new team, with a new standard to perform to, new relationships to come to terms with. Suddenly opponents were team mates; suddenly we were All Blacks.

What seemed like mountains of gear were given out, and most of it had the silver fern on it. We trained in front of television cameras, the papers previewed the tour and the players. Suddenly you were aware that the whole country was interested, not just your parents, and the flat and the club in Otago.

Under Strength – but Under Way

We left in October 1983, just after my twenty-third birthday. The team was severely under strength: the halfback, three locks, two props and a hooker who had been in the team that beat the Lions 4-0 in the test series, and then Australia for the Bledisloe Cup that year, were unavailable. Allan Hewson withdrew at the last moment with an injury. The team was captained by Stu Wilson on the wing – not a natural position for captain but he was the best candidate. Otherwise, only Murray Mexted, Mark Shaw, Wayne Smith and Bernie Fraser had any real experience at this level.

The fact that there was a leap in quality was by now familiar; I was expecting it but was unprepared for it too. You brace yourself for impact but the crash is still atrocious. My second match – against London Division – was at Twickenham.

The changing rooms at Twickenham are big, with ancient tongue and groove panelling (funnily enough, more familiar to us in New Zealand than to the British) and wooden seats worn by years of use. A separate room contains the showers and freestanding, clawfoot baths. It's a very special atmosphere; the crowd is daunting, the stands are enormous – the weather is filthy, the history and tradition associated with the pitch are inspiring.

And compounding that there was, as usual, suddenly far less time – less time to make decisions about going left or right, to kick, to make a tackle. It was not just because the players were themselves faster, they were also anticipating more, they could see the game more, they were thinking more. And they were on you like animals, fast and ferocious.

During my career, I learnt the key to managing under pressure, when there's far less time, is to use all the time available. If there is four-tenths of a second to pick up the ball, drop back and to kick – the best players know they have more than two-tenths of a second. In fact they'll use the smallest fraction under the four-tenths to complete the kick. The lesser player will rush – he'll get his kick away without being charged down but he will be compromising on quality.

They say things slow down in a car crash – it's because the adrenaline surges and you are suddenly concentrating very precisely and taking in everything around you at ten times the normal rate. That's how it is in a test match. When the scrum breaks and the flankers are fanning both ways, the number eight's going right and the fullback's coming up on the blindside – it's happening all around you as fast as a car crash and you have to take it all in without rushing.

It was on this first tour I learned about relaxation. You have to be hyped up to play rugby and you must be prepared to do things violently and to take violence, but you must also mentally dissociate yourself. The body must be fast and forceful, the mind must aspire to a form of stillness in order to avoid rushing and botching the execution of a kick or a pass or a decision.

You also have to develop a relationship with the rugby ball. This awkward-shaped thing is a puckish element in the match; and you have to love it. You need the judgment to allow the ball to live its own life and work with it. It's unpredictable, you can't dominate a rugby ball. If you don't catch it on the full you have to stop and wait for it to do what it's going to do.

The key to timing is the time you're waiting. How long should you wait? Often as long as possible. If two of you are going for the ball, you're both reading the same arc. The other guy fixes in his mind what he's going to do, and at that point he's committed, he's made his decision and you can usually discern what it is. He's committed and you still have options. That's why I say waiting is the key to timing.

Early on in my career I also learned how to build a working relationship with the referee. Halfbacks are always engaging with the ref, so it's important, for obvious reasons, to manage the ref's confidence in the decisions he's making. The captain and other experienced players are working the same strategy in their own way. It is marvellous the effect a quizzical look from a well-established player can have on an official if the moment has been chosen well.

My approach was to strike up a rapport with the ref based on our joint duty to keep the game going as it should be. So if he was penalising our players for talking back I'd side with the ref, praise him. You always side with the ref when he is clearly right. If it was possible to say so convincingly, you might comment in a voice gruff with admiration, "Picked that. Not many of them pick that." You become his collaborator in keeping the game fair and moving. Conversely, when he makes calls which go against the team I would try a quizzical look, saying: "All we're looking for is consistency" – while adopting a non-confrontational posture, hands on knees (puffing, recovering) looking up at him. Apes adopt this submissive posture all the time, because it works.

These techniques worked very well in New Zealand, I have to say, but they didn't always travel. I'd worked on our own refs for years, establishing a reputation where refs would come to expect a certain amount of lip from me. But the first time Roger Quittenton, in his Butlins shorts, heard me say, "All we're looking for is consistency" he drew a crisp blast on his whistle and awarded the other team a penalty for cheek.

"Hmmm," I thought, "these English referees play a funny sort of rugby."

Realising the nature of the culture gap between Britain and New Zealand was to stand me in good stead in later life. When I went on to Oxford, this realisation that the English and New Zealanders were very different people from very different backgrounds was largely responsible for my declining the invitation to captain the Varsity team. We New Zealanders are a lot easier with this difference than we were in those days.

We started the tour well, losing only to Midlands in the build-up to the test against Scotland. My first match was against Edinburgh. It was Gavin Hastings' first international match too. We won well, the match was fast and physical and after it I felt I was a real All Black. Not only had I been picked for the All Blacks I had played for the All Blacks; my name would appear as long as *Men in Black* was published. It's impossible to be unaffected by this: your membership becomes part of your character. I haven't played test rugby for a decade, I'll never play again, but it's part of me now, as it's a part of all of us who played on that stage.

Scotland is quite like New Zealand in play, they have coaches who have openly admired the way we do rugby, and have imitated us as far as they can. Thus, they drive low into rucks and get quick ball to their backs. The country has a small catchment area for rugby players from a small population, the only thing they really lack is talent. Not all the best individual players would get into a provincial New Zealand team. But they are tough and uncompromising; not big, but fast in the forwards, they run the ball well and play with passion.

We beat them the same way we beat most teams in the world, by taking it to them in the forwards. You can afford to be basic, you don't have to be unusual or surprising to beat Scotland. Their best teams are tigerish: you know you'll get Bannockburn at the first ruck, but you also know it won't be enough. They are, along with the Irish, some of the nicest people socially we play against.

It was in Scotland that I had my first experience of an All Black party. Invitations were handed out to any attractive women. The cards were worded formally and well printed – "The New Zealand All Black touring team invites you to a party at 8pm at the North British Hotel on Saturday night" – and a surprising proportion of the women so invited actually turned up. The practice began during a tour of France some years earlier. Younger players with no French were struggling to make a social impression: printed invitations did the trick.

It's no surprise that most All Blacks – particularly the single ones – were on the prowl the whole time. A lot of it is to do with ambition and violent exercise. This is said to increase the testosterone flow and male hormones run amuck after a game.

And because players have become prominent, famous even, and because they have acquired a new confidence, they consider themselves to be something of a catch for women. Some women find the attitude arrogant and repulsive. Others find it arrogant and attractive.

Being on tour was a cross between being a pop star and being in the army: service discipline and enormous, sometimes undeserved, popularity. Now, the players can easily be accused of dehumanising the women involved – they want little more than a warm and accommodating body and very rarely did the liaisons last more than the one night. But equally, the women were dehumanising the players – they often weren't that interested in the individual concerned any more than getting an All Black scalp on their belt. To that extent the player is being used as much as the woman.

Consider the woman, for instance, at the centre of the Roger Randle rape allegation in South Africa. She believed she had slept with Jonah Lomu that night. It was only when she found out Jonah didn't play for the Hurricanes she realised her mistake.

By and large, particularly at All Black level, the women in rugby are treated very courteously. Some people assume the players would be boorish, unpleasant and overbearing with women, but it isn't so.

However, I digress. The test match against Scotland was played and the score was a frankly disastrous, 25-25. That was very shocking. There had been a disallowed try in the last moments on the advice of a touch judge who accused Bernie Fraser of offering to punch someone (we were indignant: it was only an offer, and it had been declined, Bernie never laid a finger on him!) Scotland has never beaten New Zealand so to draw was as bad as had ever happened to the All Blacks. We felt pretty low and were relying on a win against England to save the tour. But their big, grinding forwards achieved a 15-9 victory over us. It was a shock to see the All Blacks lose, especially to England, and especially by a failure of forward power.

It was a slightly unreal experience. All Blacks don't expect to lose and don't really have the emotional apparatus to accommodate defeat. While the real induction into the power and mystique of the All Black tradition was to come the next year, it was still a wonderful experience to play rugby for the team. And into the bargain, I also deduced from Stu's brief term of office a powerful lesson about captaincy.

Stu Wilson is naturally vivacious, ebullient and extraordinarily amusing. Suddenly as captain he changed. There had been a tradition of aloof, rather stern captains established before Graham Mourie. Mourie himself added a genuinely intellectual approach to the mix but if anything he accentuated the aloofness. Andy Dalton, naturally a quiet farming type, followed suit and was only a little more open. Stu tried to fashion himself into this mould, and to my mind it was quite the wrong thing to do.

So it taught me that captains have to be natural and behave according to their real character. This is a serious principle that extends beyond the individual to national styles of play. It's a doomed mission to impose an alien style of play onto a national team – as my friend Jacques Fouroux tried to do (he succeeded, but only for a while) with France. Captains, players, teams all have to be true to themselves to be genuinely successful.

Stu actually played very well himself but had an impossible task out there on the wing as a controlling influence on the outcome of any of the matches. He'd started mixing less with the players, he tried to be stern, to do the aloof thing. He tried to fit in with the fencepost-carrying ideal – but he was a city boy, a nightclubber, he couldn't convincingly carry off the laconic country pub look.

Ian Botham seemed to have the same problem when he was asked to captain England. Through his brief tenancy his batting and bowling form fell away completely. The pressure of having to behave as other people expected was too much for him. The moment he was relieved of his command his form returned. I think he made a century in his first free innings.

I mention this to illustrate how powerful is the mental aspect of rugby. You have to deal with anxiety, fear, criticism, disapproval, contempt, anger and jealousy – all in addition to the normal internal pressures of getting yourself mentally prepared for test rugby. If you are vulnerable to criticism – if you feel your play does have weaknesses – you are mightily exposed, particularly in New Zealand.

The English, whose clobbering machine is far more sophisticated and aggressive than ours, haven't yet taught us all they know. When the English soccer team lost to Sweden, the Sun headlined the defeat Swedes 1, Turnips 0. And every time thereafter, for the rest of his career (which wasn't long), the English coach was pictured in the paper with a turnip instead of a head.

We don't get such witty abuse from the press in New Zealand, but the pressure is more intense on a more personal level.

What are You?

The next year, Allan Hewson and I took time out from the All Blacks' tour of Australia and went to the $60 million complex in Canberra, the Australian Institute of Sport, to talk to a sports psychologist. Allan was one of the most talented ball players I'd known in my career but he suffered a great deal of criticism; while he won many matches for his country he played most of his life under great pressure from the public. To many of the New Zealand public he was the All Black fullback who wore gloves when it was cold, and once wore a body stocking underneath his kit (All Blacks were impervious to both pain and cold). Like the early David Campese, he was also reluctant to hang around under high balls. The criticism was relentless and became malicious, and in the end amounted to cruelty. In his last test, the first of that year's series in Australia, he missed a goal, he missed a tackle and was dropped, six points shy of Don Clarke's record.

Anyway, we were looking around the Institute of Sport and had looked at the swimmers, the athletes and the gymnasts – and because of its novelty we also went to see the sports psychologist.

While I was increasingly of the view that sport was foremost a mental challenge I had no framework to put these ideas into. The psychologist we went to see gave us tests designed to help us identify what sort of people we were and the sort of players we could therefore become. He gave us tests over a range of situations where we scored on a scale between very bad and very good. The questions ran like, "When you are walking down the street are you sometimes aware that you've passed a friend of yours without acknowledging them?" These weren't questions our traditional coaches were inclined to ask. The traditional coach traditionally asked one question: "What are you?" Or to render it phonetically, "Whaddarrya!" The questions asked by the Australian psychologist were along the same lines, but they demanded a fuller answer.

We were asked things like, "Are you any good at jigsaw puzzles?" or "Have you had any minor car accidents?" or, "Do you think of yourself as a bit of a dreamer?" Whaddarrya! The idea was to find out how good we were at concentrating and what sort of things we could focus on. There were four categories of concentration:

- internal – how well you could focus on ideas.
- external – how well you could concentrate on things around you.
- broad view – how well you could see the big picture.
- narrow – how well you could concentrate on a single object or action.

It was a huge eye-opener to me; again, the crucial determining factors for success weren't physical but mental. To be a top player you had to be good at all the four quadrants. You had to be able to focus narrowly, internally, and analyse your skills. You needed to drill your concentration into kicks, passing and catching. You had to conceive of strategies for the team and you had to be able to see the field around you, and guide the action according to the plan. He also recommended the Inner Game concept, and the books written by sports psychologist and coach James Galway. Galway has a number of techniques to help concentration which he's applied across a whole range of sports. Coaches always tell you to keep your eye on the ball; in ball sports, keeping your eye on the ball is the first real skill you have to learn. But no-one, until Galway, told us *how* to keep our eye on the ball.

I bought the *Inner Game of Tennis* in Sydney on this tour and learned his technique of bounce-hit. That is, when the ball bounces on your side of the net you call bounce! precisely at the moment it lands. He might ask you whether you called bounce! fractionally before or after the bounce. You begin looking very carefully for the instant of bounce – already you are following the ball more closely than you ever have. At the instant it connects with your racket – not a fraction before or after – you call out hit! and you find you have followed the ball actually onto the racket. And when you tire of this exercise, and concentration is flagging, he'll suddenly ask you what side of the ball is in sun and which side is in shade. Again, you find your interest in the ball itself is rekindled.

His technique for golf putting is worth mentioning. All the action on the putting green is determined by the angle and speed at which the club head hits the ball. Galway suddenly changed the rules of the putting game. He said, "The game is not to get the ball into the hole. The game is to predict where the ball is going to end up given the stroke you have made." So, suddenly you find yourself intently focusing on the clubhead as it makes the connection. You stop worrying about where the hole is, what your partner is hoping for, or the fact that you've missed three two-footers in a row. The only important thing in the game is the clubhead and the ball. "That'll be left and short," you say as you hit it – but, amazingly, the ball appears to be guided by some other power and is only just short and only just left.

This coaching method allows players to retreat into the stillness of themselves and concentrate on the essential moment and the very limited range of things that have to be done.

The key to much skill acquisition and all skill execution under pressure is mental rehearsal. The best visualisers are the best doers. Galway's techniques focus a lot on grooving by mental rehearsal. It is a technique that is easy to talk about but hard to do. The mental image must be crystal clear and seen and felt every frame. Proper mental rehearsal is active. And hard.

The peak of the mental game is a strange condition of allowing the subconscious to override the conscious mind: to act without thinking or trying. Not to do – but to be. If that sounds philosophical it's probably more religious, a zen state. Zen and the Art of Archery is a classic religious text. Rugby is more chaotic than archery, and less contemplative and less focused, than martial arts, but some of the same principles of stillness can apply. Graham Mourie used zen koans to illustrate his autobiography. Maybe there are more zen masters than you think – or than they know – working the rolling mauls of the international paddocks.

Mini Game – Mini Revolution

Sevens rugby was an unregarded game in those days, the mid-1980s. Its status was below one-day cricket and slightly above league. We had no respect for the game because we kept losing at it.

Casually, almost contemptuously, we used to send our top provincial team to Hong Kong to compete against Australia and Fiji (and be thrashed). Finally we sent a proper national team with All Blacks to bring back the trophy. We then suffered a terrible shock: we got knocked out in the quarter-finals. Our best players did no better than our second-best players. We had sent the silver fern out into the world and lost.

It turned out to be a good example of what happens when New Zealand's rugby mana is affronted. In 1984, the administration set out to develop a sevens team that would win.

Imagine the theme from *Rocky* playing as we prepared mentally and physically. We had a week's specialist training with specialist coaches, including the indomitable Bill Freeman. We watched videos until we were square-eyed. We drilled defensive zones and attacking moves. We took the great Australian league teams as our role models and as a result we did better; we immediately got into the final – and were hammered. We still had no technique to speak of; we knew none of the shortcuts, so our only way of covering up was to run as fast as we could all the time, all over the paddock. Fiji ran us ragged – I'd never been as tired as when that final whistle blew. I nearly couldn't speak.

The following year we were better prepared, better equipped, better skilled. And when we lost to a British team in the semi-final critics were ready to say we were on the wrong track. But the trend was definitely improving. These sorts of results are not uncommon while a team is being built, before it gets to its maturity.

But building a team or learning a new technique is like climbing Mt Ngauruhoe in summer. The surface is shingle, it slides under your feet. For every five metres' progress you make, you slide back one; occasionally you slip over and slide back ten. You have to keep going if you want to get to the summit. The two biggest challenges are maintaining your belief in yourself and, secondly, persuading the public and the media that you deserve more time to complete the work.

It was in the third year that we had a combination of the best ball players in the world allied to some of the strongest players. Wayne Shelford, Zinzan Brooke, Mark Brooke-Cowden, Wayne Smith, Craig Green, Frano Botica, Mike Clamp. But we still might have lost – sevens is fast and unpredictable – however, we were favoured with a tactical insight which totally changed our approach to the game.

That year there was a sevens tournament two weeks prior to the Hong Kong Sevens. It was in Sydney. We were in a pool with Wales and felt very confident. But things didn't go according to plan. Jonathan Davies turned on a piece of individual brilliance and once again we lost. We had been holding our line, Davies chipped in behind, gathered the ball and scored; you couldn't stop him. So we sat on the bank of the Concord Oval feeling down (being beaten by Wales was at that time a ridiculous experience), watching Korea playing Fiji. We were watching Fiji closely, knowing them to be champions and because you wouldn't expect to learn anything from watching Koreans playing rugby. But, as it happened, Korea was the team to watch: they made things very hard for Fiji. They were playing an unconventional game by running forward all the time, not holding their line. It was a very original pressure defence.

The received wisdom of the time was to stand back, in a line, moving up together in a controlled way, being always careful to leave no gaps. The Koreans, on the other hand, rushed up in twos and threes on the man with the ball. It was very confusing. It was also sacrilege. And it worked. The pressure prevented the opposition getting the ball away. Unbalanced numbers in defence didn't matter because the ball never got freed into open space. We took an interest in this Korean tactic, discussed it and wondered if we could use it.

There came a point when we all thought – this really works. So we practised the principle and in it found the key to winning. We went into the Sydney Sevens finals against Australia and won by thirty points. It was in that final that Zinzan Brooke emerged as the all-time, all-round forward. We took a great team to the Hong Kong Sevens. That style of aggressive defence changed the paradigm of sevens. We swarmed. We played like fifteen Irishmen; we were everywhere. We had the ball more because we were knocking them over. We were uncontainable.

In Hong Kong we met Fiji in the semi-finals, the team that had won the last three years. They were the world's peerless ball handlers, the dancing, athletic Fijians who combined speed, power and grace like no other team, and we totally skittled them; beat them by twenty points. That victory set up a long winning streak for New Zealand sevens; and now we have the confidence and the skill we feel we have to win. And most of the time we do.

The New Zealand team had come from nowhere to being the best in the world, consistently and overwhelmingly.

I don't know why, but this happens quite often in New Zealand, this burst of accelerated achievement. We'd never beaten England at cricket but, suddenly, we had one of the best teams in the world for three or four years in the early 1980s. We'd no experience in America's Cup yacht racing – one of the most technical and expensive sports in the world. Suddenly we won thirty-eight out of forty starts in the biggest tournament in the world, and now we have the America's Cup (and easily). There's more: in 1980 our best white wine was called Blenheimer; now London wine critics say our sauvignon blancs are the best in the world. This quantum leap often happens in New Zealand. One moment we have the most regulated economy in the western world, the next we are the most deregulated. The stockmarket went higher here, proportionately, than anywhere else – and crashed lower. We have been called the passionless people – maybe we were but it's not so now. As a country we swing wildly from insignificance to excellence.

In sevens, one of the most unpredictable games in the world, we learned the game, understood it, found a new way of playing it, and established a crucial psychological dominance by which we know, and our opponents know, who the likely victor is going to be – and we did it in three years.

This re-invention of the game using a wholly new paradigm, a new vision of play, may have been the psychological origin of what later happened to All Black play. Some of the defining characteristics were certainly the same.

Bill Freeman who, along with Bryce Rope, was there at the birth of

Black and Blue

New Zealand seven-a-side dominance saw in our sevens learning the seeds of our World Cup triumph and the great teams of 1987-90. There were in fact three strands in the development of these teams – the Canterbury tradition of Alex Wyllie, the Auckland teams of John Hart and the sevens teams of the era.

As a matter of interest, the psychological attitude we developed as we learned how to win has real physical effects. A number of foreign players have said to me, "You guys are so lucky to have chosen black for your colours – it makes you look bigger." Well, it doesn't actually. What makes All Blacks look bigger is their reputation and their implacable belief in their ability to win.

All Blacks are expected to be big – quite a few people who have only seen me on television have remarked with surprise that I'm not bigger myself. My wife's father had been telling all his daughters for years that the family bloodlines needed improvement (he farms). "Bring home an All Black," he instructed them. "We need some bone and height in this family." When Brigit brought me home he was polite enough not to comment.

Ants versus Grasshoppers

Later in 1984, back in Otago, the previous year's halfback had been selected – and, again, it wasn't me. A minor controversy broke out in the letters column of the *Otago Daily Times.*

There has remained some ill-feeling from that time. In 1994, fully ten years later, Mike Brewer, captain of Otago and a fellow All Black, wrote to me (in reply to a letter from me) accusing me of bias against Laurie Mains in my writings for not selecting me a decade before.

While there are objective reasons for thinking Laurie was somewhat at sea as a selector (fifty players in two years played for his team when he coached the All Blacks) there was an element of truth in Mike's claim. I was biased against Laurie. I didn't react well to the style of rugby he wanted us to play, and I didn't at all like the way he kept selecting halfbacks other than myself. It is an unavoidable fact of the player-coach relationship. Players are biased against coaches who don't select them.

But let me suggest some other – more rational – reasons for my bias.

I thought Laurie had an essentially negative view of play. In his early years with Otago you won matches by making fewer mistakes than the opposition. That doesn't constitute a vision, or even a style of play. For virtually all his coaching career (until his final year with the All Blacks) Laurie produced a constricted, cautious and limited game. In the context of Otago at the time this was understandable. He had severely limited resources to work with. He chose to cut his cloth accordingly. The way you made progress was kicking to the corners, putting the opposition back where they might make a mistake you could capitalise on. You didn't run the ball wide yourself – that way was full of danger and potential error. His team mightn't have made mistakes but they didn't make much of anything else either.

Laurie fully recognised the limitations of the team he inherited and the style of play he developed made us more successful than we had been in the years before. The risk of relegation became remote after he took over. His strategy was a perfectly understandable one for a limited team.

The grander plans of the teams I played with later began with eliminating mistakes, but as I said before, that was just stage one. The real action was to release the creative power of the players individually and collectively. That was where the magic was. Rational play may be faultless, but without romantic inspiration and creative power it can be an awfully boring style to play, let alone watch. A good many All Black teams have fallen into this category.

I have always maintained rugby (sport, life, everything, actually) is about more than not making errors. I maintain the trench warfare view of the game was based on an old-fashioned and out-dated view of people, teams, and ultimately of the country itself. Some of these old-style values were proving to be a real impediment to progress.

A new sort of society was rapidly coming into being all around us – one in which flexibility, speed, communication and innovation were becoming more important. Pace, excitement, contact, revolution to some extent, were the new standing orders in the economy, as on the rugby field.

So Mike Brewer's charge of sour grapes was only partially correct. And there is no onus on a player to support coaches who don't pick them. Some sort of reaction is natural enough – I was on the other end of that principle when I was coaching Wellington. I got no loyalty from players I didn't select – and didn't really expect to.

In the light of that rivalry, shall we say, the 1983 final of the Speights Shield had a special significance. Otago University was in the final (myself as captain) against Southern – Laurie Mains' club, with Dean Kenny as the opposing halfback.

I love university rugby. The players take outrageous risks and win (when they win at all) magnificently. A first-five will run behind the posts to score – and at the last moment lob a basketball pass to a lumbering prop who hasn't scored in five seasons. There's a gaiety, a wit and exuberance about university rugby.

So our two teams couldn't have been more different. They came from opposite traditions. The intensely rational, diligent, rather pedestrian team on the one hand. On the other the romantics – youth and humour wanting to win but only if they could win stylishly.

Ants versus Grasshoppers

Roundheads versus Cavaliers; you know the fable – ants versus grasshoppers.

It was also a showdown between Dean Kenny and myself, the two halfbacks struggling for the provincial position.

The conditions suited Dean more than me. It was very wet and he was the physically stronger of the two of us. Carisbrook was so boggy that, later in the season, Otago and Auckland were to play a nil-all draw. You couldn't run in this swamp, or pass, or do anything very much without an outboard motor. It suited Southern's close, cautious approach.

In the event the romantic style prevailed. It was a very close game but because there was real quality in Dirk Williams, Mike Brewer and Paul Foster in the loose forwards and a ton of grit in the backs and tight forwards we did it. We staggered off Carisbrook the winners. Four years of trying and I was part of a Speight's Shield championship team.

Full Strength – Full On

In 1984 I first experienced the true power and mystique of the All Blacks. In some ways it was my first real All Black team. The year before had been a rehearsal in an under-strength team. This was the real thing. It should have been an exalted experience; yet it was among those huge grizzled forwards that I first experienced the source of the strange, negative element of New Zealand rugby I struggled to come to grips with for the rest of my time with the team.

For instance, at this time we rarely talked to the opposition (especially if they were Australian) at the after-match function. I thought that was odd, and a shame. Because, truth to tell, Australia often fields more intelligent teams than we do. They tend to be professional people in city jobs. (Not that it helps them win, I might say.)

As an immigrant country like ours, and our nearest neighbours, it is surprising we aren't more alike. But Australian rugby split early on and rugby league became the mass game in Australia that rugby union remained in our country. Union is only the fourth largest code over there, after league, Aussie rules and soccer.

Australian rugby union was sustained by the private schools and universities, and therefore players come from higher socio-economic groups, largely urban and with better educations. This has the result of producing intelligent players who think about the game, and who have good concentration. At their best they combine skill and resourcefulness with a mental toughness that borders on arrogance.

It's probably fair to say that New Zealand taught them some of that capacity – just as we learn from their cricket and hockey teams. They also have a natural propensity to run and pass the ball, to create new ways of passing by standing close and flat (Mark Ella, Michael O'Connor, Michael Hawker and Roger Gould led it in the early

1980s) instead of standing wide and passing wide.

It took them until the Eighties to develop forward power to compete with us and then they combined that power with a Gallic flair equal to the French. At their best you were never sure what they'd do next. They were always cooking something up – twice in important tests recently they have landed the ball on the goal line, a high bomb, and scored (once virtually in the game's first move) with a leaping take from one of their backs.

They also had the incomparable Campo. David Campese, in many ways through his long and brilliant career, is the glorious epitome of the amateur spirit. What did he have? He had speed; he was really fast. At international level everyone is fast but at his height he was faster by a whole order of magnitude. He could move in confined spaces in a beautifully balanced way that wrong-footed everyone, even on his own side. He invented the famous goose-step: at the height of his speed he would suddenly slow down – the defender had to slow to steady himself, Campese would then burst forward. It was amazingly effective.

He also had Zinzan's boundless confidence, that sense of no-boundaries. He'd attempt extraordinary things believing they'd work. I remember in our Baby Blacks test against Australia they were pressuring us; they started one of their set moves but it went wrong. The pass to Campo was fumbled, it dropped short. But instead of falling on the ball or peeling off and letting someone else clear it up, he hooked the ball forward with his foot, pushed it through the line and scored.

At other times his test efforts are over-reaching. He might run from an impossible position, he might try to dribble round a player, soccer-style. A few years ago I watched him playing Auckland in Sydney. New South Wales were two points ahead; it was past time Campo got the ball. Any other player would have slowed the game down, kicked deep into touch, taken the lineout. Campo charged down the middle of the pitch, chipped it over the heads of the backline, tried to gather it, failed – it put his team in extraordinary, needless danger. But then he never plays the odds, he is the antithesis of Grant Fox, it seemed to me. He only found the game enjoyable if he could beat the odds achieving things mortals couldn't get away with at test level. There was, of course, the test he lost against the Lions by trying to run from behind his line; he dropped the ball, the Lions scored and took the test (and the series too) as a consequence. But he'd done his best, which was normally better than good enough. That's perhaps where his quiet, don't-worry-be-happy smile comes from. Minnesota Fats, the professional pool player, gave Paul Newman some advice in *The Hustler*: "Don't play the percentage shot, kid, play it fast and loose."

The New South Wales incident happened towards the end of his career and I got the feeling he wasn't going to waste precious last moments on a rugby field kicking the ball off the field. The lesson was clear: the game is for playing, take advantage of the opportunity, don't squander it by kicking the ball over the stand.

As for other Australians, Michael Lynagh was the equivalent of Grant Fox (well, almost) for accuracy, but with more running skills.

Nick Farr-Jones was the best all-round halfback I played against. He was very competitive, big and strong (though not so fast), a very quick passer and with a good touch. Most importantly he was a leader and organiser for Australia.

Australia's weakness is caused by the lack of depth in their player pool. It's grown from a narrow base – only a few clubs and the private schools. If a number of their top players get injured they've got limited talent to replace them with.

When New Zealand loses it's usually because we've got too many old players in the team: when Australia loses it's usually because they've got too many young players in the team. In this country, if you're a good young player and you fail in a couple of games you rarely get another chance. A good young Australian player can play a howler and still get another go the following year.

When the Cavaliers went to South Africa the All Blacks fielded an entirely new team which played well enough to beat France and lose to Australia by just one point. The Joeys wouldn't do so well, I feel.

I have always had the highest regard for the Australian teams I've played against. In contrast to the generations before, the Australians became our toughest opponents. They challenged us, they threatened us, they brought out the best and worst in us. During the first part of my international career they were at their peak. They had beaten us in a test series in Australia in 1980 – a rare happening! They completed a Grand Slam tour of Britain in 1984. And in 1986 they came to New Zealand and won the test series 2-1. There were a lot of other things going on in 1986, but the Aussies deserved their win. We played four consecutive one-point matches in 1984, 1985 and 1986. We won three and they won one. By the end of my international career we had established a dominance that lasted nearly three years. They roared back in the 1991 World Cup and now we have pulled away again. I have a feeling we have now established something of a break on them.

But when I played, it wasn't easy beating Australia. You got nothing for nothing, you had to be good in every area. They had strong, athletic forwards and speed and skill in the backs. There's no one way to beat them. Even now you need a balance of attrition – putting the ball behind them, shutting them down, squeezing the life out of them – and at the same time creativity to make space for yourself. You must make it hard for them to play their game but be prepared to take risks yourself.

Australia will be one of those countries that rugby professionalism will help. Some of the best football players who would otherwise have played rugby league will play rugby union. Player depth will improve but, as ever, the quality and drive of administration will be the ultimate determinant of how well they do.

They've got a natural flair we have lacked in New Zealand until recently; perhaps it comes from the larger, more cosmopolitan population and a continental land mass. They've got a sort of wide raucousness that we don't naturally have. We have plenty of other qualities to be sure, but they more than us are the origins of the "wild colonial boy". I know that there used to be a prison outside Dunedin in the nineteenth century that would put working parties of prisoners out into the fields unsupervised. If they were late back at night the prisoners were punished – by being locked out. That's a character strain the Aussies would find very foreign.

So it was in July and August of 1984 that I first toured Australia. Some of the older players had been part of the loss of the Bledisloe Cup four years earlier. The memory of a victorious Australian team taking a victory lap of the Sydney Cricket Ground, holding the cup high, dancing on our grave, still burned in their Kiwi souls. This forced them into a defensive, insular – indeed, boorish – attitude at times. Only teams who are struggling and fearful of losing get defensive. The weight of tradition that bore down on the older players came to take its toll.

We had, for instance, an Australian liaison officer, a senior official in their union who naturally enough wore an Australian Rugby Union tie. For our first team meeting our senior players made him take it off and burn it. "If you're going to be part of this team you can wear our gear. Get that fucking dingo tie off." Eventually he did. But it was far from a humorous incident. I remember the expression on the man's face as they put a cigarette lighter under his tie.

Even the thought of an Australian tie in our camp was too much. Much later I understood the passion better when I read R.A.K. Mason's *Sonnet to Brotherhood*:

Garrisons pent up in a little fort
with foes who do but wait on every side
Knowing the time soon comes when they shall ride
Triumphant over those trapped, and make sport
of them . . .

The most senior players were the big forwards of the day and they were the leaders. That's been the case with the team since I've been aware of it, our tradition was built on big forward power. But I felt a sense of oppression under their de facto leadership, and came to feel they were not reflecting the longer tradition of All Black rugby.

As the tour proceeded we had a tough battle in the tests, and the laager mentality among the senior players increased.

The Australian Rugby Union was in poor financial shape at the time and asked us if we'd be prepared to wash our underwear and socks in the hotel basins to reduce costs (they didn't ask a second time). Eventually they did very well out of the tour – we filled the Sydney Cricket Ground twice, filled Ballymore and a number of provincial stadiums.

People think the All Blacks are like the Apostles, all equally close to each other, but in fact we all separated out pretty cleanly into a variety of groups. My peer groups were the younger set and the midweek team. We in the midweek teams probably had more fun – we won all our games well, and by a wide margin. The early part of the tour was notable for me in Adelaide when I assisted at an operation to put a screw in John Kirwan's AC joint.

We were looking good in the build-up, but we lost the first test, and as a result we had a minor re-run of the liaison officer's tie – only this time it was the baggage man who got it. The older players believed that four years before the baggage man had poisoned them with bad oysters. Now, here we were, with the same baggage man, we're losing – and look, there's a furtive aspect to the guy, it's more than coincidence! He'd poison us again if we let him. That's why our guys are coming down with vomiting and diarrhoea with the second test just moments away!

I felt there was a banal explanation. We'd had a twenty-four hour bug that had swept through the entire team – as they do when you are a team on tour together. You train together, travel together, drink out of the same bottles – you all get the same bugs.

But the pressure for the second test was enormous. We had to win that one or lose the series – and now people were getting ill. The baggage man started to look a little apprehensive, worrying that he wouldn't survive to carry another bag another day.

In the first minutes of the Ballymore test everything went wrong. We were well-prepared mentally and physically but inexplicably we started losing. The Aussies kicked two penalty goals; Mark Ella tried a dropped goal which bounced back off the post – Mark was following up, caught it cleanly and scored under the posts. We'd only been playing a quarter of an hour and we were 12-0 down. We eventually got up to win 19-15.

But it was a great testament to the mental toughness of the All Blacks and to those grizzled forwards. There was no sense of panic, we slowly played ourselves back into the game. The Australians' secret weapon, light-framed Steve Cutler (who dominated the lineouts with his two-handed palming), got caught on the bottom of a ruck where our Number One was lurking, and Steve had to leave the field to staunch the flow of blood. His game seemed to suffer as a consequence.

It's a frequent phenomenon, the one-test-each result. The down team moves heaven and earth to equalise; they will do anything rather than be down two-nil with one to play.

And so the road led on to the final test, a see-sawing game at the Sydney Cricket Ground in front of fifty-five thousand spectators. We won by one point, the first of four consecutive one-pointers.

The mood in the changing room after the last test wasn't one of joy at winning but of relief at not losing. That was in the days when we didn't have the mastery of the opposition we came to develop – the possibility of losing was that much higher.

It was all new to me. As a midweek player I was largely a spectator in the great dramas of the tests. I saw little satisfaction in the result – not when you suffered a sick feeling you might be letting down so many people by losing. It produced something of a bleakness on the whole. And there was still no post-match fraternisation. This was somewhere beneath sport, and only just on the right side of warfare. Feuding hillbillies would recognise the behaviour.

That was my introduction to the aching need to win the All Blacks have. They will get over the line because they have to. The contemplation of defeat is intolerable. Unity of purpose becomes paramount. We may not even have been the better team but with stronger support and greater commitment the All Blacks prevail. Was it because we were an isolated country at the end of the world that we had to do so well? We had a more defensive view of the world in those days when rugby was one of our few international areas of excellence.

Earlier that year the French were in New Zealand and I took part in the two tests (Dave Loveridge was injured and I was reserve).

In the first test, Gary Knight got a big cut above and below his eye which was caused by an elbow. If you squinted, and wanted to believe the rumours, you could imagine it had been a bite. The general reaction was that the French were animals who bit people in the eye. Again I noticed the need we New Zealanders felt to demonise the opposition – something you normally only do to an enemy in wartime. The French were animals who bit people in the eye. The Australians poisoned you and were too boorish to talk to.

Both views were foolish. We were all very good at the ways we played rugby. The All Blacks have years of tradition and depth of technique – particularly in the forwards where it really matters. But the fact remains that the Australians were generally more intelligent people and, I thought, more fun. It wasn't a view I made much of in the changing rooms.

Farewell Otago, Hello World

During 1984, my last year at university, I only played a few more games for Otago; essentially through a two-match tour of the North Island. I was in a rather odd situation – doing better on the national stage than the provincial. I had played well for the All Blacks in Australia, and had been a reserve for every test that year. I returned to an uncertain provincial future. We'd won very well against Wairarapa Bush, I played the next game against Southland. The Ranfurly Shield match with Canterbury was a disaster. Otago was thrashed by a very strong Canterbury by some forty points.

At that point I was dropped and never put on my boots for Otago again. While the games went on in front of me, I sat on the reserve bench in my running shoes (well, your feet get cold in boots). But bearing in mind that you need to get on the field quickly if there is an injury I suppose that behaviour was a little churlish – oh, all right, childish; I was sulking on the bench because I wasn't allowed to play.

It was time to move on. I remember sitting in the Carisbrook grandstand after the last match of the season looking around. I'd been here for six years, this was the end of an era. I left in a mood of frustration. I felt I'd not had the chance to play enough. I'd never really made the contribution I'd wanted or got established in the team.

However, I did know where I was going. My application to Auckland Hospital had been successful. With some anxiety, and in some trepidation, I was leaving the deep south to go to Auckland, the best team in the country.

Notwithstanding the trepidation I felt I knew it was important to put myself in a position where I could fail as well as succeed, to go down as well as up. In Auckland it's easy enough to get lost; you might easily end up the fourth halfback instead of the second. For instance, Steven Pokere was in Auckland and was an All Black – but not a regular member of the team. John Hart had a particular style of rugby he wanted to play and Steven didn't fit the Hart need for a centre in his team. In the same way, I didn't fit Mains' need for a halfback.

I'd spoken briefly to Andy Haden at some stage about coming to Auckland but not much more than polite interest was demonstrated by either side. But I felt it was inevitable. If I wanted to move up to the highest level there was nowhere else to go. Auckland was exercising its awful magnetism and its pull was irresistible.

There was an end-of-season All Black tour to Fiji which was enormous fun – and very tough. Fiji has the most superb athletes, perhaps the best rugby athletes in the world with the largest physical capacity and wonderful ball-handling skills. They are tall and strong – but fortunately for us they have never established their forward technique. Mostly they fail in the forwards because they don't drive low; in addition, most haven't mastered their desire to grab the ball rather than drive over it, knock the opposition down and leave the ball for the halfback. Nor do they have an instinctive desire to be in a scrum – they more naturally want to be out in the open field running and passing and having a great time. This is perfectly understandable because they have the fastest runners and most elusive side-steppers in the world. Their ability to change pace and direction at speed – their swerve – is incomparable. But, as I say, they haven't mastered the dour, uncompromising discipline of forward play.

There are no Indians in the team. The ethnic Fijians have rugby sewn up as they have other parts of national life. Later on, after the coup, Colonel Rabuka (who had propped for Fiji) was asked in a newspaper interview about discrimination against Indians and he said, with a candour few politicians have matched, "Just because Indians are more intelligent than we are, and just because they work harder than we do does not mean they shall own more than we own." The interviewer questioned whether this was a racist policy. Rabuka replied, "Only insofar as it applies to Indians."

The Fijians are passionate rugby players and when selected for a representative team will come paddling in from the outer islands.

They are known to be headhunters on the field and can often be injudicious about tackling high. They commit themselves to a tackle early – and once they've lined you up, the fact that you've passed the ball makes no difference. They are one of the most physical teams – not in the sense of punching or kicking but by using their whole body as a weapon. One of the scariest moments I ever had in rugby was playing against a Fiji selection. A lineout ball was tapped back – but upwards instead of down. As I watched it arc up I knew there'd be three Fijians on top of me directly, with the whites of their eyes showing. It's one of those moments when you want to escape – to the changing rooms if necessary, but there's a convention about halfbacks not actually running away from the ball. So I got smashed to pieces.

But their wonderful smiles and friendliness afterwards makes you always keen to come back and play again.

The way to beat Fiji is through forward technique. The rule is not to open it up and allow them to exercise their hope and optimism and sense of fun. You drive it in the forwards for the first twenty minutes until you've bored them into submission. You may or may not have scored but they will have started to lose concentration, they're missing tackles, they're starting to arrive late to rucks, they're leaving one man back, they're losing cohesion – and suddenly you can do what you want.

Tactics are more important against Fiji than against any other team. Exactly the same two teams might play two different tactics and have two very different results. If you played their game from the outset – running, passing and enjoying yourselves – you'd come off with a five-point margin and delighted for the final whistle to release you to attend to your bruises. But if you, the identical team, spent the first quarter of the match boring them into submission before loosening the reins you will win by fifty points.

I remember sewing up Alan Whetton's ear at the hospital in Nadi. He didn't want the locals doing it. This was a curious sensitivity in Alan. He now sports a pair of huge great slabs of meat I remember thinking then what unfortunate pieces of flesh they were, and I'm sorry to say that they haven't got any better.

John Hart happened to be holidaying there and he came over to watch the match (which was, incidentally, Grant Fox's All Black debut).

He asked me jokingly when I was coming to Auckland. I replied dead-pan that I should be up there towards the end of March. He immediately went into organisational overdrive. "We've got our first match against the Wasps and then the Barbarians at Eden Park . . . I've got very good halfbacks that demand my loyalty . . . " It was pure John Hart. He was encouraging me to come to Auckland but seeking to establish at the earliest opportunity the relationship he wanted – giving me a come-on, but letting me know he had other options. Later on I told a journalist I was moving to Auckland and the die was cast.

Nineteen eighty-five was the year of enormous ups and downs, of wrenching dislocations, of anger and accusations and a sense of betrayal. It was the year of my first test, of an aborted tour to South Africa, of the great Ranfurly Shield challenge. It was the best and the worst of times (and, as it turned out, it was nothing compared to 1986).

The year began very upbeat. We started on a New Zealand Universities tour to England, Ireland, France and Italy. The two halfbacks were Tim Burcher and myself, and we shared the captaincy duties. We had sort-of test matches against Irish Universities, French Universities and Italy; we also played in Sicily where we won. We were young, we were a universities side with all that implied. We had fun, we played hard, played to win but tried to do so with style.

In the level of organisation and player enjoyment it was very different from an All Black tour. When we were travelling from Cork to Dublin one of our forwards didn't turn up for the bus. He'd gone back to a flat after a party and overslept. This would have appalled any serious tour management. He would have been stood down for several games. He arrived in Dublin by train some hours later but to miss the bus was a great crime for a New Zealand touring side. The player had a chat with the coach and all was forgotten..

The New Zealand Universities tour was my first tour as captain. When we were on the field – training or playing – I was firm in my desire that people fronted up. The All Blacks have a thing called "tour balance". That is, for players on tour to have the ability to adjust to hotels, to travel, to drink and go out with girls – but let none of that interfere with their ability to train and play well.

I was also determined we'd win all our matches. That's the New Zealand thing – even at the height of the amateur tradition it is vital to win. We had to win, I felt at the time, there was nothing else to do.

But as it turned out, there was. The game we played against Cork and Galway Universities – probably the worst team we played – was a draw. That rocked us. The only consolation was that we did better than the last All Blacks who'd come through this way. The 1978 All Blacks had lost to the province of Munster (the newspaper clippings still adorned the walls of every pub we went into). Of that day, Bryan

Williams memorably said, "We lost twelve-nil and we were lucky to get nil."

Cork scored a runaway try, aquaplaning over the surface of the bog where the cornerflags seemed to float on buoys. The field was called the Mardyke, but the dyke obviously had a hole in it. Luckily, it turned out to be the only game we didn't win.

The Irish are great competitors. They are very similar to the Scots except they are less organised and significantly madder. They don't have a style as much as a capacity to swarm. They play at a hundred miles an hour and the match resembles a thirteenth century tribal battle. Though it's a berserker experience, you wouldn't describe them as dirty players – though they can do damage, they aren't spiteful.

The Irish also play hurling and Gaelic football as well as union. Gaelic football is one of those games that seem to have no rules to speak of and is only played by the Irish. Hurling is unusual because alone among contact sports, the players are armed (and many players have lost fingers as a result). Maybe these games, so truly expressive of the Irish temperament, have influenced the union game because they have relatively little skill in handling the ball (with some glorious exceptions like Michael Gibson, Tony O'Reilly and Tom Kiernan). They have tigerish rather than skilful forwards (again with some notable exceptions – Fergus Slattery and Willie-John McBride) but the standard is generally not high. A reserve for Auckland goes to Ireland and within three months he's playing for the national team. Both Scotland and Ireland are the antithesis of England – each plays to their potential, and beyond. England promises but so often doesn't deliver.

It was a great tour and some great players emerged – Sean Fitzpatrick, Mike Brewer, Emosi Koloto, Mata'afa Keenan. Others who didn't make it on to the international stage were top provincial players – Tim Burcher, John Collinson, Tony Lewis, Mark Cameron. Through it all, Mike Cormack and Alan McRae handled us just right.

In France, because we were a university team at a formal dinner, we had a food fight in front of the dignitaries. A cake was passed around with firecrackers on it. A table was turned over and used for a barricade behind which we could throw more French food at each other.

It may interest urban intellectuals in this country (one of whom wrote disparagingly of the All Blacks in a French newspaper) that there is an admiration for New Zealand rugby and for our rugby players across a wide range of French society. The French call rugby players “les rugbymen”. They mean it like it’s a good thing. Philosophers, gastronomes, artists they may be, but as a culture they also respond to the camaraderie of a hard, physical tradition which is equally boisterous off the field (i.e. food fights – which may be why French cuisine is, in addition to all its other qualities, aerodynamic). And the further south you go, the tougher the play, the more approving the people are of “rugbymen”.

It’s a bit the same in New Zealand.

It was, despite the onus of winning, a light-hearted tour.

Into the A Team

Back in Auckland, John Hart named me in his representative squad. This was another breakpoint in my career. Steve McDowell and myself were the two newcomers from out of town. We played our first game for Auckland on the same day. There it was – a place in the great team. If I couldn't fulfil my potential in this team, I couldn't anywhere.

My first match in the team was against the Barbarians on Eden Park. I had my first lesson during that game; the ball fell loose, I kicked it forward and chased it. One of the loose forwards did not attempt to conceal his frustration. "Don't kick it away." he said, "Get it. Grab it. We want the ball."

There in a nutshell was the difference between Auckland and Otago. One theory said, "Kick for the corners, box them in, let them have the ball and wait for them to make a mistake." Auckland believed they could do better with the ball than anyone else. This was the new world of positive rugby. It was a world of technically superior players who were striving for a perfection that other teams didn't realise existed. Their performance with the ball was exhilarating. On one level the play was efficient and error-free, but it was also explosive, dynamic, creative. They also made a nonsense of relying on the other team making mistakes: Auckland didn't make mistakes.

At one hour and twenty minutes the training was much shorter than I'd been used to. But in that concentrated period there was total discipline. You were expected to be there warmed up, practising skills that were relevant to your position a quarter of an hour before practice officially started. That sounds like commonsense but many is the team I've known where the props spend their warm-ups practising dropped goals, and the halfback is throwing to a lineout.

The other difference was that Hart talked all the time. I was used to the old school that prized the monosyllable. John Hart kept up a constant real-time commentary on the action. Telling people what they should be doing while they should be doing it, he'd guide and mould moves as they were happening. Add to this the premise that you were supposed to be doing these moves perfectly and you get an idea of the immediacy of training and the concentration it demanded.

Before my second game for Auckland (against Sydney, in Sydney) Andy Haden twisted his knee, an injury that was to put him out of play for a few weeks. Something very unexpected happened then, something daunting. John Hart asked me to captain the team. I had gone from reserve in a poor team to captain of a very good team. This took some time to get my head around.

My initial feeling was that I hadn't earned it. They were a great team full of great players and they didn't even know me. I didn't know why Hart had asked me to do this. I presumed there would be a whole line of potential captains waiting to take over the Auckland reins. In fact, good leaders are uncommon, and there were few other obvious candidates.

In one sense it didn't matter much who captained a team as good as this. In another sense the position I played in helped – halfbacks, riding on the ball-joint between scrum and backline, are best placed to guide the on-field action.

But then I got a piece of advice from a man who had (how can I put it?) a wide experience of the world from many different perspectives. Lindsay Harris said to me: "You don't have to be obviously in charge of this team. They know what to do. As captain you can keep their focus, say the right things to keep the concentration up but you don't have to try too hard."

Actually, there's no easier team to lead than a really good one. They've already got ability, cohesion and discipline. The most important thing is not to get in the way.

It is important to be good at your own position. Authority comes from the ability to be respected as a top player. Above all, the team wants to win; the players which most help it do that gain respect and, thereby, authority.

There's always a need to set standards – setting the example in punctuality and dress and so forth. More importantly, the captain needs to stand above the fray a bit; to help individuals but let them know how crucial to the team they are. He has to make sure that players understand that they must draw out their individual ability but ultimately submerge themselves in the group. He has to build other leaders; a leadership which is dispersed so that each player leads their sub-group – front row, the tight five, the midfield, the back three are all led from within and support each other.

On the field, the captain chooses the moments to influence the pace and rhythm of the play. He decides when to drive for a time in one direction, then slow the pace for a while; he calculates what risk/reward balance to play to. Shall we play a tight, controlled game for a while because the opposition are getting anxious and are about to crack? Or shall we pick up the pace because the opposition are running out of mental energy, they want a break to gather their wits. And because we're very tired, the opposition must be close to exhaustion and now is the time to apply the real pressure.

It's easy to talk about it but you only learn by doing it. You can read and agree with it, but there's a physical and emotional reaction between the people concerned that requires experience. Sometimes I look back and wonder what I would have done differently? I would have liked to be more prepared, more meticulous, more methodical. My instincts were to be more off-the-cuff, more spontaneous. I would have been more of a professional and less an enthusiastic amateur, less spontaneous and more distant. I probably would be trying, like Stu Wilson, to be a different person.

But finally, you've got to be true to yourself. You can't say, "How should I act to be a leader?" There's no answer to that question. You must be yourself in a leadership role.

They were a wonderful team with the generosity of spirit that comes from excellence. The players were totally self-motivated. And such individuals can be an inspiration to play with. For instance, when I first moved to Auckland I had problems kicking into the box – both in direction and length. Kirwan on the right wing would suffer from that. If the kick was too long – as it frequently was – Kirwan would have run down the pitch for nothing. The fullback would have cleared the ball with time to spare. But every time, JK faithfully chased the ball as hard as he could because it was his duty to do so. That I'd made a mistake didn't, in the spirit of that team, absolve him of the necessity of chasing the kick. In some way he was doing it for me – to try and turn the bad kick into a good one; but also he was doing it for himself, his own pride, his own compulsion to do the best he possibly could. And he'd jog back every time with a resigned look on his face and some cute remark for me, but never any hint of exasperation or resentment.

So, in this new arena was a new sense of team work, a new sense of individual excellence that I'd never experienced before.

It is true that the ability to win matches generates a group psychology and that can help sustain you when the individual psychology becomes brittle. When you worry about losing, when confidence fails, the group sustains you, the tradition comforts and inspires you.

But in great teams this sustenance wasn't necessary, the tradition becomes irrelevant. The great players in the great teams are living in the present and the future – not the past. They have their eyes firmly fixed on their vision of rugby success. And they are living in every present moment as they seek to play the best rugby they possibly can. The two great teams I played with weren't drawing on tradition, they were creating it.

Actually, it came to the point where the old guard and their interpretation of tradition became something that held the team back. Systems, methods and programmes had to give way to inspiration, risk and fun. More penalties had to be tapped and run with, more attacks started from inside our own twenty-two. Forwards were looking for passes to give and take – they weren't just thinking about when to hit a ruck.

We never felt we played wildly; our play was based on a secure and well-founded confidence that we would score. This fortune-favours-the-brave attitude became cumulatively more effective. It produced ever-increasing depths of reserves. If you play with that relaxed, confident approach you make fewer mistakes – and there is nothing more intimidating than a relaxed opponent. Other teams have looked at All Black and Auckland teams and seen that we knew we would win. That was a matter of knowledge, not belief. If you can secure psychological dominance before the game starts you have won the most important part of the game. It's better than clean lineout ball.

For instance, England came to play a test series in 1985 and Auckland felt entirely confident about beating them. A perfectly good international team would be well-beaten by our provincial side – and we all knew it. We all knew what the result would be, if not the score (24-6, in the event). It was Andy Haden's first match since he'd twisted his knee in Sydney, and he played a blinder. I played myself into my first test match. Dave Loveridge was back after injury but I was the form player. I had served my apprenticeship (three All Black tours and reserve for the previous eight tests in a row). I was ready.

Into the A Team

I have to say that playing my first test for that All Black team was – incredibly – to move down a level. There were a lot of mistakes made, the match was slow and ponderous. In retrospect it is easy to say that many of the players were on their last lap. It is true to say of the All Blacks as of any other top team – it is often harder to get out than in. The team hadn't lost and our selectors have never been good at improving teams by degrees. They wait until losses pile up and then they sweep out a generation of players. This is a weakness and a strength. We won't get rid of an individual player unless his form is manifestly bad. There's often no strategy to gradually bring younger players through at the expense of established players – irrespective of their relative merits. That's why there is a strong cycle observable in All Black teams. It's a strength too because we don't mess with success.

In the tour to Australia the previous year you could see an All Black team nearing the end of its cycle. Later in 1985 we played the Australians again in a one-off test. It was the second of the one-point difference test series. It was a game where two teams who knew each other well nullified each other. Both were good enough defensively to close each other down. It was an old guard game where the team that made the least mistakes was going to win.

In the event we broke that pattern for a moment. We were awarded a penalty and instead of the expected place kick we tapped and ran. It was so unexpected – the only surprising moment in the match – that they let the mysteriously elusive Craig Green through to score.

We won, but there was no sense of mastery, no sense of playing our style and imposing it on the other team, no sense that the way we played was inherently superior and that we would, as a result, inevitably win. The sense of our own style of football was bubbling below the surface of the New Zealand team; that is the Canterbury and Auckland teams under Wyllie and Hart were continuing to apply pressure upwards. Auckland (and previously Canterbury) had started to play better rugby than the national team.

That trend was in evidence all through this period.

My first test, against England on Lancaster Park, was a sombre affair. We kicked six penalty goals, they scored two tries. The ground was wet and heavy, our play was wet and heavy with no rhythm or joie de vivre. We ground out a victory. I really felt quite disappointed that my first test match had been such a dull affair. At least we had won.

Birth of a Rebel Tour

Nineteen eighty-five was the year of the scheduled Springbok tour. It was in Wellington before the second test against England earlier that year that I first realised the implications of the opposition to the tour.

This was to be the first contact with South Africa since the extraordinary convulsions four years before when the Springboks toured New Zealand. The tour split the country in half like an apple. It had the status of a minor civil war. It was a traumatic dialogue between two generations, between two political sides and between the two races that largely account for our national identity. The aftershocks were still strong. There were many demonstrations – and the public hostility to rugby was intense among a large swathe of New Zealand. As a result, before that Wellington test we had to sit in the convent school opposite Athletic Park for fear we wouldn't get through on the bus.

Brian Lochore told the players that unless play improved there would be changes – irrespective of the result. This was a tacit recognition that the team was nearing its use-by date. And it had a powerful effect. The team exploded on to the field; within the first few minutes punches were thrown. Andy Dalton, normally the mildest-mannered player, swung at an English player (he missed and hit Steven Pokere instead). The tension that had developed translated into a passion to physically dominate the opposition, to drive them back harder, to knock them off the ball. It is always the case that cornered, desperate teams will resort to very hard, physical play. We saw it again playing the French a year later in Nantes. The French team were playing in desperation – they'd been pilloried by the press for the new style of play Fouroux was imposing and they'd been told if they didn't win they'd all be booted out. Sean Fitzpatrick was kicked badly in the head that day and Buck Shelford left the field with a ripped scrotum. The French did win that match as a result, and in the same way and, for the same reasons, the All Blacks beat England by 42-15 that day in Wellington. We had to.

It was a real All Black test performance, the last top match of a generation of players. The unrelenting intensity was overwhelming. It was windy in Wellington; we played into it in the first half. We kept the ball close to our awesome forwards, we ran close to them and fed it back into them whenever we could. John Kirwan scored his first test try that day and started his journey to the record number of test tries – a record he still holds.

When we changed ends and got the wind we became progressively more dominant. The disappointment of the previous week was erased in this performance of power, control and unbeatable determination.

It's curious how a team that is essentially past it can still produce a great performance. The ability is still there, it just can't be accessed as often. The psychological intensity has gone. It needs the fear of failure burning bright to create the need. It was nearly the last time the old guard played successfully together, and the last time they did so in New Zealand. It was a fitting finale.

It was the rebel tour that put an end to that generation, the Cavaliers going to South Africa. It happened in three stages – first, the official tour was cancelled, then there was an aborted rebel tour, then the rebel tour itself.

We were scheduled to go later that year. I remember one afternoon listening to lawyer Kit Toogood telling us that there had been a legal challenge to the scheduled tour. It had been brought on the basis that the union was not acting in accordance with its mandate. The constitution contains a clause that says the union must always act in the best interests of New Zealand rugby. The objectors claimed the tour was not in the best interests of New Zealand rugby; therefore, the union was acting illegally.

It seemed a fairly technical objection to us players at the time, and that it would be unlikely to succeed. How could the constitution of the New Zealand Rugby Union be used to stop the All Blacks playing the biggest series in a decade?

But the objectors were well-informed and well-briefed and, as it turned out, they were right as well.

There was a huge amount of publicity surrounding the issue. As a player I didn't really know what to think. There were entreaties from all sides. Many rugby supporters saw it as a simple case of sport and politics. Rugby was rugby, and political systems existed in a different moral universe. The anti-tour people argued that everyone had an obligation to do whatever they could to show opposition to the South African system. Rugby tours were a succour to the South African government; they reduced the momentum of progress to a more democratic system. I received many letters and the benefit of a wide spread of opinion. The most moving plea came from an African UN defence force officer who wrote directly to all the players selected to go on the tour.

I didn't agree with the politics of South Africa but thought that sports teams had little effect on governments or government policy. (I've changed my mind on that – an empty gesture is still a gesture.) Nor did I know then about providing succour to the enemy, but I didn't think touring or not touring would make any difference to the political system of South Africa.

As it transpired, the court case was successful. The injunction succeeded. The judge decided that for a New Zealand side to tour South Africa would not be in the best interests of New Zealand rugby. The tour was off and for many players – including me – it was a huge disappointment. The South African tour is the height of the game. If you're an actor you want to win an Oscar, if you're a novelist you want to win the Booker Prize, if you're in rugby you want to go and play against the rugged, brutal, humourless South Africans and hang them out to dry.

We'd never won in South Africa and while in retrospect that All Black team was unlikely to beat the Springboks (who were not particularly good at the time) the experience would have been incalculable.

The players were all called to Wellington to be briefed on the situation. The New Zealand Rugby Union was not able to send a touring team to South Africa because it was illegal. However, some of the senior players – including Dalton and Haden – explained the real purpose behind the call to Wellington: individual players could go any time they wanted without legal impediment. Just as long as we weren't the representatives of the New Zealand Rugby Union. That started a long debate about whether we should form an unofficial team and go as a so-called rebel tour. We were told some members of the New Zealand Council (who were breaking the law by doing so) supported the idea. There was a deafening silence from others.

There was also a lot of discussion about the best interests of players – would it be good for us personally if we were to go? And there was a pragmatic discussion about whether the public would support us. What would be the effect of the memory of those riot scenes in 1981? Also, for the first time, money was mentioned. Andy Haden said there were interests in South Africa who were supporting the tour and if we wanted to go we would be paid. A feeling gathered in the room that we would go.

We went back to our provinces; we were under the impression it was all on, that there would be a rebel tour, that we would go cloak-and-dagger to South Africa, and that travel agents would act as intermediaries to book our flights. Shortly afterwards I was rung up and I confirmed that I would go if it came to it. We got to the point of assembling in a house on the North Shore, but by then a different mood prevailed. You could feel the wind had gone out of our sails. A confused discussion and lack of conviction dissipated the sense of purpose.

It was partly the fact that the original plaintiffs had got wind of the plan and they had gone back to the court to clarify the original injunction. Now it was clear that any agents of the New Zealand Rugby Union – that is, the captain or representatives on players' committees – could be deemed agents of the New Zealand Rugby Union, and so senior players like Haden and Dalton, suddenly in the firing line, started to wonder whether it was the right thing to do.

We left the house under the impression it was all off. In fact, that wasn't true either. The idea for the tour marinated away. The real action was yet to happen. It wouldn't come to a head for another year.

My feelings about South Africa were mixed. I'd been there two years previously in the university summer holiday hitchhiking through the country (not something you'd do now) with a New Zealand emblem on my pack to take advantage of the "special relationship" that existed between our two countries.

I saw how a people's cultural essence is reflected in their architecture. There's the Dutch architecture transposed which isn't particularly interesting because it's not theirs. The modern public buildings of Afrikaner South Africa express the reality: they're huge slabs of stone, concrete and granite – parliament, libraries, major office buildings – they're bunker-like, fortified. It's not for practical reasons but they make a statement about stability and permanence.

I met up with two Indian Muslims beside a pool and they took me for a drink they probably shouldn't have had. We couldn't go to the nearer bar because it was for whites only. They took me discreetly into a coloureds-only bar where I sat at the back of the hose-down area.

Petty apartheid was everywhere – seats in public parks that only whites could sit on, public toilets that only blacks could go in.

Another time I was the only person sitting in my whites-only carriage. The black carriage was full, but more fun, so I went to join them. The conductor moved me on: "It's not for you in here, boy. It's for blacks. Get out."

You were confronted with the magnitude of the problem. The enormous majority had so little education, so few prospects, I couldn't see how one-man-one-vote would work with P.W. Botha in charge. He was the uncompromising dictator, firmly entrenched in the Boer myth. It's an enormous tribute to Nelson Mandela that they made the transition so peacefully, without economic meltdown like there was in Zimbabwe (where, I can remember, ten years after independence, in the central post office there wasn't a single phone that worked).

The world and its dangers were remote from us in New Zealand in those days. There may have been forty murders in the whole of New Zealand the year I went to South Africa. That happened on one otherwise uneventful day in South Africa.

Friends I made in Zimbabwe told tales of terror. They were people who had lived through the reality of other people running over their paddocks, firing assault rifles and machine guns into the house. So often the transition to democracy is heralded by civil war. These were dangers that we in New Zealand were largely unaware of.

I was a medical student. I spent a night at the Accident and Emergency Department of the great Cape Town hospital Groote Schuur. The whites went one side and the blacks the other. There was usually no-one in the white side, the black side was full. Many of them were badly hurt.

In Auckland Public Hospital, where some of New Zealand's most extreme cases of violence end up, I saw one stab wound in three months. In one night in South Africa there were six stab victims. Johannesburg is now the acknowledged murder capital of the world.

One Sunday in the Orange Free State I got a ride with a

characteristic bigot, and couldn't stand it after a while and told him to let me off. He saw the blacks as incapable – "bloody animals" as he put it. He was a chilling Afrikaner who had a supervisory role over these "bloody animals" – but this was the only country in the world where he'd be anything other than unskilled labour, working on the roads.

After a couple of hours in the Sunday sun, with a towel over my head and no cars passing, I nearly regretted my decision, but got picked up by a Dutch matron. She said she'd only picked me up because she thought I was a soldier and that I hadn't any business hitchhiking on a Sunday. She was almost as bad as the buffoon I'd just escaped from.

But then again, there were those white South Africans who spent time and money educating, training and employing black South Africans. They knew they couldn't solve the problem themselves but they were doing what they could. Most of them lived in Cape Town or Natal.

A family friend, Lionel Wilson, Springbok fullback of the 1960s, was a good friend of Morne du Plessis. I went for an early evening run with the great man. I had cursed him as I admired his ability as he led the 1976 Springboks to victory over the All Blacks. He turned out to be a very liberal Afrikaner who was offside with his white tribe. He was personally endorsing reform and continued to do so.

How these economic and racial forces could ever be reconciled was beyond me. It took individuals of the stature of de Klerk and, finally, Mandela to bring about the transformation of that country.

As a matter of interest, the mana of Mandela in New Zealand is probably the highest of any visiting dignitary. When the Duke of Edinburgh was guest of honour at a business function in Auckland his entrance was hardly noticed by the gathering. When Mandela appeared in the doorway at his luncheon the conversation in the room immediately dimmed and then stilled. As he stepped into the room the two hundred business people, in silence, rose to their feet. They didn't even applaud.

In the 1981 tour I played the curtain-raiser (on another field) to the Springboks-Otago match. The Otago match against the Springboks was the only one I watched live. Michael Laws had started SCRUM, a small group of university students supporting the tour, in colourful opposition to most university opinion.

At the time, I was agnostic on the moral question of whether the Springboks should be touring New Zealand or not – but in practical terms I did think that nothing was worth this violence. There was a body of opinion that held that Prime Minister Robert Muldoon was using the Springboks for his own political purposes, to divide the country, to divert attention from his economic management, and to mobilise his supporters. There are those that say Mrs Thatcher used the Falklands in the same way.

I didn't have an answer about how to remake South Africa. Apartheid was a horrible human construct – but in a *This Is Africa* way, universal franchise might create more violence (it had in Zimbabwe between the Shona and Matabele tribes). Beyond that, I hadn't thought it through. Rugby was here and now – I watched it on television.

For New Zealanders the tour was probably the most powerful national experience since the Second World War, more comprehensive even than the Waterfront Strike thirty years before.

Families divided over it all over the country. At first, professional activists only were involved. But as the conflict escalated there were policemen with long batons beating up civilians and women. Rugby crowds were baying for the blood of protesters: "Kill them!" the fans called out. For their part, the protesters typecast all rugby supporters as ignorant, selfish racists. It was deeply damaging to rugby's good name and popular support for our national game.

Some players, notably Graham Mourie and Bruce Robertson, disconnected themselves from the tour; most thought that the politics of it were nothing to do with them.

Rob's Mob, as Muldoon's supporters were called, came out in force. The events developed into a struggle well beyond the rights and wrongs of rugby. Talented Maori activism had turned it into profound dialogue for all New Zealanders: "Don't feel comfortable about protesting against South African injustice," they said, "look next door and you'll see Maori suffering too."

All this, the 1981 tour, my South African experiences, a cancelled tour and an aborted rebel tour were all stewing away. Emerging, too, was a more balanced approach to the question of team and individual. Coming into the team I had submerged myself in doctrine of team solidarity, the garrison feeling of comrades in arms. I had enormous respect for the All Black tradition, and the belief that the team always comes first was unquestioningly accepted.

Now that view was beginning to change. There were clearly individuals in this All Black team who were running a different agenda from the one demanded by All Black mana. I think I knew even then that South Africa was going to be the testing ground. I had no idea how deep a divide it would drive between me and some of my team mates.

That was also the year Auckland challenged Canterbury again for the Ranfurly Shield. They were looking to establish a record of tenure for the shield and we were looking to stop them. They'd held it for three years, they were hungry for victory, there had been a huge build-up in the area, they were playing at home, they'd smashed Auckland two years before, Auckland had thrashed them the previous year. The whole country was waiting for the decider.

It is difficult for visiting teams to win at Lancaster Park. When the West Indies play cricket in Christchurch the local supporters have been known to throw bunches of bananas at them. More than spectators, they're participants. It's an atmosphere that you don't find anywhere else – and perhaps it's just as well. They're more like French villagers than anything else, and you breathe a little easier after the plane wheels actually leave the tarmac of Christchurch airport.

Towards the end of the game, when Canterbury had scored in the corner, I was pulling myself out of the turf when a spectator burst out of the crowd. He grabbed me by the front of the jersey and shouted into my face: "We're going to beat you! We're going to beat you!" I feel that even in his exalted state he wouldn't have chanced his luck grabbing Andy Haden or Steve McDowell by the shirt and shouting into their faces.

It was the biggest crowd I'd ever played against in New Zealand – people were crammed into the stands, they were hanging from trees. They were very vocal.

But we knew we were good enough to win, and so it proved. We rolled them back to 24-0 by halftime. We played well, we rode our luck, and we took advantage of our opportunities. Just after halftime we scored again. We were going to romp away.

And then it turned, as matches can turn – on a mood, on a feeling, on a lapse in concentration. Only for a moment we stopped playing to get further ahead. We stopped constructing the belief that the score was 0-0 again each time we scored (that was the way you kept the threat alive, that's how you keep going forward).

We took our foot off their throat for a few moments and they came back like lions. It was the most impressive comeback I'd ever been involved in. If you lose control against a team as good as that Canterbury team it's very hard to get it back.

They scored, and they scored. Then they ran it down the wing and chipped it over our heads into the corner. There was no way the kick could succeed, three of us were there, the danger was well in hand – and the ball with its schizo personality kicked up and bounced back over our heads into the hands of the Canterbury man chasing. He touched it down for the try that took them to our gates.

They had caught up to within five points of us. The momentum was with them. They had the power, they piled on the pressure; in the dying moment of the game they came down the field, put up a kick into space; it bounced once, over the line, high into the scoring area; it floated up there; Canterbury were swarming, Craig Green was leaping – and John Kirwan appeared out of nowhere to tip the ball one-handedly over the deadball line. It was out. The whistle went. The game was over. We were shattered. We had won but we were wrecked.

A week later we played Otago. We were the shield winners, Otago was an indifferent team – and we lost. This was a personal blow for me. When you go back to a team that has rejected you, you want to win handsomely; you want to run around the field at will throwing one-handed passes and scoring freely. But we were beaten, no two ways about it. This was a particularly galling lesson – at the height of victory you are at your most vulnerable.

The defeat was a wake-up call for our next few games. We thrashed Waikato, but only just scraped home against Counties. For a couple of games after our shield victory we were at our most vulnerable. At the height of our victory we were at our least competitive. Physically we were victors, mentally we were pudding.

Going to play the fascist state of South Africa would have brought the New Zealand Rugby Union into disrepute, so as a consolation prize we were sent to play the fascist state of Argentina. We didn't incur the disapproval of protesters, perhaps because the persecution over there wasn't racially apportioned, but was indiscriminate. Everyone was in the gun in Argentina.

The nightlife in Latin America is interesting and varied. I

remember finishing an evening debating with the locals in a bar with Robbie Deans at 2am. This wasn't late; the country operates on Winston Peters' European hours – a siesta in the middle of the day, work in the morning and early evening, dinner around 10pm and night-clubbing until four. Anyway, it was early at our bar, but I remember the publican making a phone call when our discussion about whether it was "play your own ball" on the pool table or not had reached a certain point of intensity, and shortly afterwards policemen arrived who bundled us into a police car at gunpoint.

This was out of the ordinary run of things for All Black tourists. We were more usually asked where we'd like to visit, and who we'd like to meet and whether we'd like another drink. "They're not taking us back to the hotel," I remember thinking as we were driven through Buenos Aires with the sirens going. The car pulled up outside a hopeless looking building and we were marched through enormous wooden doors into a police station. The evening was becoming quite melodramatic. If you wanted to summarise the situation you would include the following: the Falklands War was only recently over and the death toll was still fresh in people's minds. As we remember, the country was a fascist state with the army still in charge. And then there were los disparadoes, those innocent civilians who disappeared into the back of death squad vehicles and were driven off into the night, never to be seen again.

It was in this context that we stood in front of a desk and watched a variety of South American policemen shouting at us in Spanish. Then we saw them all walk out of the room. Then the door opened and one paunchy character came back in to slam a truncheon pointlessly on a table, favour us with a meaningful look and leave. Then another came in and stared at us, laid his revolver on the table in a gesture full of film noir significance and also left. We didn't say anything. We looked at the gun. What were we supposed to do with it? Were we supposed to pick it up so they could shoot us for stealing police property? Were we expected to think they were coming in to use it on us whether they had an excuse or not?

I remember being told about Kit Fawcett being bawled out by the coach during training – in South Africa I think – and the nonchalance with which Kit walked away ("What's his problem?" his demeanour suggested) was magnificent in its way. He was dropped shortly afterwards for surfing the morning of a match, sunbathing and eating ice-cream while a reserve in the stands. While his attitude was not quite the thing for a match-fit All Black, it was a fine example for circumstances like these.

After we'd left the country, an Irish footballer, Willie Anderson (whom I got to know some years afterwards), stole a flag from an Argentinian building and for his display of high spirits was kept in prison for three months and threatened with execution – that would have taken some substance on his part, keeping his spirits up. Three months is a long time to suffer the threat of execution. We weren't having a heart-of-darkness experience – but it was a small step into the shadows. We were sustained by the fact there were two of us and we were only in the police station for three-quarters of an hour. Eventually one of the ridiculous officers came to the point with a banal question. He said, "Have you got any money?" Money? You want us to give you money? What creeps; had all this been about a five dollar bribe?

We gave him some of what we had (I was pleased with myself that I didn't give him everything I had), and walked out of the station. We considered carefully what we should sensibly do. Then we did the opposite. We went back to the bar for more bravado argument ("I'm on overs!") but caught a cab this time, before the owner could call the police again.

We had a glimpse of how life is organised in another country where history is still working itself out, and I felt grateful that most of the great convulsions are behind us in New Zealand.

As for the tests – we did well in the first one. It was some of the fastest rugby I'd ever played. We were all physically drained by the running, covering and the need to tackle. We won it, but didn't gain real control until late in the piece.

Then for the second, for the only time in my All Black career, Brian Lochore dropped me. And we drew it. This was Dave Loveridge and Wayne Smith's last test. The Argentine captain, Hugo Porta, scored all their points (three dropped goals and four penalty goals). He was, I think, the best first-five I ever saw. He is now an ambassador-at-large for his country; a most urbane, intelligent architect and potential president of Argentina. I'm sure he'll do something about the police pulling argumentative rugby players out of bars, if he hasn't already done so.

The Argentine social context of rugby is very interesting. It's more advanced down there than many South American countries. There is a strong, wealthy European element in the game. In the cities the scene is dominated by two or three sports-cum-social clubs. These clubs have tennis courts and swimming pools. It's an upper-class game (which is partly why they stay firmly in the second division). But though they lack crucial strengths and technical endowments they are marvellously entertaining opponents, and as tough as anything. It might be something to do with that gaucho strain (you see the same sort of thing in rural New Zealand).

On-field the backs play with a Latin flair and pace; they play with enthusiasm to be part of a spectacle. In the forwards they are extremely hard and tough with a reputation for being some of the best scrummagers in the world – not so big but very powerful.

Their traditional rivals (apart from England – whom everyone wants to thrash) are France, and there are invariably quite serious punch-ups during the French games.

Their attitude to professionalism has hobbled them internationally – they are (as only the wealthiest sport can be) fanatically amateur. Any player who played in Italy in the northern season (and was paid for it) was banned for ever from playing for Argentina. Professional rugby will be good for Argentina, but because it's not a mass game, and because children aren't started at six and seven years old, they'll never have the fundamental grasp of technique that we have in New Zealand.

This tour turned out to be the swansong for a lot of the old guard, though we didn't realise it for over a year. It was the last test for players like Mexted, Loveridge, Smith, Haden, Ashworth, Simpson, Deans, Fraser who would not play for an official All Black team again. The rebel tour of South Africa – the Cavaliers – that finally took place the following year saw them off. But it was in Argentina that Andy Haden canvassed opinion of the squad, going round the hotel rooms before the last test, again raising the potential of a tour, and again raising the prospect of money.

It became real when a South African banker made contact with us in New Zealand. I was called to a meeting in Andy Haden's house where a representative of the sponsoring bank came to solicit our expressions of interest. The squad of thirty who had been invited the year before were invited again. Colin Meads was to be the coach and Ian Kirkpatrick later signed on as manager. There was a document – a letter of intent they wanted us to sign. The banker was going to use the document to raise the money for booking grounds and organising the tour. It was made quite clear that this wasn't a legally binding document but an indication that players would be prepared to come.

There was also mention of the sum of $100,000 – a lot of money ten years ago (a lot of money now, come to that), about a quarter of a million dollars in inflation-adjusted terms.

The game was afoot. The rebel tour was on. Security was in place, plans were laid to get us out of the country unobserved and unobstructed. We were all asked more formally in March to give a firm commitment to go.

That was the point at which I withdrew. I didn't give that commitment. In March, I said I wouldn't go, and I stuck to this position – which became a difficult one to sustain, even though there was no overt pressure on me to sign up. The senior players never rang to say I'd be letting them down; the pressure was all in my own head – that these, my intimate colleagues, whatever I felt about their style of play or attitude to the game, were some of my most powerful human connections. And they were all (except John Kirwan) going.

Why did I refuse to go? First: it wasn't an All Black tour, it was a rebel tour. The fact that there was a large sum of money involved was the best and worst thing about it. Who doesn't want money? For yourself, your family, a cash injection like this is always useful. But there is a downside to money as well. It sticks like tar. You could proclaim that you were in South Africa to play rugby – but if you'd taken the money no-one would believe you.

I didn't worry about the fact that all thirty players might be banned for life (how does the union ban all its best players?) But if only there weren't money involved I would have found it easier to go.

So finally it was a moral decision. I had always been uncomfortable about these contacts with South Africa. I was coming to think that maybe sports boycotts (like trade boycotts) did hurt the regime, and that going there did give comfort to apartheid. I remembered jogging with Morne du Plessis and how he stood apart from his tribe because he felt it was right. I had the role models of Ken Gray, Graham Mourie, Bruce Robertson and (in a most unobtrusive way) John Drake.

So, putting that in with the financial inducement, and putting both of those in with the fact it wasn't an All Black tour, made me decline.

But I swayed – first one way then the other. On the first occasion I became further committed to staying behind. We were coming back on the plane from the National Sevens in Palmerston North and John

Hart – normally so involved with the team, so concerned about winning the matches – seemed distant and indifferent. He made an oblique comment about the nature of loyalty, and I said, "What do you mean by that?"

"What you guys are doing," he said.

"Like what?" I said.

"Going to South Africa," he said.

"I'm one of the few people who's not going." To him it was a revelation. He knew nothing about the tour arrangements, about who was and wasn't going, he had been excluded from everything (in a society as small and close as ours that was quite an achievement). It surprised me too. He was very close to Andy Haden, his Auckland captain. I presumed Andy would have confided in him.

It was that secrecy which cut him to the quick. He had developed and nurtured a close relationship with the team and their individual careers and he felt very let down by the exclusion. His view was that touring South Africa was not in the best interests of New Zealand rugby or the players involved and Haden, his captain, organising the very thing he most disapproved of was hard for him.

John Hart was an important mentor of mine. His creative, cerebral coaching style had been an inspiration to me. He had trusted me as a leader of his beloved Auckland team after just two matches. I was his man. He supported my decision not to go a) because he thought nobody should go, and b) on a less exalted level because he needed someone at home to keep the team together. His support, which was the only support I'd had, encouraged me to stay.

But then, in the second event, I was swayed the other way. It was the team thing. I was reeled in by my close bonds with my fellow players, my colleagues, my mates. It's a solitary position out there on your own, and I came to feel it.

We played the New Zealand Barbarians in Auckland, and after the game (which was exhilarating, as only Barbarians games can be) we went out on the town. Everyone knew I wasn't going on the tour and those who were close to me argued strongly that I should go. They didn't bully me or even apply heavy pressure; I wasn't blackmailed or coerced. But their thrust was that if we were to go then we should all go. It was an offer for me to come back into the fold, into the solidarity of the team. They believed strongly that the public would support the tour, as they had the year before, and if we won we'd come home heroes.

That night I slept on the floor of a Regent Hotel room.

By Monday something had changed in me. I was back inside the team. In spite of the fact that I didn't really think it was a great team, and that I didn't really appreciate the rugby they played, and in spite of my reservations about the motives of some of the players, I decided to go along with the team decision. I put the commitment to the team before my decision to follow my own instincts.

I rang the travel agent who was organising visas and told him I'd changed my mind. I wanted to go. He said, "I think I can get the visa – they're rushing them through for you in Sydney." New Zealand had sent the South African Consulate General packing years before.)

All that week I was going. And as soon as I'd made the decision to go I started feeling sick about it.

I felt so bad that in retrospect I knew it must be the wrong decision. I didn't speak to anyone about it. During all this period I was working at Carrington Psychiatric Hospital among some of the most unpleasant – and, frankly, disturbed – people I've ever had to deal with (I mean the nurses and social workers, not the patients).

I'd never worked in a more hostile environment. The support staff would ignore me or make hostile remarks about rugby, rugby players, rugby politics. The doctor in charge asked to see me once to enquire whether the atmosphere among the staff was affecting me. People I actually loathed were treating me with real bigotry and my colleagues and friends with whom I had a deep bond were depending on me. If I did what I thought was right I would be doing what people for whom I felt deep distaste wanted me to do. At the same time I would be selling out people I felt something akin to love for.

Eventually I asked my family. It was a measure of how much I had created my own little world of moral dilemma and self-absorption that I took so long to speak to my family. I had convinced myself that unless I made the decision myself, alone, it would not be fully my decision. I kept telling myself no-one could make the decision for me. This was right, but to translate this into refusing to ask for advice was taking the old boarding school self-reliance altogether too far.

My mother deferred. "Whatever you think is best," she said.

My father took a different view. "It's a mistake," he said. "I think it's a bad idea and the public will never forgive you."

My brother rehearsed the arguments for and the arguments against (he's a lawyer). On balance, he advised me not to go.

The passport had come back with the big South African visa. I walked around the lovely grounds of Carrington.

You never know – I never knew – about that decision, what tipped me over the edge. The smaller decisions in life you can work out with a pencil and paper and two columns. But big decisions emerge in a more mysterious way.

I remember looking up at the trees and seeing the light play through the deciduous leaves, and in that moment of stillness the decision emerged that I shouldn't go, that I wouldn't go, and that this was the final decision.

I rushed home from work and rang the travel agent to tell him I had changed my mind. His only comeback was to ask who I thought should go in my place. I suggested a name, said goodbye and hung up. And that was the last conversation I had with any of them. I was never rung, and while I didn't immediately feel excluded or ostracised, I had left the fold, the team, the deep solidarity, and gone out on my own. That made me vulnerable to what came later. There is a close sense of contact, of the group, of collective endeavour in New Zealand. It's deeper in New Zealand than in larger societies.

I resigned my position as House Surgeon at Carrington the next week. I didn't give any reason.

I still believe that if the tour had been a success (which it wasn't), if they'd been televised (which they weren't), if they'd been supported (and that didn't happen either) they wouldn't have felt the animosity towards me they later developed. It was a defensive reaction because they'd made a wrong decision and they projected that anger and frustration onto me.

In the first instance there was no hostility, no anger, no sense of betrayal. Later on, the hostility was real, and so was the sense of betrayal and anger. It was failure that aroused these emotions, failure to win, failure to find approval in New Zealand, failure to be televised for their covert supporters.

Until the tour actually took place and spawned the string of failures, we were amiable, even comfortable. For instance, we all went off to the Hong Kong Sevens. It was very relaxed by and large. We played great sevens, we had finally made it as a sevens nation. We smashed Fiji in the semi-final and went on to win the Hong Kong Sevens for New Zealand for the first time.

Then we went to Lancaster Park and the Canterbury match in the South Pacific Championship. This was the last match before the Cavaliers took off.

Canterbury is not the team to be playing when half the team is thinking about something else. I didn't know anything about the players' leaving arrangements but I guessed when the final whistle blew on our 9-16 defeat, and the Auckland All Blacks literally sprinted off the field, changed into jeans and T-shirts in front of the rest of us and, with scarcely a word, loaded themselves into a waiting minibus. They looked as though they were making an escape, as though they were doing something disreputable, a dine-and-dash, perhaps.

Then again, they wouldn't want to have done it any other way. I was spat at by demonstrators at Auckland airport on my return, and as I walked into the terminal a man came alongside abusing me and abusing rugby in general until my companion, Peter Fatialofa, quietly advised him to go away. He went away.

Anyway, those of us who weren't going to South Africa went to the post-match function in Christchurch where Don Hayes said to me, "I never thought it would be two Auckland players who didn't go." (It was a reference to Auckland's appetite for money, I think.)

I felt – wrongly – that I'd let down my team mates, that I'd broken ranks with them. That's the power of a team, and their unanimous feelings. The rules of the schoolyard go on well into adult life. There are said to be nine degrees of separation in the world. In New Zealand it's more like two. Everybody knows someone who knows someone who knows the man who sells the pies at the Turangi service station. So the opinion of your close colleagues gets retailed out into society and can quickly acquire the force of public opinion. When you're the odd one out you feel more than uncomfortable. If you turn away from your close colleagues you feel disloyal – whether it's right or wrong to do so.

The forgotten people were the non-All Black team mates who weren't that thrilled about their colleagues running off to South Africa in the middle of the season.

The next day, the story broke in the media. John Kirwan had been playing in Italy and had gone on to play a centenary match in Britain – so I was the only All Black in the country who hadn't gone. I thought long and hard about saying anything to the media. It's one thing not to go, it's another to publicly defend not going, and, by implication, criticising those who have gone. Also, skilful journalists lead you into comment that can be misinterpreted, I knew that. But it also would have been perverse to remain totally silent. This was a public issue, a matter of legitimate public interest and concern.

I didn't want to proselytise for the anti-apartheid movement; I wanted my decision not to go to be respected as a personal decision as I respected theirs. So I answered their questions frankly – but my fears were well-grounded. Some of my colleagues came to see me as a Machiavelli who had conceived a plan to take advantage of their absence to promote my own career.

The interviews enhanced the animosity of the players and their families. One wrote to me saying she thought I'd let the team down. "I thought you were a friend of my son," she said. I replied that friends should be able to differ. She wrote back accepting my position, which was gracious of her. And, indeed, I subsequently had the support of her son, eight years later. He said he should never have gone, he wished he'd never done it and that it was a mistake.

The Cavaliers assumed that at least half New Zealand would support them; as in the 1981 tour. They assumed New Zealand wanted to see New Zealanders playing the Springboks. And, as the polls had said the country was still split fairly evenly over the aborted tour the previous year, they assumed they'd have at least a million New Zealanders on their side. But research is an unreliable guide to what people are really thinking and feeling, and in the end it didn't turn out like the statistics suggested.

The notion that they would be soldiers fighting for New Zealand's honour on foreign soil never came to anything. My father was right. It was a pack reaction from New Zealand; there weren't so many shades of opinion in those days. The public all went the same way. Very few people spoke out for the Cavaliers, even rugby stalwarts. They didn't see the team as honourable. How could they be fighting for our honour when they had their back pockets stuffed with cash?

And of course, to add injury to insult, they lost. Many said the Welsh referee at the end of his career had been susceptible to a cash offer from the South Africans – but that struck me as our Kiwi pots calling that Welsh kettle black.

The final humiliation was the television stations deciding not to broadcast the matches. Even in defeat they found no glory.

Perhaps the memory of the angst and violence from the previous tour had an effect. For all that grief and moral self-examination to be reduced to a mercenary exchange – it hit the wrong note.

They ended up, I think, with about $60,000 each, though it was possible the organisers got more. I don't know this for a fact. No-one ever spoke to me about it; I never saw a contract. But these things have a way of emerging. The strong rumour was that the money was not to be picked up until the last player being paid had retired – round about now, that would be. This was to protect the younger players who had a whole career in front of them.

There were enquiries; the government made a statement that they knew what was happening and David Lange implied he knew money was involved; he was outraged, and as a result he snubbed rugby for two years, holding no official functions at all for the World Cup. He later formed the view that rugby union was some exclusive, old boy's club and that the true, egalitarian game for New Zealand was league.

Jim Bolger was able, as Leader of the Opposition, to step into the vacuum Lange had left, and as a very genuine supporter became prominent in union circles. He was given his reward during the final of the World Cup when Mike Moore, as government representative, came up the stairs with the French Minister to the officials' box to claim his pride of place – a seat in which Jim Bolger happened to be sitting. The administrators had only a moment to decide which politician to back – the representative of the government that had steadfastly ignored them until it looked like they'd win the competition or the Leader of the Opposition who'd stood by them loyally? In the event, the union sent the French Minister to the very end of the row of seats and then sent Mike Moore way off to the other end (he had to go down steps and up steps to make the journey).

Eventually there was a New Zealand Rugby Union enquiry. But enquiries of this nature find what they want to find, and the players gave the board to believe that they were paid the IRB allowance of $36 a day. And yes, there may have been a specially bountiful team fund because the South Africans were so pleased to see them. (This fund is built up largely from the free tickets the team is given – you sell them – and from other donations.) Team funds can build to quite large sums. In Australia in 1984 I had been the banker and was carrying a bag around with $12,000 in it. The sum was not inconsiderable, but rather short, I think, of the 1986 team fund.

The union's finding was thought to be a masterful compromise, punishing without assigning blame. They said they had not found anything particularly wrong but because the men had deserted the All Blacks in the middle of the year they were to be banned for two tests.

Birth of the Baby Blacks

So that's how the Baby Blacks came into being. Ten new players were capped to represent New Zealand against a powerful international touring side.

The French were coming on from their tour of Australia for a single test. They had flair, a large forward pack, and the experience and strength of international veterans of the world rugby scene. The sum of our experience was a handful of players who had played test rugby. As for the captaincy, it was really between John Kirwan and me, and only I had had that sort of experience. So it fell to me.

I was very proud. That extraordinary thing had happened again. I'd captained Auckland after three matches and the All Blacks after four tests. Even though the conventional wisdom was that the best we could do was to be heroic losers, it was the chance of a lifetime. We would lose, but I had heroic examples to live up to: "Tiber Father Tiber, take my soul today."

It didn't help relations with some of the Cavaliers that the television did a documentary on the Who Is David Kirk? line. Because my instinct is to be open about things I let them come into the changing rooms where they photographed and broadcast my rear end going into a shower (a Cavalier said his wife was disgusted). And I talked about what the All Black shirt meant to me. That must have grated on the old guard's nerves. They were five-year veterans who would never have perceived me as their captain. I wasn't of their type, their size or their generation.

Having said that, it's also worth noting that not all the Cavaliers felt this animosity. In fact, the Canterbury players who had toured sent the Baby Blacks a pre-match telegram (for which we were very grateful).

Anyway, as the match turned out we got pushed around in the forwards and we threw it around in the backs. Sean Fitzpatrick, playing his first test, probably still hasn't retreated quite so fast in an All Black scrum. Joe Stanley made some great tackles; Greg Cooper kicked an opportunist dropped goal from way out; Frano Botica got two. He also chipped ahead with nothing on, John Kirwan leapt up to reclaim the ball and fed it on to Brett Harvey who in-passed for Mike Brewer to score. We won 18-9. The crowd, who had turned up to see us lose valiantly, went wild.

This was the start of a new style coming into the national team. It turned out to be a largely Auckland style as the World Cup unfolded the next year, but the Baby Blacks were drawn from all over New Zealand. And it was very new. Prior to the game, I remember being asked on television what tactics we'd play. I said that because they had big forwards we'd have to keep the game fluid. The other commentator in the programme – Norm Wilson, a forthright individual and something of a character both on and off television – said words to the effect of, "I don't know about this 'fluidity' stuff." And then in that ponderous, get-your-head-out-of-the-clouds way the older players sometimes had, he said, "They've got to knuckle down, work their forwards, make their tackles and hope for the best."

And he was quite wrong. That wasn't what we had to do at all. What we had to do was to keep the game fluid because they had big, but comparatively slow, forwards who would have liked nothing better than to spend the afternoon in some deep dark scrum with our test virgins, far from the referee's eyes.

Until then I'd just been an ordinary member of the team, and suddenly there was a reason to talk to me. And the fact I handled the media so openly, and the fact that we'd won, helped the public get engaged with this new side. The fact that I was beaming in the post-match interview was very unusual – I'd go so far as to say that such a stretch had never been seen on an All Black captain's face. I was so pleased we'd won, so pleased that an unproven team had given so much and been so rewarded. And my joy was infectious, people responded.

But then I said something to a radio journalist which came back to haunt me. They asked about the new players and how they measured up against the older players. I said I hoped many of them had laid the foundation for long All Black careers. Error, error! My endorsing these new players, being seen to want them in the team, was a provocative thing to say in the atmosphere of fear and paranoia that some of the older players were giving off.

Auckland, my Auckland. Above: Trying to get a pass away in front of Canterbury defenders Steve Bachop and Bruce Deans, 1986. Below: Leading Auckland into the fray. Behind me are John Kirwan and Terry Wright.
Peter Bush and Leon Hamlet, Fotopacific

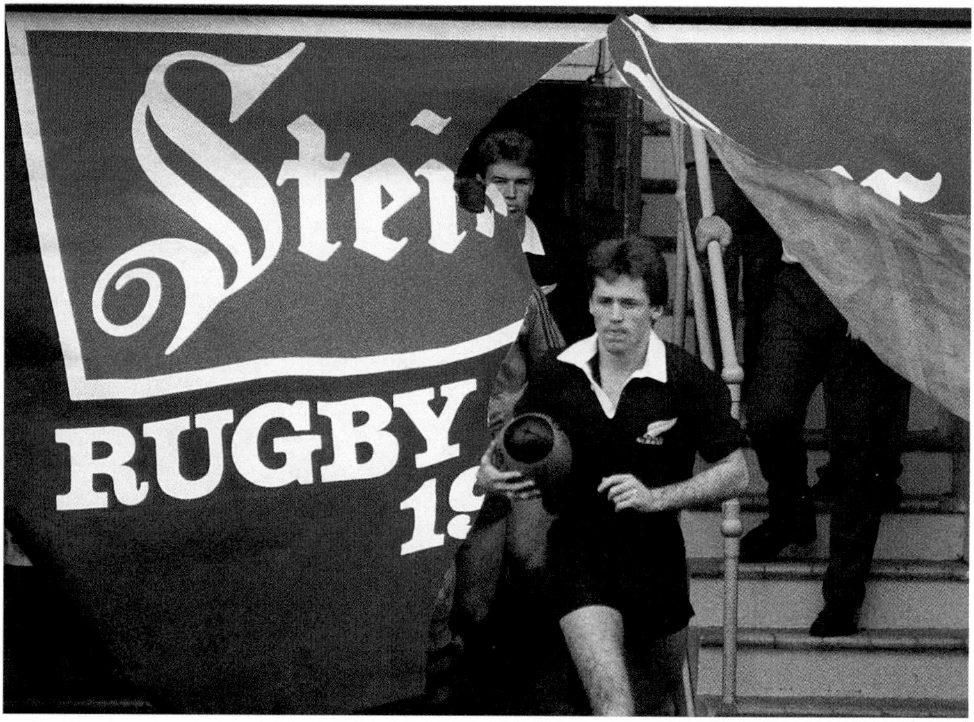

Only a point in it – twice! Above: Leading New Zealand out for the first test of the 1986 series against Australia at Athletic Park. With the Cavaliers under suspension we lost 12-13. Below: A bloodied nose, but this time a one-point win, 13-12, over Australia in the second test at Carisbrook. The Cavaliers were back, en masse, for this match. *Ross Setford, Fotopacific*

Full of confidence after our 70-point romp against Italy in the 1987 World Cup opener, we took on Fiji at Christchurch. The result? Another win, another 70-pointer. Above: I've got John Kirwan in support and Fijian winger Serupepeli Tuvula in front of me. Decisions, decisions . . . Below: Fijian halfback Paulo Nawalu is unable to stop me diving across for a try wide out. *Photosport and Fotopacific*

The Argentinian goal line beckons during New Zealand's final pool match of the '87 World Cup at Wellington. Other All Blacks in the frame are Kieran Crowley and John Kirwan. Los Pumas No 15 is Guillermo Angaut. *Fotopacific*

Harassing my Welsh opposite Robert Jones during New Zealand's 49-6 World Cup semi-final win at Brisbane. *Fotopacific*

A special – and well-publicised – moment with Andy Dalton after the World Cup presentation in 1987.
Fotopacific

The French have been split asunder and Buck Shelford (with headband) will be on hand to take my pass and put John Kirwan in for a try in the 1987 World Cup final at Eden Park. *Fotopacific*

So long, Buck. My last game in the black jersey – Concord Oval, Sydney, 1987 – and the All Blacks have beaten Australia 30-16 to win back the Bledisloe Cup. *Ross Land, Fotopacific*

Turning out for the French Barbarians in 1988 was an interesting experience, especially as the opposition was New Zealand Maori. For the record, NZ Maori won the game, played at Mont-de-Marsan, 31-14. *Photosport*

But what could you say? "The guys played well but so what, they've got one more match so they better make the most of it"? That's not what captains say about their young heroes, their giant-killers. You wouldn't say that about Sean Fitzpatrick or Frano Botica or Joe Stanley.

We had one more test before the Cavaliers emerged from their test ban, and that was against Australia.

We'd had a couple of injuries but it was essentially the same team that beat France. My view was that if we could repeat our performance we could beat the Australians too. As it turned out, we played better. We played on a windy day in Wellington. Australia scored first – a try coming from Campese's individual brilliance and not indicative of the run of play. We turned 9-0 down at halftime and played the half of our lives. Australia responded in kind. Greg Cooper kicked a couple of penalty goals and Mark Brooke-Cowden scored a great try after a big build-up from a long way out. With five minutes to go we were camped out on their twenty-two, looking for a way through. I tried a snap dropped goal but it skewed away. We tried everything, we gave everything, and it wasn't enough. The whistle went. The score was 13-12 but in Australia's favour.

In the end we weren't clinical enough, not dominating enough. We were a far-flung team without psychological dominance. We'd played better than against France but we needed better than that to beat Australia. We had been unable to reproduce the emotional intensity of the first test and we didn't have the advantage of surprise.

Nonetheless, I learned a real lesson there by experience. The All Blacks really are far bigger than any individual player but, more surprisingly, they're also bigger than any individual team. We beat the French with only a few test players; we lost to Australia by one point with virtually the same team. The tradition, the example and the aspiration to the national team carried the rest.

What a difference a point makes.

Some Pretty Cavalier Treatment

A week later the selectors dumped ten of us, although Mike Brewer was brought back in after Wayne Shelford withdrew with an injury. They were out. John Kirwan was left, of course, and I (bizarrely) was left as captain. It was an invidious position: I was leading a team that disliked me personally, who felt no loyalty to me and who felt I'd betrayed them.

Why did the selectors keep me? As I said earlier, I wasn't the right size, of the right style, or of the right generation to be their captain. I'd also jumped their ship, as it now looked to them, and left them to the humiliation of an unofficial tour.

When looking for a leader, the first thing you look for is someone with legitimate authority. And that wasn't me. I had all the legitimate authority you could want among the Baby Blacks – I didn't have a shred among the rest.

The All Black selectors have traditionally been astute at picking captains. The legend is that they wanted Wilson Whineray to captain the team – but they had to put him in the team first to find out whether he could actually play rugby at the required international level.

But in my case they were less perceptive.

The build-up to the next test was pretty average. I didn't have the respect or confidence of the team. I never met with overt disagreement but never any overt support either.

The second test was in Dunedin and played in cold, wet conditions. After ten minutes we had a scrum and executed a move Auckland had used earlier that season against North Harbour. I'd pass to Kirwan, he'd take the tackle and flip the ball to me as I looped outside him. It worked and I scored in the corner, the only try of that match.

In the second half, Australia went down the blindside and probably scored – the ref was unsighted and didn't award it. When I referred to it in a post-match interview I said, "He may have scored, I didn't see it." The headline was, KIRK SAYS TUYNMAN SCORED, and I remember being abused by an elderly lady. "You should keep your mouth shut!" she said. I could see the sense in her advice, but it didn't make any difference.

The scoreline was the same, 13-12, but with us winning. And so we went into the crucial final test with everything up for grabs.

We should have won it; we hadn't lost a series to Australia in New Zealand, not in my lifetime. But disunity had become worse. The forwards in particular wanted to exclude me. Forwards always have their own bond and the Cavaliers had their own special bond on top of the normal one. They'd go into huddles and find their own things to talk about.

We played at a hundred miles an hour, as if we were all on speed, as if to exorcise the demons. This was wild, this was Irish, this was risk-filled and hysterical. It wasn't the sort of game the All Blacks play. We had them cut to ribbons but we never got the ball over the line. All the cross currents of loyalty and anger blocked our rhythm. The stress and the frenzy wouldn't allow us the clinical finish we so desperately needed.

And Australia did to us what we would have done to them. They made their tackles, they scrambled it from three metres out, they held the line. And when our emotional energy had been expended they came back at us with power and precision. It was the tactics we used to beat many Latin teams; it's what you do with over-emotional opponents.

At 12-9 with a quarter of an hour to go we were still in it. However, two penalty goals by Michael Lynagh put Australia out to 18-9, and we had to score next. In desperation to score we tried to run the ball from our line. It was kamikaze stuff. Arthur Stone was tackled, the ball spilled, Campo picked it up and scored.

It was the first time Australia had won a test series on New Zealand soil for thirty-seven years – and that put me in a pretty exclusive club of All Black captains.

I didn't play particularly well either as halfback or captain. There were a lot of unforced errors, and the wild, uncontrolled play – very different from normal play – was so unsuccessful it could have given a bad name to the new approach of running, passing and continuity. It was uncontrolled – but, more importantly, it was being tried by the wrong players.

Some Pretty Cavalier Treatment

Things weren't going well, not at all. My youthful idealism was increasingly frayed. I'd come into the All Blacks with the idealism of any young player coming to the world's greatest team. It was a great thing to aspire to, one of the pinnacles of New Zealand – indeed, world, achievement. And you go in with a sense of warmth and mateship – a feeling that grew stronger when the South African tour was cancelled. I found the excitement and pleasure at being chosen had a dark side too. When it turns out that you might be threatening the status quo, the team can turn on you.

Though these were the same players who, it seemed to me, were lying freely to the public about receiving money, they were also making me feel I had done the wrong thing. This team that you revered suddenly rejects you. You have an untenable position as captain, you lose a series against Australia, you are dumped as captain – that's when you end up in the pits reading Dostoevsky's *Crime and Punishment* (the single darkest book in the library).

It's worth rehashing all this because there are parallels today. The failed attempt to shanghai the All Blacks into a shonky World Rugby Corporation was surprisingly similar to the Cavaliers tour. Both were led by players towards the end of their careers looking for a cash bonus. Both applied considerable pressure to the younger members to sign up (one-in-all-in). Both had a couple of dissenters (in the WRC case it was Josh Kronfield and Jeff Wilson). And finally, both were rotten ideas.

If the World Rugby Corporation had succeeded, those players would be nonentities in striped jerseys playing for Townsville. Instead they are the All Blacks, the finest rugby team in the world, and its players are the stars of world rugby. And they owe it – as we all owe it – to the All Black tradition formed by the five hundred or so players since the beginning of this century.

It wasn't wholly dark. John Hart kept me as Auckland captain – which Andy Haden didn't particularly resent, and that was good of him. He would occasionally re-assert his authority on the field – probably more out of habit than anything else, and I didn't make an issue of it. Grant Fox was a little more peremptory with Greg Cooper, the kicker for the Baby Blacks who had come into the Auckland side. I remember Greg was about to take a kick when Grant ran over, physically took the ball out of his hands and took the kick himself. Well, it was only an idea.

Black and Blue

For the All Black tour to France I heard that I'd been dropped as captain on the radio. In spite of the fact that I'd lost the first home test series to Australia since the 1949. I was both surprised and disappointed to be dropped. It's a big thing to captain your country and it's a blow to be fired. But at the same time there was an element of relief in it. And also the character of the All Blacks was changing more rapidly than before. The winds of change were picking up.

Some of the old guard were retiring and some Baby Blacks were coming through again. Haden, Mexted, Dalton, Smith and Ashworth had finished in South Africa, Knight retired after the third Australia test.

Jock Hobbs was captain again, as he had been in Fiji in 1984 and Argentina in 1985. Jock was making a specialty of end-of-season tours. He took me aside and said that he hadn't sought the captaincy and he wanted to heal any rift, and he asked for my support, which I willingly gave. I withdrew into my shell, began to play better and became quite happy (insofar as you can be happy halfway through *Crime and Punishment*).

There was an amusing incident in Strasbourg (for those with strong stomachs it was amusing; I can't imagine our mothers laughing at it as hard as we did). Mark Shaw was reserve watching the pack train on the scrum machine. The pack went into the machine hard and low and slammed the block back on its industrial springs. They hit hard and kept the pressure on – "Hit! hold!hold!hold! Coming in" and we'd shove even harder, "*Break!*" the coach's call goes. They'd been holding for fifteen seconds and just before "*Break!*" was called there was a scream from Mark Shaw. He'd got his fingers caught in the machine, trapped between the block and the metal backstop. They were seriously messed up, crushed and torn and oozing blood. "Why didn't you let us know your fingers were trapped?" we asked him, amazed.

"That was a great scrum, you had a good hit on there," he explained.

After my indifferent form at home I started to play better. I scored three tries in Perpignan and played well in the first test at Toulouse. I made a break which was almost a carbon copy of the one in the World Cup final a year later. But this time I got the ball to John Kirwan. He was tackled in the corner but we scored from the scrum which followed.

Then things got darker when we went into the second test at Nantes. It was certainly the most violent game most of us had ever experienced.

The French were on a losing streak and were going through a lot of division about the style they should be playing. The French media and public have always enjoyed the thought of big, physical forwards, they like the sense of power, but they also have to see the ball being run, they want the game played with flair and intuition. Winning alone was not enough – they had to win with style. But Jacques Fouroux was a student of All Black play and wanted his team to play like we did – or like he thought we played.

The ferocity with which they played was too much for us; they collapsed the scrum and a French forward stamped on Sean Fitzpatrick's head and dragged their sprigs through his scalp. He just carried on. His capacity to play while injured and to bear pain is extraordinary. Wayne Shelford was concussed early and later retired with a ripped scrotum. Gary Whetton left with a leg injury. Drake and McDowell had calf injuries, Hobbs a bad hamstring.

I visited the French dressing room after the match. They had won, and won well, but there was little joy there either. The match had been a war. The result was without honour.

The All Blacks are not good at losing (not enough practice) but we're particularly bad at being defeated physically.

The next morning a drinking session started around 10am. There wasn't a good feeling in the room. The sourness of defeat crystallised the larger anger of the rebel failure. And when alcohol had loosened people's tongues some of them found it easier to be direct with me about my part in the fiasco and what an inadequate individual I was. There is a cumulative power in these sorts of attacks from your team mates; they know you intimately, you trust them at an important level, their attacks have the power to damage you that enemies' don't have. I was surrounded. And the long and short of it was that after a while I couldn't take any more and I ended up – what's the technical term? – sobbing in my room. I hadn't done that for twenty years. I never asked the rest of the team how many times they'd ended up doing that but I thought it a very unlikely event in most All Black careers.

Three of the team came to support me, and I've always been grateful to them for that. You remember that.

So I was very sensitive and vulnerable and generally down. The guys had been able to produce in me this overwhelming sense of guilt that I had betrayed not only them but the whole All Black ethos: I was a pariah now and forever.

Most rugby players don't take views on these things. Even Brian

Lochore – great man, great player, great coach – even he wasn't equipped to handle the situation. Maybe I was expecting too much. I felt ostracised and deeply unhappy. I wanted to quit.

It was at this time that I made a definitive break with my past. My life from boarding school had been one of needing to fit in. My intellectual curiosity and ambitions and my need to feel I was doing the right thing by my own lights didn't always sit well with needing to belong to a group of my peers. This problem was going to get worse for me, I could see; you could get so used to being a popular rugby player that you could come to value the popularity for its own sake and, for the sake of not upsetting anyone, never say anything again.

I resolved the tension finally and decisively by accepting that I couldn't have it both ways. If I was to live by my own lights I had to accept that this would put me offside with some people. I took that on board, and suddenly felt strong again. I started to look forward again.

John Hart was very supportive when I told him what I was thinking. He said, "You think too much, you've got more support than you realise." Maybe I had, but no-one was letting on. But I was very hyper. I was thinking hard about quitting, even though I'd deferred a Rhodes Scholarship to play in the World Cup the following year.

I went to the beach that summer feeling as low as I ever had, and then, walking along Pourerere beach it occurred to me how sick I was of feeling depressed and guilty. The point about guilt is that it steers you away from wrong actions – but there was no positive outcome from this guilt at all. There was no upside to the depression. I decided to put it to one side. To stop allowing anxiety to have its way with me. To stop worrying whether some players liked me or not. There would never be a satisfactory answer to that question and it was time to take John Hart's advice and stop making things hard for myself.

And as I thought these things through a great weight lifted from my shoulders. And luckily the time was right. Two weeks later I met Brigit.

My wife, as she became, is less interested in rugby than anyone I've ever met. Eight-year-old girls are more interested in rugby than Brigit. She had heard of the All Blacks. But she had no idea that I was in them when we met at a beach party in Hawke's Bay. Nor did she believe it when she was told (the one thing she knew about All Blacks was that they were big). Her only real reaction was irritation at young girls who kept asking me to autograph their arms or their books or their plaster casts. For my part I found it a great relief to be with someone who had a life totally outside the game with friends interested in completely different things.

Actually, it wasn't for a few months that I realised quite how little she knew about the sport – it was when I introduced her to John Kirwan. "Brigit, this is John," I said.

"Hello John," she said and they chatted for a while. When he left, she asked me, "Does John play rugby too?" I have to say that when I recounted this to Kirwan he didn't believe it. It's not that he's conceited (he's not), it's just that every other adult in the country knew who he was. It was in this one way he resembled Mrs Thatcher. When knock-out victims were coming round overseas doctors would ask them, "Who is the Prime Minister of Britain?" to determine whether they had any memory left. In New Zealand they'd be asked, "Who plays on the right wing for Auckland?"

As I say, added to Brigit's many qualities was her distance from the game that was causing me so much grief.

This new relationship gave me strength and independence maybe because I stopped worrying about them – and things also started to move my way in the rugby sphere.

That year began with the administrative body changing the selectors. John Hart and Alex Wyllie took over from Tiny Hill and Colin Meads. Colin Meads was a classic of his generation, of course; it showed the depth of feeling against the Cavalier tour (he'd been the coach) to dump this lion of rugby. It was a profoundly significant move.

Meads in the traditional mould was largely uncommunicative. Tiny Hill had enjoyed a distinguished career as a professional soldier and still carried a military attitude to the world. A thoroughly honourable and charming man, he still could not hold out Wyllie or Hart.

Times, though, were running against the old ways. The whole structure of authority had changed over the last decade; you could see it everywhere. Matrons no longer ruled their wards with the rod of iron; airline pilots no longer barked orders over the flightdeck; army officers and surgeons relied on informed consent rather than blind obedience. Society had changed.

Physically and psychologically Alex Wyllie was of the old guard, but he also had a modern vision. He was committed to fifteen-man rugby, the running game, the new game – and he got a lot of loyalty from his players. He knew the game very well and was a very good selector. Brian Lochore was a much more obviously amiable man, but, like Alex, all his contacts and colleagues were from the generations he played with. However, his rugby style also was modern. Brian Lochore's management skill was more modern too, and didn't include large-scale assault and battery in its technical array.

For a glorious single year, these three giants of coaching took New Zealand rugby into the new era, they oversaw the huge change.

Progress was unstoppable and broadly based. The reputation of rugby had been publicly tarnished by the infamous 1981 Springboks tour and the subsequent Cavaliers. The argument that the game was brought into disrepute was being given weight. There had been a significant drop-off in participation in the game since the tour.

Another factor was coming into play: women's influence on rugby was becoming stronger. Women had defied their husbands to demonstrate against the South Africans, and anniversaries of the 1981 tour had become something of an item on the feminist calendar. Women were influential in whether their sons played rugby or not, and they brought a new attitude to bear on regulations concerning injuries, for instance. The rise of touch rugby and new image rugby was also occurring around this time – the impetus was to build skills rather than physical power. The whole spirit of the game was lifting out of the trenches and into the fast running game.

From the Bottom to the Top of the World

The 1987 season began like any other – but it was not like any other. It was the first Rugby World Cup. This was a new and exciting competition which had only just scraped through the international ruling body. There were eight members of the International Rugby Board, and they were evenly split. The northern hemisphere (against) and the southern hemisphere (for), with France siding with the south. The opposers said it would interfere with the traditional four-test tour, and would also become the inevitable harbinger of commercialism. The next step would be, they felt, the Kellogg's Lions, the Fisher and Paykel All Blacks, the Wattie's Wallabies. But, at the last moment, one country switched its vote and the competition was on.

Actually, there was quite a lot of creeping professionalism at the time. For years the All Blacks had been advertising products like rub-on cream for muscle strain, clothes, cars, a computer. This had picked up round the World Cup. Andy Dalton was promoting a three-wheel farm bike on television and there was something of an outcry about professionalism. We scooted around that by saying Andy was a farmer and a farm consultant and was contracted in this private capacity. A degree of animosity was developing from some other teams that we were benefiting in this way from rugby.

Anyhow, the World Cup would hasten the advent of professionalism simply by lifting rugby's profile. Most people felt it would be a great boost to the game in New Zealand but after the year before (a series lost to Australia and a heavy loss in the Nantes test in France) there wasn't a lot of hope we'd win it.

Personally, I was concerned for my place in the team. I hadn't played well the whole previous season. So for the first time in four years I thought it would be better to decline the opportunity to play sevens and dedicate the time to preparing to compete for my place. You can calculate this quite carefully. You set goals through the trial matches and preparation matches. You have to play well when selectors are watching – they don't rely on hearsay; they believe what they see.

The Auckland season unfolded in its usual way (we won all but one of our games). The North-South match had been remade as a competition between three regions with two North Island teams. All matches in the pool counted as trial matches, and from those games they selected two teams for a final trial. Auckland was part of the North Zone; we played Central in Pukekohe where I marked Andrew Donald, the test player I'd been reserve to a couple of years before. Bruce Deans played halfback for the South.

North won both matches and the competition but, as ever, in trial matches there were no great spectacles. I wasn't picked to play in the final trial in Whangarei. I was a reserve. Either they wanted to find out who should be All Black reserve and I was firmly in; alternatively, I was in the reject pile. I honestly didn't know which it was.

But my mood had lifted. Brigit's magnificent lack of interest in the game was inspiring. She was treated as something of an outsider by some of the other wives and girlfriends in the team (and they knew how to make newcomers feel uncomfortable), and this had the curious effect of lifting me out of the claustrophobic sense that teams can build around you. She told me that the queen bee in Auckland, in charge of handing out tickets for the after-match function, resolutely refused to remember her. "Now, Brenda (or Barbara or Bertha), who are you with again?" She used to feel uneasy enough to wait outside the players' entrance after the game, for me to take her up to the reception room. It put my relations with the team into perspective because I was able to think that this behaviour from the women wasn't a hundred miles from the earlier behaviour of some of the guys.

I was feeling pretty chipper, really. Andy Dalton had captained the North Zone and it seemed pretty clear that the selectors were intent on having him as a sort of reconciliation captain.While we were waiting for final trial to be played Craig Green and I went riding in the hills and eeling in the river across from the hotel (we caught an eel which we didn't kill but left in the washbasin of one of the rooms). I'd been dumped as captain so I felt I needn't behave like a captain. They put me in the team, notwithstanding the eel. I was in the All Black squad for the first World Cup.

We appeared in the very first All Black poster, our first experience of professional marketing. The Saatchi and Saatchi poster became a collector's item. We were shot in twos and threes and they stripped the photos together under a dark and threatening sky split by forked lightning. We were instructed to look proud and dangerous – that smiling thing we were starting to do, that was out.

Jock Hobbs, in particular, had argued cogently earlier in the year for television advertising so some of us were taken down to Wellington to dive around in a warehouse for an afternoon, to jump off trampolines, make tackles on gym mats, apply what looked like camouflage paint (was this war? well, yes, it was, in a way). They cut all that together in the editing room and put Stand By Me on the soundtrack for a highly effective plea to New Zealand. I can't help thinking that we'd never have asked New Zealand prior to 1981 to *Stand By Me*. It would have been more *These Boots Are Made For Walking* or *Old Man River* – something else celebrating power and suffering. The advertising brief specifically instructed the agency to include an appeal to women – that recognition was increasingly important to a traditionally conservative administration.

The team got together. It was a very well selected team, designed to play a certain style. The coaches understood what they wanted to achieve in strategy and tactics and therefore how we would play the game, and therefore who they needed it to be played by.

Given the confines of the rules, they had aspired to a style that was unbeatable. It was a style that was comprehensive, it touched every player and every aspect of the game, but it was also adaptable. We could arrange for tactical adjustments against England's very heavy pack, or France's powerful running forwards and fast backs. But the key thing was the conceptual base into which everything fitted. And this concept of rugby was the Canterbury/Auckland analytical one.

There were fourteen Aucklanders out of twenty-six on the squad, ten of whom subsequently played in the final. The influence of Hart was clear, though Lochore as the convenor must also take credit for the new wave.

Brian Lochore was a key figure in the World Cup and he successfully managed the expectations and ambitions of his lieutenants, John Hart and Alex Wyllie. He played a very canny game plan by suggesting that, of the three of them, only two should have executive power at one time. That is, he, Brian, and one or other of the lieutenants. His was a position of age and experience and the other two fell in with the proposal. Lochore had a wide range of managerial abilities, including the ability to ignore unhelpful antagonisms. He'd come back from the French tour satisfied that everything was cosy in the team. "There were no cliques on this tour," he proclaimed. "It went a long way towards healing the rifts and restoring unity." Personally, I had a different experience of it.

Rugby changed for me at this time. We had always played to win. That was our constant purpose, our strategic objective. But then, in training, in discussion, out of our collective spirit, another aim evolved. Our ambitions increased. There had been a goal of winning the World Cup. It changed to become a larger one – the goal of playing the best rugby in the world. This distinction may have seemed slight at the time but ended up becoming a whole new philosophy of play. We stopped playing to win, we stopped playing against our opponents. We began to play against the game itself, pushing back the boundaries of what was considered possible. The opposition simply became the means by which we brought our vision of rugby into the world.

It was a reincarnation of the amateur ethic. Winning was not the most important thing any more. Winning wasn't the point. Playing the best rugby was the point, and winning was the by-product. The distinction is real.

The World Cup began relatively low key. We had been ostracised by the political establishment and enjoyed no official function, not even to welcome the overseas players (remember, this was David Lange's revenge on the New Zealand Rugby Union).

We convened in Auckland, as ever at the Poenamo Hotel, and began our team preparation. The question of captaincy was settled. Jock Hobbs had received serious head injuries and had to bail out. Out of his misfortune Michael Jones got his first chance to play. We had a new team; it was an amalgam of Cavaliers and new players. The generational baton had been passed. Wise, calm Andy Dalton was chosen as captain. In some ways it was a relief to be out of the running. However, I couldn't help feeling a pang when Andy got the call to lead us into the World Cup, but there were larger concerns to occupy us.

Our training operated on the new philosophy – less time, greater intensity; quality not quantity. But, perhaps ironically, we were doing

Hennie Mullers – a mindless training routine running diagonals on the pitch – when Andy Dalton twinged a hamstring. This brought in Sean Fitzpatrick as hooker – he'd played for the Baby Blacks against France (owing to another injury, funnily enough). The change was good for the team because Sean was a better hooker than Andy, as Jones was a better loose forward than Jock Hobbs – but there was still every hope that Andy would be back to captain us. Meanwhile, we trained without a captain.

On Wednesday morning, in the final days before the Italy test, we were training unopposed when, five minutes in, Andy stood up saying his hamstring wasn't up to it. Brian Lochore must have been considering what to do in this eventuality because he turned to me crisply and said, "You take over." And without further ado I did.

Why was the 1987 team so successful? There were many reasons; the coaches, the management and the non-playing members like selfless Andy Dalton made an enormous contribution.

But finally, a lot of success comes from having the best players.

We had players endowed with extraordinary physical capacity. Even at international level, when everyone is in the top bracket, the best physical specimens outperform their team mates decisively. It's like watching Michael Johnson running the two hundred and four hundred metres against the best in the world and seeing him win by five metres.

Many of my playing colleagues were the greatest in the world. Some could rely on breathtaking physical capacity; others needed to out-think their opponents; others just wanted it more than most of us could have believed possible.

Top of the list would have to be Michael Jones. He exploded onto the world rugby scene in the 1987 World Cup and brought a whole new dimension to rugby – that's an amazing achievement for one person. His power, speed and explosiveness have been unmatched; he has exquisite hand-eye co-ordination. In club rugby he was good. I remember from experience. At that level I was often able to sneak past the loose forwards close to a ruck. But Michael never took dummies. That is, he did take dummies, but had such reflexes and responses that even if he did take a dummy he was fast and ferocious enough to retrieve the situation. He concentrated on the game like a hunting animal. He had the speed, and he also had the vision, the foresight, the ability to anticipate. In his first match for Auckland, in a midweek game against South Canterbury, he scored three tries – the most memorable of which came from his being outside the winger.

In the Baabaas tour earlier that year, we played Leicester. I was running a small, tight blindside. Realising there wasn't a hole, or a gap, or any way through at all, I threw the ball to Michael on the wing thinking that he was bigger than me and he could take the tackle. He didn't take the tackle. He chipped the ball over the winger's head, caught it on the full and bolted away to score under the posts. "I wish I'd thought of that," I said to myself, and felt put in my place.

Michael has all the physical attributes, but more of them than anyone else. He's about 1.85m, powerful and with a great leap. But, equally important, he has the emotional resources for a great player. He works hard, he comes back from disappointment, he continually learns.

John Kirwan was the other extraordinary player of my time. I had a rule of thumb when blindside running: if you can't think of anything to do, give it to Kirwan as quickly as you can. Such was his ability in two or three metres he'd beat two or three players and, at the very least, make ground, stand in the tackle and get his pass away. John was our first really big winger; he combined speed and elusiveness and the ability to stand people up. For someone his size he's remarkably nimble in small spaces.

These were the greatest two players for combining mental and physical qualities. They turned experience into improved rugby. They both had an explosive start to their careers when they were very young – nineteen-odd – and began by playing as well as anyone on the field. But their crucial difference was they continued to get better. They learned how to read the game better; they got fitter, their work rate increased, they got more involved in more parts of the field.

Sean Fitzpatrick is extremely strong, stronger than most props. I remember three of us had an archery contest in Fiji one year. I struggled to get the big, professional bow half bent. John Drake strained to get it back the full way, and he was shaking with the strain. Sean pulled it back like a piece of chewing gum. Training helps him, and the physical work he used to do, but it's largely natural. He was born as strong as an ox. And his strength is enlivened by a ferocity of spirit. Sean was also the first of the big hookers. They used to be small, to swing forward on their props in the old days. But when power-scrummaging began, size became important – and Sean is built more like a prop than the hookers of old.

No-one's in the league of Michael Jones for skills and physical capacity (not even the extraordinary talent of Zinzan Brooke) but in all my career the two toughest players would have been Sean Fitzpatrick and Mark Shaw.

They hit rucks (and more than occasionally other players) harder than anyone I knew. Shaw hit them like he expected to move them. His physical power was of another time. Towards the end of his career the game moved away from him; he didn't have the running and passing abilities you need now, but at close quarters he was peerless.

As for brain over brawn, John Drake was a classic example. He was a big tighthead prop, the anchor of the scrum, the biggest man on the field. But he was highly intelligent too – and this isn't always the case with props. He also played a lot of touch, and dropped goals occasionally in a very tidy way. But because – for all his size – he wasn't the strongest prop he'd arrange the scrum to suit himself. He'd never let the scrum go down until the ball was ready. So he'd be hard on me to get the ball there. He didn't want to go down for a protracted wrestling match with tougher, better equipped, hardmen. So he'd get his body into the perfect position and the scrum would be over in a moment. He was the consummate tactician.

He was a great support and coach to Sean. The two of them would drive in with their weight perfectly deployed to put pressure on the opposition hooker. Drakey would provide the technique and positioning, Fitzy the power. A lot of opposition hookers emerged with legs turned to jelly-tips after scrumming against these two. On the other side was the most explosive prop of a couple of generations, Steve McDowell. Not naturally a big man for a prop, Steve was a successful judo expert (in fact, a Commonwealth games rep) and with long years of weight training he was extremely strong. More than this, he was fast – particularly at running; he exploded with the ball in hand.

Andy Haden's time had passed by 1987, but he was one of the most dominating players of my era. He was a player who could rule a game. It was true he was big even by the standards of big rugby, but he dominated by the power of his mind. He used to talk to referees a lot. And while he had none of the explosive athleticism of Gary Whetton (who'd suddenly appear in open play to take a pass or be out wide on the wing to make a tackle), Andy had a way of controlling the game with his presence. He had a sort of physical charisma that drew the ball to him. Playing against him in club rugby you wished he wasn't there. He put a pattern on the game, he imposed his will and his purpose on the whole match. That's a remarkable achievement. Being a ferocious ego maniac helps, of course, and you probably couldn't do such a thing without that quality. In an All Black trial I played with him, he, as usual, made the calls in the lineout, and that determined who'd get the ball. Whenever we were in front of the stand, in front of the three selectors, Andy would invariably call himself. It was the sort of benefit he deserved, given that he was the best player. Entrusted with the lineout he figured, like Tuku Morgan, that his mana rightfully allowed for a few unscheduled benefits.

Alan Whetton's greatness wasn't based on his physical capacity. He was half a blindside flanker and half a lock (locks are slower and more powerful). He bridged the gap through sheer willpower. He had this enormous drive to be everywhere the action was. He'd be supporting wingers running for the line, he'd be back making last-gasp tackles, he'd be the last up off the ground when the ruck cleared, but he'd always be right there when the next ruck formed. He wasn't the fastest, or the most agile, but he was always there.

Wayne Shelford also brought a new quality to the game, and it was power. His secret was the denial of the tackle. When most players are hit by a 90kg opponent, they stop a bit – if only to set up the pass, or wait for support. But Buck used to run through the tackle, his legs kept pumping; he'd always make those extra two or three metres, he'd always get over the advantage line – and that made a huge difference because it allowed your pack to move forward rather than do momentum-breaking U-turns.

Grant Fox had the same ferocity of spirit, tremendous self-discipline and determination. He practised continually. He was never subject to whims or flights of fancy, but he invariably did what was statistically most likely to do well. He introduced a level of cold analysis to first five-eighth play, and that was his secret weapon because it was new. On the ten-metre line he'd put a kick up and it would land one metre short of the opposition twenty-two. From another place he'd put the ball just over the winger's head and bounce it into touch. He gave nothing away. He kept asking the questions of opposing defenders – and if the answers weren't exactly right we'd win.

Today when people compare Foxy with Andrew Mehrtens and Carlos Spencer he will always suffer in the comparison because he didn't have their dash or vim; he scored only one try in his long test career, and will always look less of a star runner with the ball. But his strengths far outweigh these relative weaknesses.

And interestingly, while Foxy wasn't quick enough or elusive enough to be a great runner himself, he was a very good runner for others. He picked a line, ran it hard and made space for other players.

And while the newer players occasionally approach Grant's precision, they haven't demonstrated the awesome consistency which was his legacy to the game. The new guys make ten times the mistakes Fox makes. Mind you, they try more things, they score more tries, they're bound to make more mistakes. And in the new climate they are attuned to the new game. You can't manipulate the match any more like we used to, from set piece to set piece. Under the rules of a decade ago you'd have an even chance of getting possession, even with an opposition throw-in. Today the rules put a premium on running and passing and keeping the ball in play. It's a different game and comparisons are invidious.

The double-A-plus category from my playing career is not a big group. Michael Jones, Sean Fitzpatrick, Grant Fox, John Kirwan, Wayne Shelford and Andy Haden. They were the best players in the world at the time, but they were also the great players of their generation. They all had rare physical talent, but what made them truly great was their ability to dominate mentally. They dominated their number, they were the masters of their game.

Zinzan Brooke followed Shelford, and he was set apart by his extraordinary ball-handling skills. He played the ball like a basketball player. He has substantial (but not as substantial as he thinks) kicking skills. He has missed many a dropped goal, and we tend to forget those efforts. But everyone remembers when a number eight drop kicks a goal, and he has done that enough to get a name for it.

The great thing about Zinzan trying for goal is the confidence to do such a thing. The only real boundaries are the ones you impose yourself. Most players would expect to fail dropping a goal from forty metres out, so they don't try. Zinzan can't see why he'd be likely to fail, so he tries.

I should say that Craig Green was a player with a mysterious ability. He wasn't the fastest, biggest, strongest or most slippery player – but he had the remarkable ability to run without being tackled. He was a very gifted ball handler, he could chase a ball and time his leap to take it in mid-air. He also had a subtle feel for a pass. And he was always appearing when it counted. He, like Haden, had that physical charisma, an occult ability to make things happen around him.

The World Cup had a very modest opening ceremony, but when the first game started it was electrifying. The team exploded into action for the first time. None of us knew exactly what was going to happen. We were powerful and unpredictable, we were very cohesive. The new wave burst on the Italians and they were shocked, shaken and bewildered by it. Michael Jones scored the first individual try (as he did four years later in the next World Cup). Immediately, there was a sense of power and precision about everything we did. When you were checked on the run there'd be half a dozen black shirts fanning out in passing distance. The contact and support play was exhilarating. It wasn't just that we were on form, it seemed suddenly that we didn't have to strive; we had slipped into the inner groove that coach Galway had written about.

The matches went as follows.

First, Italy: People say that Italy weren't a good team (and there's some truth in that) but they weren't that bad. They beat Fiji later in the competition; and four years on they held the All Blacks to within ten points. They weren't brilliant but that All Black team made them look inadequate.

John Kirwan scored what still ranks as one of the most memorable tries of all time. He took a long pass close to our tryline; he accelerated, chopped, swerved, twisted and ran the whole length of the pitch and scored.

When Italy kicked off on the full we chose not a new kick, nor a scrum back, but a lineout. The Italians were trudging back for the scrum they assumed we'd opt for; I made a quick throw-in for Kirwan, he took it to the line and got me over with a last-second pass. It was a comprehensive victory with a thumping scoreline of 70-6. The Italian captain summed it up to the media in his broken, but expressive, English: "We tried. They have always the ball."

We played Fiji in our second match. To be fair to them they had decided they couldn't beat us and weren't going to try – they were going to save themselves to beat the others enough to make the quarter-finals. The score came out at 74-13 with some fantastic tries, ball handling and backing up.

It was then on to Argentina; Zinzan played his first match. We didn't field our strongest team but we scored over forty points to go into the quarter-finals. I actually got knocked out in that game in the last seconds, being taken early in a tackle. The local ground doctor, Bill Treadwell, wanted to examine me for concussion (an examination I would have failed). John Drake ushered me off the field, and Gary Whetton, from the heart of the Cavaliers team, protected me from being seen to. The management closed ranks outside the changing room and wouldn't let Bill in. Concussion probably was evidenced by the rambling and garbled interview I gave after the match, and the next day's training was a turgid experience for me. There was a lot of very demanding running and driving, of rucking, scrumming and mauling – it didn't stop for seventy-five minutes, but I remember very little beyond the fact that I shouldn't have been doing it.

Perhaps that was why I didn't play well against Scotland, my least successful game of the tournament. But the pattern was the same. We absorbed extra pressure and then started piling on the points. They got three, we got thirty.

It was after this match, I heard later, that there was a move to have me ditched as halfback (and as captain). The team was firing, the game had never been played better, and Alex Wyllie was putting up team manager Richie Guy to canvass support to dump me, put in Bruce Deans at halfback and I don't know who as captain. The idea didn't fly in spite of my mild concussion – Brian Lochore squashed it – but the complicated way Alex put the manoeuvre in train contributed to the disintegration of his relationship with John Hart.

Now matches were a week apart. Lochore took the team to train in the Wairarapa and billeted us out in ones and twos. This was a very good move – it gave the team a break from the routine of living in hotels, we had real people around us, and we were given a psychological boost by being taken to the heartland of New Zealand.

We trained also in Napier prior to travelling to Brisbane. We were to play Wales next, and though they were a far cry from the height of their form in the Seventies they were still one of the Five Nations that formed the inner circle of international rugby. In Hawke's Bay, some of us went riding – Craig Green, Gary Whetton, John Hart and I. None of us could ride much, and John's horse bolted. He owns race horses but I don't believe he's ever ridden one since that day outside Waipukurau.

We had dinner with friends, and a beer at the Tavistock Hotel in Waipuk on the way home.

There was a blanket feeling of quiet confidence in the team, a sense of enjoyment (and goodness knows it's hard to enjoy playing international rugby). But we were expecting to win, we had that confidence, even though the stakes were getting higher the further into the tournament we got. The public had high expectations of us and our winning reinforced those expectations.

For the semi-final against Wales we had drawn a Sunday match (so Michael Jones couldn't play). What did we assume Wales would be like? It was a country that had gone through the huge emotional crisis of being one of the best teams in the world to being a shadow of their former selves. In the Seventies they had the likes of JPR Williams, Gareth Edwards, Phil Bennett, Gerald Davies – wonderfully fast and elusive players. And they had top forwards too.

And it should cast a fear into rugby playing nations how fast a demise can happen. The Welsh blame it, I believe, on teachers suddenly deciding not to coach rugby at school – a sort of work-to-rule in the early Eighties. And rugby league hasn't helped by taking the cream of their players. Their administration isn't that flash, either, dominated by an old boy network – a poor model anywhere; in Wales, disastrous. The decline of Welsh rugby happened fast, within a decade, and is an awful object lesson of what can happen to a national side.

Wales hadn't been playing well for a while, but their failures were relatively inconspicuous until they met the All Blacks in the semi-finals of the '87 World Cup and were beaten 49-6. The dry, brittle core of Welsh rugby was laid open, and they went into a real decline. They came back to New Zealand the following year and were, if anything, worse.

However, the good news is that they are now starting to recover. But they play with one eye on the past, trying to play as the great old teams used to play. This is futile – unless you can run through tackles like JPR Williams, or jink like Phil Bennett, or pass like Gareth Edwards; you should find your own way of playing in which you can succeed.

Professionalism may help them; they should get their league players back. Reasonable money will come into the game and their clubs will improve (as long as they resist the temptation to buy in washed-up Aussies, Frenchmen and New Zealanders).

However, others will go ahead faster; they will not be bereft in the new world of professionalism as Scotland and Ireland will be, but they won't match England either.

A good Welsh team is very hard to beat. The good ones are like Australia, skilful and tough. They are also habitually some of the dirtier players in international rugby (more so even than the South Africans). They also have a reputation in Europe for being rotten winners, for rubbing your face in their victory in a self-satisfied way. But, not having experienced this myself, I can't comment.

The whistle went for the semi-final against this once-proud rugby country and – and their tradition was turned on its head.

We scored two tries in the first ten minutes. A drive from a lineout and a pushover try. Our forward power imposed total dominance on their pack. Their scrum effectually disintegrated. Then we wound things up a notch. We played a first half that was both great and appalling, driving up the guts, splitting them out wide. It was a very physical demolition. We hit halftime. Then there was a flat patch in the second half; we were throwing the ball around casually; we had to get back to our strengths, to summon up our concentration and then it was all on again, punching holes in the fringes of the rucks, opening them up with our passing and support play.

As is often the case with Wales it was a niggling match – elbows here, rabbit punches there. There came a moment when the niggling stopped. One of the Welshmen reacted to Gary Whetton's elbow with some misplaced punches; they were two ineffectual blows but his error, as he was walking away, was deciding to come back and try and land something more substantial. Wayne Shelford, in a spirit of comradeship, drew a punch up from his heels which had the Welshman arching backwards and out cold before he hit the ground. He was woken by smelling salts and the voice of the ref in his ears informing him that he was being sent off – sent off for fighting. I had to support the ref in this perceptive decision; Wales had started it and Wayne had functioned as a peacemaker (he therefore escaped any retribution).

After the match English commentator Nigel Starmer-Smith was as morose as an Englishman could be about Wales being beaten. The only cloud in his sunny mood was the fact that Wales had beaten England the week before, and easily.

Over in Australia, we had watched the best game of the tournament the day before; France beating Australia in the last seconds with a typically Gallic try – props bursting down the field, flinging the ball back to have it plucked out of the air by their loose forwards, they slipped it to their speedy centres; defenders were sized up and drawn one by one, and finally the incomparable Serge Blanco scored in the corner. It was a try to rival the famous Gareth Edwards' Barbarians achievement in 1973, but with far more at stake. So we knew it was France we'd be playing in the final. We went home to prepare.

In one sense there was nothing to do – no controversy, no selection issues, no injuries.

The French were very worthy finalists. They have the Latin temperament against which all other Latin temperaments are measured. They have enormous flair in the backs and an unusual ability to combine as a team. The fullback might start a run and suddenly the whole team ignites. They all have an uncanny sense of lines and angles, an ability to be in the right place at the right time to receive a pass. The big, Foreign Legion forwards grow up playing touch at training and pass like backs.

France is a nation that does not prefer the fancy backs over the pack – they love the power as well as the glory. The rugby public wants mystery, elegance, intelligence. There is a Corinthian view of players there; they want the human dimension expressed, they want to see personal character on the field, and the press creates myths around the strengths and the background of the players.

The French have always been a team that demands good leadership if they are to perform to their potential. The captain is crucial and spends the match constantly gesticulating, shouting, encouraging, praising, abusing, pushing and arm-grabbing – in equal measure back-slapping and face-slapping. Top French captains have the ability to be very robust and vocal with their players, nagging and harrying them – but the team still, overall, lacks discipline.

In the late 1980s France went through the same sort of identity crisis as we did in the 1990s, with the decline into the '91 World Cup, teh rejection of John Hart and the tenure of Laurie Mains. Jacques Fouroux's determination to play like the All Blacks, in order to win, ultimately failed because it was not an approach consonant with his society. They demand more than relentless power (as, actually, do we), they want panache, joie-de-vivre, elan (Eskimos have a lot of words for snow, the French have a lot of words for flair).

How do you beat the French? They're often so big, hard and ugly in the forwards you're better off out of it. You must play precisely and relentlessly – and rely on their Gallic flair to lead them into the errors that will give you the breaks. Our job was to impose our own rhythm and style on the match. It wasn't to negate the opposition – if we played our own way opposition impotence would be a happy by-product, it would happen automatically.

We didn't train hard that week; the last session was a walk on the beach. That in itself was a masterstroke of coaching before the most important match of our careers. We thought about making history, and recognised how fortunate we were, so rarely does this happen, and there was an overwhelming sense of never having the chance again. Of course, many of the players from that final have gone on to play in subsequent World Cups – Fitzpatrick, McDowell, both Whettons, Jones, Fox and Kirwan all played in the next World Cup. Fitzpatrick played in the third one. But still, this World Cup was the first, it was at home and we knew we could win it.

I've been in teams that were overconfident, and that's a serious character flaw. It results in a lack of attention to detail, a lack of ferocity, a lack of the appetite to win – a false confidence that a win would appear. That team was quite different: we had a total understanding of what it took to win.

It hadn't come easily for any of us. We had all set ourselves the goal of playing for New Zealand and winning the inaugural World Cup, in some cases, the year before. We had all been through the emotional strains of the previous year when much of the solidarity and the essential goodwill of the All Black tradition had broken down. I have talked about my suffering, but everybody suffered in their own way. We had gone through the normal physical rigours of training, injury and playing to make that final. But no-one gave that a second thought – we were there.

We went out for that match carrying the hopes of our families and the expectations of the country. We knew we were ready. From the first minutes in the first match we had found a fluency born of simplicity and confidence that had surprised us as much as anyone. We had woven a spell. We were going to win. We believed it.

But then again, matches at this level are unpredictable. The French felt they had a good chance of winning – and whether they did or not, they certainly played like it. In matches like this, passion counts; indeed, it can be decisive. They weren't the better team, but the better team doesn't always win.

It was a little wet which didn't suit us. Again, Michael Jones scored the first try. I flipped it from a bad lineout, a good clearance, a dropped goal attempt which came off a Frenchman and floated wide, spinning back into the field of play, spinning away from Patrice Lagisquet as he bent to pick it up. He looked up to see Michael Jones bearing down on him, he fluffed it, fumbled it and Michael scooped it from under him.

But they were tough; there was no sense of easy, fluent play. Tackles had to be made, they ran hard, bursting forwards close to mauls and their backs ran hard and straight. It was grinding.

The rain came in squalls. We were 9-0 ahead at halftime – it didn't seem enough. The French received a penalty in the first minute after half-time. If they get this, I thought, it's going to be tough. They didn't.

We kept at it, eliminating errors, making tackles. The French lacked discipline; Foxy kicked the goals.

Down their end, our throw, I moved Michael Jones up the lineout and had it thrown to him. It came back to me. I scrambled it to Foxy, he gave it to Joe. The ball emerged quickly, I went right to Foxy, we were headed for the line. Michael Jones burst through on Foxy's inside, took the pass and, in a flash, threw it to me; two tacklers crashed into each other, I dived over them, through them, I felt the tryline passing under me and, as I hit the ground, I knew we were going to win. We were far enough ahead, it was late enough in the game and psychological dominance had finally been established. We would be world champions. I came up smiling.

At the kick-off the ball came to me, someone came to charge me down, I ducked under him and looked up and, my God, all I could see was open space; I ran and ran; where was JK? Too slow again, I thought; what about Michael Jones on the inside, he's got the reflexes and the pace but he's not there either. There was only Serge Blanco to beat (only!), but the cover was coming across too. The hooves on the cobblestones were drumming in my ears. Do I chip over Serge? Too risky, I'm not Michael Jones, and the ball is everything, keep possession, that was the first lesson I'd learned in my first game for Auckland; too late now, take the tackle, there'll be someone there, that's what it is to have the best loose forwards in the world. In the tackle, only thought, place the ball, make it available, think continuity, "Hey Norm, it's fluidity!" Hit, down, place. My bit finished. Buck picked it up and gave it to John Kirwan who scored in the corner. Two tries in two minutes.

The French, to their credit, came back and back. Another long movement gave them a last-minute try but we'd won the World Cup by twenty points.

Andy Dalton played a very important role off the field, motivating players, and that took a lot of the burden off me on the field. He was a reluctant hero, reluctant to be there at all, but I pulled him out of the crowd to hold the cup with me, a measure of the depth of gratitude from all of us. Some commentators saw this as symbolic of the healing of the rifts. A symbol it may have been, but in its own right it was an uncomplicated human gesture. It was a personal moment on a very public stage.

Downstairs in the changing rooms there was a melee of photographers and managers and players; among all the steam and the mud we savoured the satisfaction of that moment. It didn't matter that South Africa hadn't been there, they wouldn't have won, they wouldn't have beaten that All Black team. It was the best team in the world playing some of the best rugby anyone there had seen – and they went on for another two years never losing; the second longest unbeaten run New Zealand had ever had.

De Gaulle wrote about the cloak of melancholy which hangs around great achievers. There in the moment of triumph when things can't get any better – that is when you are at your most vulnerable, that is when the emptiness of ambition is most revealed. In the very moment of achievement you feel – is that it?

Well, is it?

What makes a Champion Team?

This was a great team we'd made, and I thought about it a lot afterwards. What makes a great team? How do you recognise a great one – and how do you set about creating one?

Great teams are rare; we all know the ones at the peak of their cycle as they dominated their time. Australia's rugby league teams of the 1980s, the West Indies cricket team in the Seventies and Eighties, the McLaren Formula One racing team, the Williams Formula One racing team, the San Francisco 49ers, Liverpool Football Club in the 1980s, Manchester United in the 1990s.

When you're in these teams you know it. They have a sense of ease, of relaxation. Individuals feel at ease with themselves and their ability to win. This feeling wasn't there in any of the All Black teams I played in except the 1987 team. Year in, year out the All Blacks are a great tradition; only at certain times are they a great team. The only two great teams I've played in were the '87 All Blacks and Auckland. There have been exuberant teams, careless teams, earnest teams, teams full of joie de vivre but only these two were great teams.

So what are the signs of a great team?

First: they make very few mistakes. The players seem to understand each other so well that unforced errors are eliminated. This is partly the result of a sort of divine discontent, a sense of eternal dissatisfaction, a lust for perfection. They have that restlessness on the one hand and extraordinary relaxation on the other. It's a mix that produces a real enthusiasm, a sense of fun at the same time as a desperation to achieve. It's hard keeping these opposites in balance. It's not easy to have fun playing rugby at international level. Only the great teams earn the right to do so.

When teams get to a certain level they start to win by big margins. International teams expect to win by five to ten points – not thirty, forty or fifty points (Auckland once beat Thames Valley by almost a hundred points; the All Blacks beat Italy by seventy and Wales by forty-five). Because truly great teams are rare, you don't often get two such teams playing against each other.

What do these teams have inside them? They've got a vision, they've got something to achieve, but more important something to become. Now, everyone and every team has objectives – but a true vision is something bigger, and it's outside the team, and it isn't rational.

There's no point in having an unachievable vision – but it has to be big enough to be a little frightening, big enough so that there is a fear it won't be achieved.

Ours wasn't to win the World Cup. It was to be the best team in the world, to set new standards, to play better rugby than had ever been played. Winning the World Cup was something that would happen along the way. The aim every time was to play the perfect game. That was the vision. Big and bold (and easy to fail at).

I wouldn't call any of the aims of the earlier All Black teams I played in visionary. The aim in those days was not to lose to the opposition, a very different ambition to winning which was, in itself, a limited sort of ambition. Unless you have a vision bigger than victory the team will remain in the box it has built for itself. If winning is enough that's all that will be achieved. The team that concentrates on just winning will inevitably start to lose. And the team will have to lose in order to start growing again. Only with a wider vision and the leadership to make it real will it be possible – even necessary – to change a winning team for its longer-term health.

And there are greater losses than not winning a match. There is the loss of potential, there is the loss of achievement, of what might have been.

In my day, test matches were precious to most rugby players, we played so few of them. Then, most internationals wouldn't play more than twenty tests. Every time you went out onto a test pitch you had used up five per cent of your playing career. After ten tests you were halfway through your international life.

Even today, unless you have a vision of what you are to achieve it's too easy to descend into just needing to beat the opposition – and you've missed one of life's biggest opportunities.

The first qualification for greatness, then, is having a positive vision. All the best teams have a positive vision. But there is always the underlying dark side of that ambitious goal, the fear of failure – the fear of letting yourself down, your family down, your clubmates and supporters down. There is the fear of going back home from a tour and knowing you've let your country down. When you go over to Australia there are an awful lot of people who want to beat the Australians. If you lose you feel you're letting down that twelve-year-old boy you were yourself, as well as the All Black history of success; that long, hard slog of every All Black team since 1905. If you lose, you chip away at the legend; if you win you make it easier for the next team to win. Winning is important all right, but it must be kept in its place.

But fear is not only the dark side of the positive vision: it is the driving force behind the negative vision. The Baby Blacks were a much less capable team than the All Blacks they replaced, but they had a positive vision, and played as though they had everything to gain. They were outsiders, and here was their chance to make the most of their rugby lives. They weren't going to creep around fearfully, but seize the moment and make it their own.

Second: you also have to have a vision of the team as an entity. The opposition is no longer what you are competing against but the means by which your team expresses itself. Under these conditions you find out what rugby is capable of, what really is possible.

The third characteristic is ability. You can't have a world class team without world class players. But you need more than brilliant individuals, it needs great players who complement each other.

For instance, Kurt Sherlock played second-five most of the years I was in Auckland. He was a talented, solid, dependable player. John Schuster was more brilliant but he stayed in the reserves because Kurt fitted the game plan Hart wanted to play. He didn't want brilliance everywhere – he wanted someone who'd reliably keep the backline straight and ensure that our running fullback and wings received the ball in space. He was the guy who made sure John Kirwan got the ball. Schuster moved to Wellington and went on to play excellent All Black rugby himself – but in a different team.

The very best teams are chock full of really great players. I always thought the 1987 team had ten or more players who were the best players in their position in the world (incidentally, I wouldn't count myself in that ten in the '87 team). Six or seven of the forwards and four or five of the backs were in that category.

Rugby is an amazingly specialised game. Every position has a different set of skills – halfbacks need special, spiral passing skills, to be able to kick high into the box, to run and draw players to you and create gaps.

Propping is a technical position; props have to be able to position their weight as carefully as sumo wrestlers; they need to get the ball off other players in mauls, to block and, these days, lift in lineouts.

Modern number eights need all the skills of a loose forward in tackling, going back and taking high kicks, driving with the ball in hand, but also the passing vision and anticipation of a centre.

More and more players in all positions are masters of their speciality – but at the same time they are developing general skills to a higher level, too. Forwards are becoming more adept at running and passing. Forwards tackle, and backs are getting bigger and better at rucks and mauls. If the first-five gets tackled, the second-five claims the ball and waits for support. If the fullback is caught, the winger comes in driving from behind to support. Forwards read defensive lines.

If players have all these skills you can do an extraordinary amount on a pitch. Why would you want to waste the possibilities in closing down the game just to be certain of winning it?

Also, this way of play brings a sense of wholeness. If I know how centres have to draw a man and make a pass I am much more able to live his game with him and, therefore, predict which line he's going to run. It becomes easier to complement players because you know what they are thinking about doing.

Players in great teams generalise their attitude. They're more able to do their job because they're thinking about team patterns; they are feeling responsible in part for other people's performance. The jigsaw piece, as they see themself, doesn't have any meaning until it's in place as part of the whole. Then they become owners of the team output. They all become leaders, rather than just plodding around doing their own job.

The fourth characteristic of great teams is a restless desire to improve. Auckland came to the point where, after every game, we'd spend five to ten minutes thinking about our mistakes. The atmosphere in the changing room at the end of the match was often meditative; we'd run over our mistakes and lament our errors. The better the team became the less we celebrated. It was so much harder to get to the further stage of improvement. At the end of every match there was always something you could have done better.

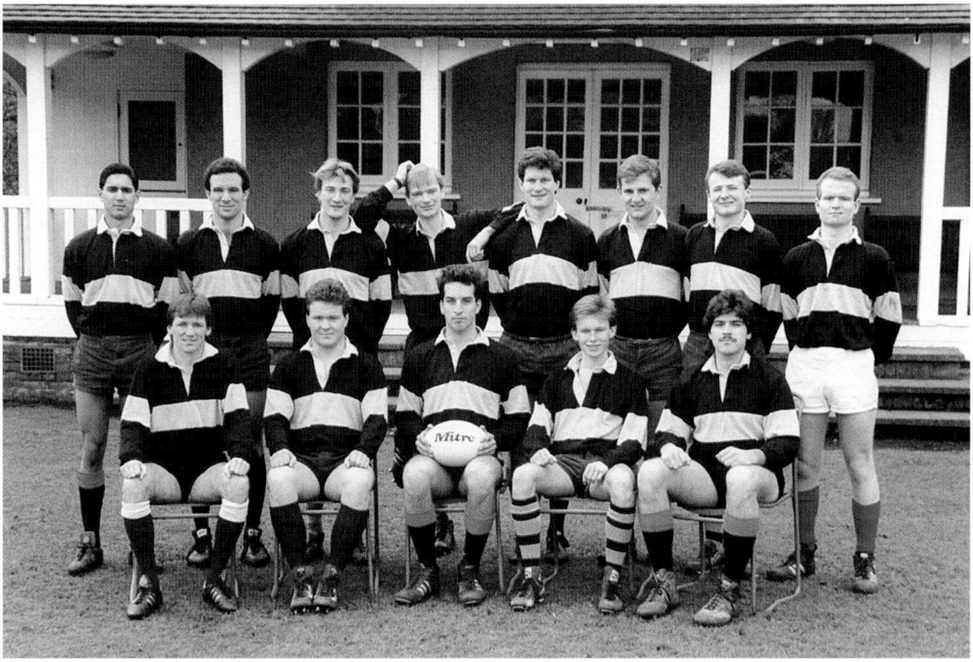

There are six different sock styles, one pair of white shorts, a phenomenal hangover in the back row and, apparently, a 14-year-old in the front row. University rugby at its most characteristic.

Kirk collection

The guy behind me in the bow position was the only person in the boat lighter than me. Our Worcester College eight didn't do well enough to 'burn the boat'. *Kirk collection*

Brigit in front of Worcester College, Oxford, one of the university's fortified colleges – very elegant on the inside.

Kirk colletion

"Good argument, I don't believe a word of it." My politics tutor at Oxford with his million-page library.

Kirk collection

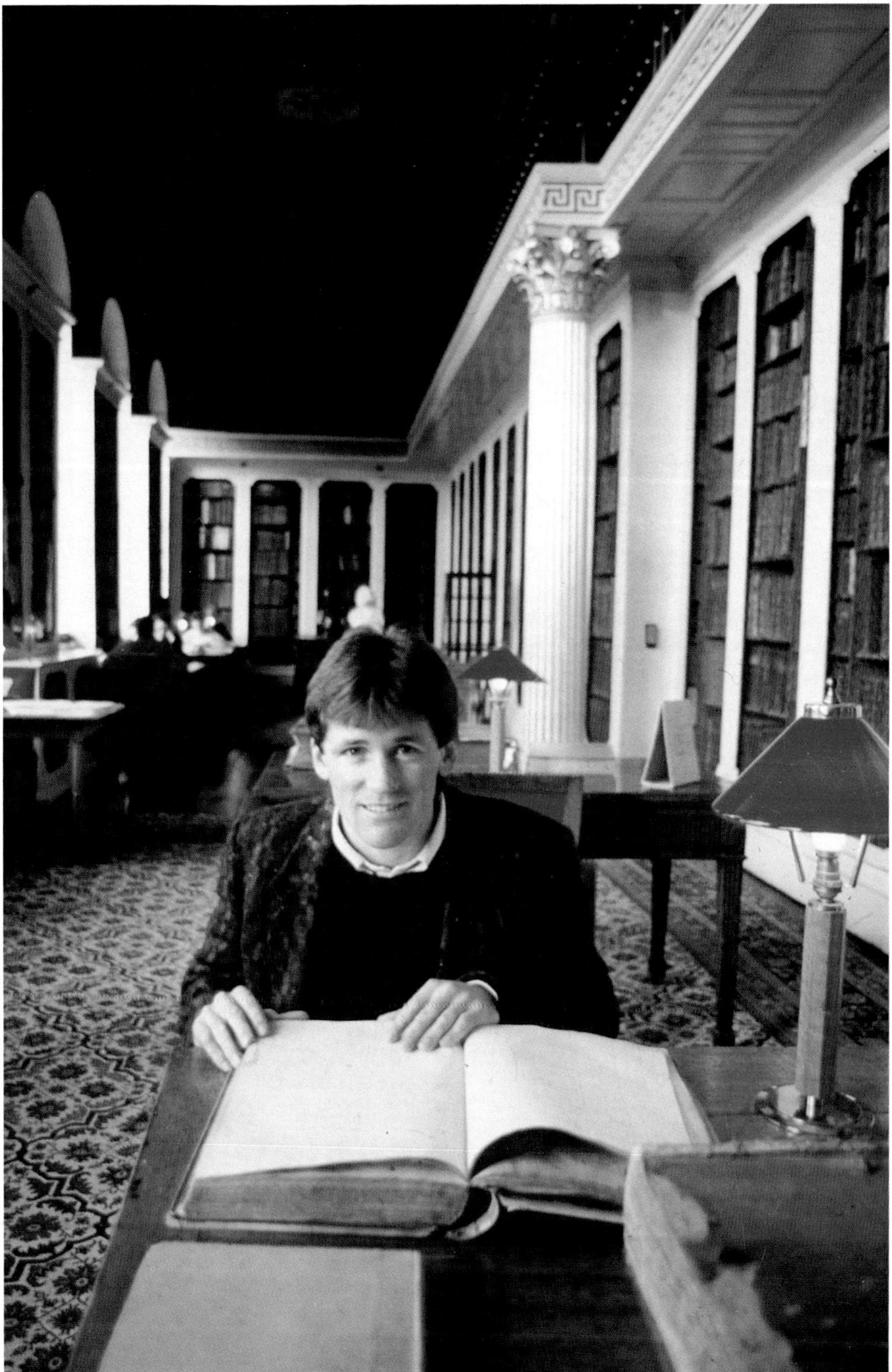

The library at Worcester College (practically deserted, but very impressive). *Kirk collection*

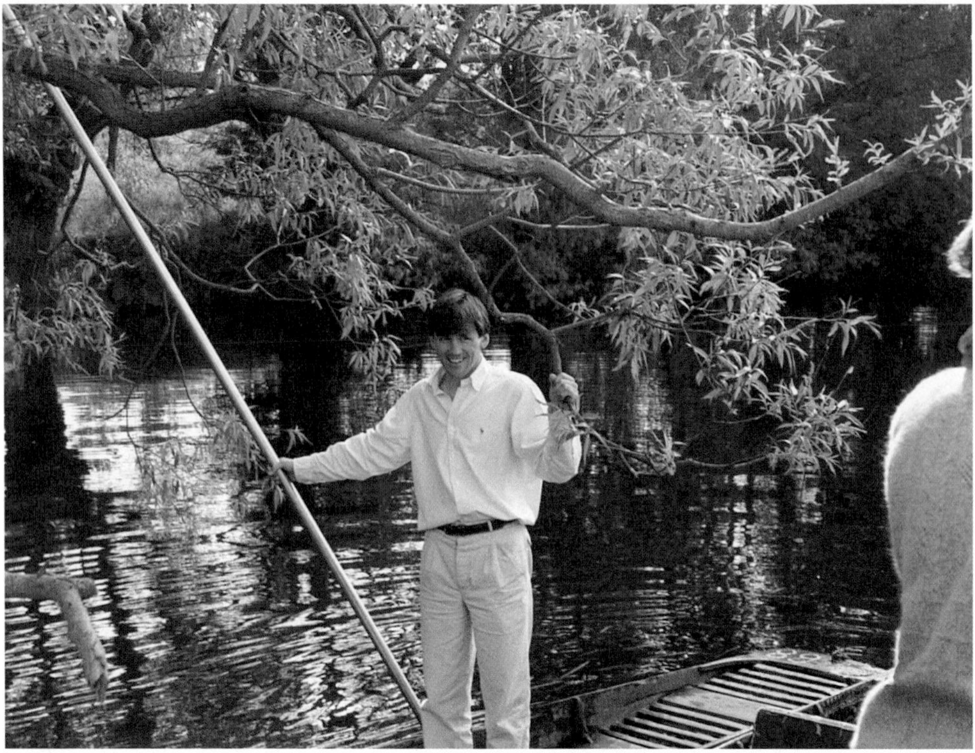

Oxford stands at the correct end of the punt. At Cambridge they pole from the other – incorrect – end.
Kirk collection

Aussie Oxonians Brian Smith and Troy Coker who paid the penalty for not turning up to training.
Kirk collection

Emerging from an 18th century hole in the wall for training at Oxford. *Kirk collection*

Outside Buckingham Palace with Brigit and brother Peter – and an MBE. John Kirwan and I were the only All Blacks to be awarded one by David Lange (perhaps because we were the only players not to join the rebel tour to South Africa). *Kirk collection*

The bride was beautiful – even by Hawke's Bay standards. *Kirk collection*

Celebrating the night after Finals. English crayfish taste very rubbery compared with New Zealand's.
Kirk collection

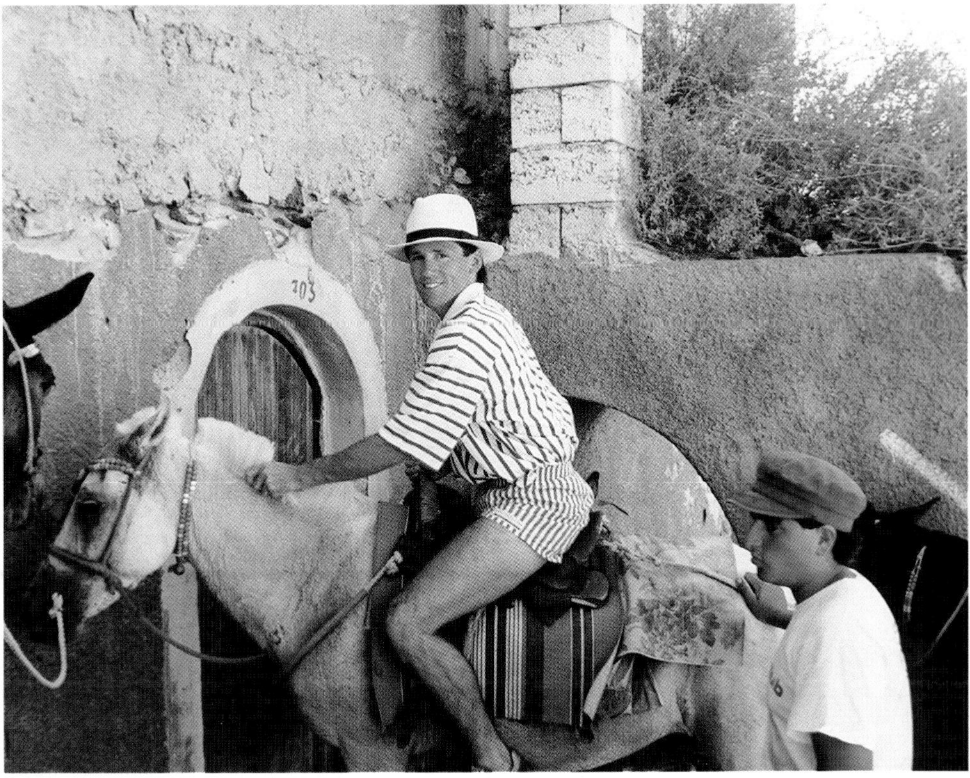

On holiday in Greece – the beginning of my equestrian career. *Kirk collection*

New Zealand childhoods don't really change – sun, beach, swimming and that long swing on which you sail out over the river . . . Brigit with Hugo, Harry and Barnaby.

Kirk collection

It was quite the opposite atmosphere in Otago; when we won we'd yahoo and fizz the beer. Later on, when I was coaching Wellington we played Waikato, the current national champions, in the third match of the NPC campaign in Hamilton. We had lost to tail-end charlies King Country the week before but here, totally against expectations, we won. Our joy was unbridled. We hugged, we danced, we sang – Waikato was beaten, wasn't it great that players could be so happy? But amid the bright sparkle of victory was my thought that we were so happy because we'd never do so well again. There is a special joy for the underdog that wins, but for the coach the knowledge of being the underdog rather spoils the pleasure.

To outsiders, this attitude of top teams can appear churlish, refusing to accept a compliment. We're like those women you can't compliment. You say, "That's a nice dress." She says, "This old thing?" You say to a prop, "You crushed the opposition." He says, "I had my weight too high in the rucks." It is important to recognise that you can go into a morbid descent if you go too far down this track. The process should be confined to that period of post-match meditation and then relegated to the back of your mind.

So if those are the elements of great teams, how do you go about creating them?

It starts with the administration and the coaching. Basic things are done correctly. Training sessions always start on time and are run crisply with a sense of discipline and organisation. Nothing's as demoralising as not knowing what's required. The coach must be very specific about what's required. Punctuality and dress standards are important. The team that observes the little things off the field will do the same on the field.

External disciplines become internal standards – which is when people become truly self-motivated.

I believe most players, even top players, aren't capable of maintaining disciplines without coaches to drive them. Contenders can't push themselves to the max because they don't know what the max is without someone to push back the boundaries – just when you think you've hit the wall they tell you there's a whole new level you have to rise to.

In the 1987 World Cup we constructed a simple analogy for ourselves in order to lock in the commitment to relentless improvement we needed. We visualised ourselves on a staircase.

Every match we played was an opportunity to take a step up the stair; every match was a vital opportunity to keep moving, locking in the gains we had already made, and preparing for the next step. I made this analogy to management consultants at McKinsey and Co later on and they built it into their theory of corporate growth.

Teams also have to manage the politics of interpersonal relationships. This usually falls to coach and captain. Sometimes the challenge is larger than others. Players may look like bruisers but many can be quite highly-strung.

The positions have an effect on the characters who play there. It's something of a chicken and egg argument; I have never been sure which came first, the position or the personality. But Foxy, for instance, was one of the more self-absorbed players. His contribution was very specific and very precise. He wasn't given to extravagance of any sort; boundaries were understood. Wingers are generally more creative and exuberant, out there on the edge of things, and you think of the characters on the wing like Stu Wilson, John Kirwan, Grant Batty, Jeff Wilson.

Props are more silent, bigger, quieter, more agricultural. Halfbacks are bossy, chirpy, talkative, verbal people – as their position requires.

If you don't manage the personalities you run into problems. The reason we lost the third test against Australia in 1986 was because of the unresolved personal conflicts in the team.

On a more individual level, Foxy was very tough on himself and on people around him; he'd criticise openly those who didn't come up to his level. So, he'd tell people what to do and get annoyed with them for not doing it. But then, that wasn't unusual. Everyone had opinions about tactics and didn't want to be contradicted – though they would invariably subsume their opinion to the final decision.

Thinking Early Retirement

After I collected the World Cup and completed the photographs and interviews I went back to the the friendly, comfortable home team changing rooms at Eden Park with the rest of the team. We were ecstatic. But somehow, even in that moment of triumph it wasn't that much different from many big matches. There was joy, huge satisfaction, and pride. And there was something else, another element as I changed and showered: my retirement. I am usually one of the slowest showering after a match; I tend to sit around, think and talk a bit. However, this time I moved through quickly. I had duties to do in the press room, but I was also moving on, looking ahead, barely pausing to say goodbye. Sometimes I think I live too much in the future; the present is the place to be, after all. Especially then.

The day after the World Cup final, not twenty-four hours after the final whistle, I sat down to write an article which appeared in the French paper *Liberation* explaining why I was leaving rugby.

I explained that while I loved the All Blacks, the culture of the team and the demands of the tradition were too demanding. "The need to conform and to accept a system of behaviour and values that are not your own, but those of the rugby culture is known as 'discipline', and it is a quality highly prized in New Zealand rugby.

"It is true that discipline is an essential element of success on the rugby field. It too often becomes a tyranny of the majority off the field. Those who refuse to conform are seen either as undisciplined, or as selfish and egotistical. The price of conformity is too high for some and perhaps I am one of those."

I was remembering the drinking session after the Wales match; I got cornered on the floor with the drink!drink!drink! routine. I'd felt both that I was growing out of compulsory drinking games and that the team itself was above this. I remember hearing about one of our big drunk forwards coming out of a pub and seeing a donkey tethered up; he punched the animal so hard it fell unconscious to the ground. I remember another of our forwards whose party trick it was to bite the heads off budgies.

I didn't get so specific in my *Liberation* article, these incidents didn't strike the tone of rather melancholy grandeur I was after. And my reservations about the All Blacks were larger than the fact that they sometimes committed errors of taste and judgment. Every large collection of individuals has its reprobates. Essentially, I felt it was time to move on; I had the Oxford scholarship to take up, that involved travel, study, new horizons. I was on a high – after all the tribulations, the depression, the rejection, here was tangible victory in its fullest and most public sense. And maybe underlying the desire to leave at the top was the fear of coming down the other side of the hill, step by step, until the inevitable fall off the edge.

There was another element in this feeling. For some time now I'd been standing with John Kirwan waiting for kick-offs, thinking the game was getting boring. Sometimes we'd be thirty points up with twenty minutes to go and I'd feel that we'd lost something. Every time we tried the same move we'd get the same result – a try. We were in the best team in the world; our system of play was unbeatable. We were not only bigger and faster, we were more accurate, more dominating and far more certain of victory.

It was at that point that I knew something had gone. If you execute a certain move and score nine times out of ten, some sense of fear, of anxiety is lost. At twenty-six I had the need for constant stimulation and there was none in seeing perfect moves working perfectly.

John Hart wrote in his book that I was the most unsentimental player he knew, that I was ruthless in terms of wanting to win and once ahead wanting to win by a lot. But he also picked that I was unsentimental about leaving the game and walking away from the deep bonds established in the cauldron of international competition. And I did walk away almost without a sense of loss. The only symptom I can pick from that time was that I didn't watch the All Blacks play for two years. And I don't know why.

Having said all that, I would never have written the article at all for an English-language paper, let alone a New Zealand paper. I doubted a French paper would be translated. I also thought the French would understand, and judging by some of the conversations I'd had with French people about the article, I think they did.

The pressures to conform were enormous – and for good reason. The culture that has built up is the result of years of figuring out how to win. Layer upon layer, year upon year, team upon team have taken on characteristics that reinforce success. It's our national secret, our national style. In rugby, the greatest contributor to winning is conforming to team patterns. The reason why our forwards arrive closer together is because they all conform to the one discipline.

People are happy to conform if it produces a win. For some of us the problem is conformity off the field. The way All Blacks do things is not necessarily the way you'd like to do things yourself.

The drinking sessions, for instance, are amusing at first. The team drinks together, there is a judge and a prosecutor. People commit minor crimes – not wearing a belt, or talking when there is a no-talking rule, or drinking with the right hand when the left has been stipulated, or crossing your arms when you're only allowed to cross your legs. It was all good fun, it only lasted an hour and it was an exercise in team bonding. You see each other under an unusual sort of pressure, and it applied to all of us equally – good players, weak players, new or seasoned, all subject to the same penalties. It has its egalitarian virtues in building a team.

But after some years you think that a quiet drink at a bar with your particular friends would be nice, rather than something that has become a drill for the sake of it.

The same applied to training. In the Otago team, the drill could be mindless. In Auckland you were applying your skills to playing the game with as much creativity as possible. The older players got stuck in their traditions; they felt that you couldn't get flash or you'd make mistakes and lose games. That's a suffocating way to play or to live.

In the later Eighties players started to want to express themselves rather than bury their personalities and grind out a victory. They wanted to win, but win memorably – gloriously, even. We got immense satisfaction in perfect moves and scoring from sixty metres out, pushing back boundaries of the way the game was played.

There is always an element of averaging down in conformity. This is where the tension is. You have to act in concert to succeed – you have to act with others – but you also want to be different from the crowd. New Zealand has a hard time accepting that's normal. But that's hardly surprising as we've all had experiences of being different at school and being pushed firmly back into our box with teasing and bullying.

I noticed that at Oxford a lot of the public school boys had much more individual assertiveness – at times bordering on arrogance. This was very different from New Zealanders of the same age – we're pleasant self-effacing characters who say "Don't look at me, I'm nothing out of the ordinary."

In New Zealand, conversation with people you don't know very well can have a sense of holding hands in the dark – people search for names in common. The New Zealand game some people call it in England. "Oh, you know Bugs' cousin? She's Muff's aunt, we met at Huffy's fiftieth." Maybe that's why people take things very personally in New Zealand, we're all so intimately involved. But sport is a useful tutor. You get a lot of comment, a lot of criticism and you learn to take remarks as one person's opinion – no more, no less – and your task is to find a stable of people whose opinions are worth taking seriously. The best person to ask is the one who'll tell you the truth. Brutal honesty from someone who cares is the most valuable thing for a sports person who wants to improve.

It wasn't an immediate retirement. A couple of club matches and a test formed a coda to my New Zealand career. Our club – Auckland University – was on the borderline of being knocked out. We had to win the next five matches to make the play-offs in the top five of the Gallaher Shield. Ken Baguley rang me up on the Tuesday saying, "You probably feel like a break, David, but the fact is we need to win every game on our fixture list. And you *are* the University halfback, after all." I went to training that Tuesday and I played in the next two games for the club (Mt Roskill and Suburbs) before injury took me out. We made the play-offs, won the semi and went on to win the final. That was satisfying, but it remains one of the deepest regrets of my playing career that an injured knee kept me out of those matches.

The last test was coming up and it had a very important dimension for me. It was the first time I'd been selected in my own right as captain. We were going to Australia. We'd been beaten the year before. We'd lost the Bledisloe Cup and I'd been dumped as captain. It was my last-ever game for New Zealand.

They picked a good team against us. Alan Jones had made some mistakes during the World Cup, but this time we were convinced he had got it right.

I had a very sore knee throughout the training; on the morning of the match Brian Lochore came to my room and said to me, "You shouldn't stay on for the sake of it, David, you don't have anything to prove here."

I didn't tell him what I really felt, which was that I did have quite a lot to prove, and particularly to him. Sometimes Brian had had a lot of faith in me. At others it was marginal. He'd dropped me in Argentina two years earlier when I'd been playing well. He'd dropped me as captain the year before. I hadn't heard then that he'd kept me in place during the World Cup just gone, but I felt I had something to prove, and nothing was going to stop me.

It was a bloody hard game.

We were away from home, everyone was a bit creaky. As we now knew, at the point of greatest success you are at your most vulnerable. Australia scored from some penalty goals, Michael Hawker kicked a huge dropped goal – suddenly they were six points ahead. We weren't making it. Finally, in the second half, from a shied kick, Sean scored in the corner. We were about to get into gear and move past them. And when their kick-off failed to go ten metres we all recognised the moment: this was when we turned the screw, we'd get ahead and watch them crack. But the chance was blown by a stupid mistake – that was bitter. And the worst of it came from the fact that it was I who blew it. Instead of putting the ball in John Gallagher's hands I kicked for the corner. I kicked too early. I wasn't in the gap (what had Jim Wallace always told me about being in the gap?) The ball bounced off Brett Papworth's legs. He gathered and raced away to score for Australia in the corner. We'd slogged for two thirds of the match, it was just starting to come our way and I'd made the mistake which put them ahead again.

The team didn't bat an eyelid. There was no sense of disappointment or resentment, no criticism under the goalposts, just the resolve to keep doing the work.

I have always believed Craig Green won that match for us. We had a penalty on our twenty-two. Instead of waiting for Foxy to kick to touch on the halfway, and the inevitable slog for the ball in the lineout, he grabbed the ball, tapped it and ran. Eventually it was kicked into the corner but we were on attack and we never looked back. It was as if he'd said to himself and the team, "Let's take this by the scruff of the neck; let's change gear, speed it up, run it, take some risks, and just beat these guys. We know they're not as good as we are." That's what he communicated by tapping the ball and running with it, and he changed the whole collective psychology of the team. It was a fine intuition.

The dam broke in the last fifteen minutes. The pressure finally told. We scored three times in the last period. John Kirwan scored a great running back try from a lineout. Craig Green got over by the posts and a John Drake pass put Fitzy in for the last try. Warwick Taylor had another legitimate try disallowed right on fulltime.

Australia was cleaned out in a way that only that team could do it – the score closed at 30-16.

My knee was blown up like a football. It was restrapped twice during the game. It didn't survive the match, but it was worth it. I struggled through the last two games I played for Auckland, the Ranfurly Shield match against Taranaki and the Wellington match. The only two games I left the field before the end were these last two, in the last moments of my playing career.

It was a badly-scripted end, but a moving farewell nonetheless from Auckland. I owe the rugby people, players, coaches, administrators and supporters, of Auckland more than it is possible to explain. Brigit, on the other hand, was cheerfully looking forward to a new life, and that cheered me up, too.

Dreaming Spires, Aspiring Dreams

So it was Oxford. Another standing start. Another example of the principle that nothing you have done counts when you move from one pond to another.

Oxford is, as we know, venerable, intellectual, ancient, surpassingly beautiful etc. It isn't a university as we think of it in New Zealand. There is no powerful centre from which radiates administration, appointments, financial grants, admissions, teaching – all that is run by the colleges. Oxford is a federation of self-governing colleges which are financially autonomous and run by the dons. They might even be the owners of the college and could, in theory, sell the asset to the highest bidder. Commercialism isn't that strong a danger in Oxford, however.

There is little observable hierarchy when you arrive; although, it being England, everyone has their place. Everyone wears a distinctive gown. The commoners wear a short, black waistcoat-style gown with two tapes hanging down the back. These were said to be for the convenience of creditors – giving them something physical to catch on to when chasing debts. Exhibitioners and scholars wore longer gowns – they were all worn on quite routine occasions like tutorials or dinner in college. The most obvious feeling was of being in an environment where people were more intelligent, more ambitious, more academic than oneself. It was to fit into another great traditional body.

Oxford's special magic is described in many books. But the colourwash that goes through the most evocative descriptions is one of youth, and lost youth. You go punting; you get up in the dark on May mornings to listen to the choristers singing from the top of Magdalen tower at dawn; you go for Sunday lunch at the Perch; you buy books at Blackwell's; you visit friends in their colleges and marvel at the gardens of Worcester, New College or Trinity. And you remember it all like a secret place, hidden from the world.

Boarding schools were supposed to knock the nonsense out of boys – Oxford was there to put it back. I noticed here that people didn't get dragged out of their rooms in the small hours to be thrown into a bath of slime, but this was partly because we were less young than we had been. Undergraduates at Oriel and the other rowing colleges used to burn their eight (the boat, not the team) in the quad if they won the annual regatta. Revellers would jump through the flames and very often emerge unscathed. Vincent's dinners are an experience by turns beyond and beneath comparison. And there were stories of deplorable achievements – the Bullingdon Club that shot out every traffic light on the Great West Road with shotguns one night. The Hellfire Club was banned from Brasenose (for the noise rather than the diabolism) – but that was going back a bit, two hundred years or so.

The sense of the past is strong in England but never stronger than in cities like Oxford or Cambridge. Quite a number of the colleges were built seven or eight hundred years ago; their steps rounded from many generations of student feet, their narrow doorways, their barrel vaulting.

So, for me, once more a forbidding entrance – the great gates of Worcester College, its pocked, eighteenth century walls, its porters, its fabulous walled gardens (including quite a substantial lake round which torch bearers ran and fireworks flew, and young voices called Illyriaaaa! in a famous production of *Twelfth Night*).

You ask the porter where you find your room; you climb a twisting staircase; you open your two doors (one a fortified oak slab studded with iron, inches in front of a conventional study door); you find your cell with its desk, angle-poise lamp, bed and Parker Knoll unsprung chair.

The colleges are built as though fortified against a hostile world – a sensible precaution.

The university had enjoyed a long history of violence, particularly in its relations with the city – it was quite unlike the cordial relations enjoyed by Otago town and gown. This troubled relationship boiled over in 1357 in the St Scholastica's Day riot – it began over an argument about the quality of beer in a tavern and three days later sixty-odd scholars had been hanged, shot or thrown into dunghills. The king sent in troops to restore order and the town (held to be the aggressor) had to pay restitution of sixty-three pence every St

Scholastica's Day for five hundred years (one penny for each scholar killed – not a lot of money even in the fourteenth century).

There is a long tradition of rivalry between Oxford and Cambridge, and while I am too far out of it to suffer from it myself, I have been close enough to have observed some of the symptoms.

Oxford prides itself on its worldliness and contact with the great, gay world of television and journalism (they are helped in this by being on a motorway to London). They think of themselves as cosmopolitan. Cambridge think themselves to be cleverer and more logical. Oxford prides itself on its dash and daring – and accuses Cambridge of wearing pens in the top shirt pockets. Cambridge is said to pride itself on precision and believes Oxford to be intellectually inferior. Oxford is the city of dreaming spires, but both are of aspiring dreams.

Like the great centre of learning it has been for nearly a thousand years, Oxford has a great body of diffused tradition. In no particular order here are some observations on the Oxford mystery.

Oxford has been royalist, loyal to the Monarchy; Cambridge has a Cromwellian streak. Cambridge was on the side of the Roundheads during the civil war while Oxford gave refuge to the fugitive king. Cambridge is the source of most of the post-war traitors (Philby, McLean, Burgess and Blunt). Oxford is quick to point out that Oxford is that part of the country associated with Merrie England and Cambridge part of the more dour, damp fenlands where Hereward the Wake led the invaders of the time into the swamp.

In the Bodleian Library, a marvellous Gothic building built in the durable yellow sandstone of the area, there are the medieval examination halls. You were examined viva voce; that is, out loud. Oratory, argument, articulacy turned the sedate and silent tradition of exams into a form of single combat.

In those old days, the very old days, most of the scholars were from relatively humble backgrounds – the upper class had private tutors and retainers to educate their children – and there wasn't a middle class to speak of. Graduates would go on to seek a career in the church – which was the main sponsor of learning in those days.

In the last century, the dons lived in their own world, originally rather a monastic one. They weren't allowed to be married and they lived in college, taking a close personal interest in their pupils. The remnants of this survive in the tutorial system by which you are individually taught by your tutors. Undergraduates have what is called a Moral Tutor (to look after your personal problems) as well as an academic one. I didn't find I called on my Moral Tutor for help, but my academic tutor revealed a new dimension of education.

Surprisingly, tutors seemed to know everything – everything from the general rate of inflation in the nineteenth century to the heretical reforms of Akhenaten in ancient Egypt. One of my colleagues came up for his admission interview to try for a place. After the English literature part of the interview he was asked two questions: i) what his interests were outside English literature (he said the north-eastern railway system in the 19th century) and ii) what he'd brought to read on the train (he said Farewell, My Lovely by Raymond Chandler). One don then asked him why the Hull-Grimsby sidings line changed gauge in 1844, and the other said, "Chandler uses many of the same visual devices as Dashiell Hammett in his prose, but to rather better effect – or would you disagree?"

Tutors exercised an extraordinary level of courtesy with us, their ignorant charges. They would rarely contradict you. If you used a word wholly incorrectly they might say, "Are you using that word in, perhaps, a special sense?" It wasn't their purpose to prove us wrong or tell us what was right. They wanted to improve the processes by which our minds worked. They didn't want to argue but to establish in our minds that there were right and wrong ways of proceeding, not that there were right or wrong conclusions to arrive at. "Jolly well argued," one said on an essay I produced about the international gold standard and the exchange rate, "don't agree with a word of it myself." This was an approach we in New Zealand don't follow locally; most argument is taken personally, and to disagree with a person's argument is taken as a criticism, and ultimately as an insult.

Their courtesy was of a different time and place. If they detected an error of logic or reading they would ask a series of questions to lead you further into the cactus until even the most cloth-headed of us would understand we were wrong.

Oxford undergraduates aren't required to attend lectures. You are invited to attend – but you aren't required to send your apologies if you can't make it. Your only fixed duties are one or maybe two tutorials a week. Here you spend an hour with your tutor, reading for the first ten minutes an essay you have prepared on a set topic. Then you discuss it and debate it and learn.

My closest tutor was in the last of his sixties, had worked for British Intelligence during the war and kept goal for the Sudan. He had one leg and a library of ten thousand books from which he could remember de Gaulle's point or Churchill's view and go unerringly to the one page in a million where the quotation lay.

I was immediately drawn to university rugby, but was still recovering from my last injury. It took a New Zealand doctor to diagnose it as a ruptured pectoralis major muscle. In my first college game (against Balliol) I put the ball in and our scrum started moving backwards faster than I could chase them.

Bedford was my first Blues game, played against a team with huge beer guts. Their strategy – a good one in the circumstances – was to take it very slowly, try to get the opposition on the ground and then sit on them. It was my only match before the Varsity match that year. The second Tuesday in December came round quickly and we trooped off to a packed Twickenham. I managed to score in the first ten minutes but we never fired and Cambridge – not the better team – beat us.

That first Varsity match was a let-down. Injured all term, I wasn't engaged with the team or the occasion. I determined to contribute more next year. There had been a big expectation that I'd captain Oxford but I decided not to, and it was a good decision. I wanted to play and make my contribution but I didn't know enough about the culture and ethos of Oxford rugby to perform this very intimate function. I didn't have a feel of how to make people respond in the right way – that's how you know you're in a foreign country. And for all our deep bonds of history and trade, the differences between us are important and probably getting larger. I saw that going to England more easily than the English see it coming to New Zealand.

The captain in my second year was Rupert Vessey, a Varsity match veteran. He did an outstanding job.

I suggested that the administrative role be separated from the playing role of the captain and that they bring in a coach (a job that had hitherto been done by the captain), and an administrator to get in close with the colleges and help build their teams. The captain needed to be free to concentrate on playing and leading the training and on the matches themselves rather than worrying about clean jerseys for the players on Saturdays.

Because the colleges have greater autonomy, politics is important – the captain is elected by a fine, longstanding tradition. The fifteen players who gained a Blue by playing in the last Varsity match vote independently for the following year's captain. We met in the house of the Dean of Christ Church, in the house where Charles Dodgson (aka Lewis Carroll) wrote *Alice in Wonderland*. The papers were collected up and the winners announced.

The glamour that accrues to the captain of Oxford is quite disproportionate to the stature of the team. But this was the university, after all, that elected its own members of Parliament within living memory.

There is the equivalent of an arms race between Oxford and Cambridge. That's why they ruthlessly recruit good players from around the world to beef up the teams – but there is still a majority of British players among the burly South Africans, Australians and New Zealanders. It's worse in the Boat Race where people express surprise that the boats stay afloat under the weight of monstrous Americans.

But because most of the players are British it needs a British captain. The British communicate in a unique way. They are more oblique, less straightforward. At our ends of the world we are more assertive, more definite. Danny Hearn, the English centre who came to grief playing against the All Blacks in the Sixties, tells how he was over in New Zealand and was asked whether he wanted another drink. "Oh, I don't know," he said. "Are you going to have one? Is there time? Shouldn't we be moving on? What's everyone else doing?" And the New Zealand official had to interrupt him to say, "Do you, or do you not, want another drink?"

(I also remember laughing at a friend's story about how a Fleet Street editor cancelled a Thursday lunch with the words, "Dear boy, a cloud no larger than a man's hand hangs over Thursday." Huh? Isn't that the day we're having lunch? Should I bring an umbrella? Are we eating outside? What?)

Rupert put his heart and soul into his year as captain and set up a whole new structure. We won all three matches against Cambridge (Blues, Greyhounds and Whippets) for the first time, and in the Varsity match won by the widest margin for eighty-odd years.

The Varsity match is a very important institution, particularly for the players. It's usually their only chance to play in a big game at Twickenham – in front of 55,000 people – and will be their most important sporting memory. Blues applying for a job in the City find it a great asset. Sometimes the interviewer has a varsity blue as well – it's an immediate bond. So, understanding how it affected people, and how important it was for them, it became important for me as well.

Therefore, for the last time in my playing career, I set goals; in the northern summer of 1988 I looked forward to the second Tuesday in December and decided the Varsity match was important, and that I had to play well in it. It was back to the old routine of running and weight training. I'd never got fit for its own sake in my life, there always had to be a reason for it; this was the hardest it had ever been because I didn't have the hunger any more.

Fortunately, there was a Japanese tour before the term started in October and that helped. Rugby is surprisingly big in Japan (there were quite a number of top players from around the world playing for steel rolling mills and car manufacturers and other big industrial teams). They'd also been the main sponsor of the World Cup so I had quite wide name recognition. As I was getting into buses, strangers used to come up to me and give me things; if they didn't have gifts they'd touch me.

It was a typical university tour – it was terrific fun. We were joined by three very good Australian internationals, friends and proteges of Alan Jones, the Australian coach who'd encouraged them to go to Oxford – Troy Coker, Ian Williams and Brian Smith.

Two years later, Brian assumed he'd get his man in as captain and that created quite a few problems when Mark Egan, an Irishman, became captain. The faction had a go at the Constitution to get one of their guys in as President next year to try and sew the thing up. Even then they didn't succeed; Troy and Brian didn't turn up for training and were both booted out, taking an American international with them. This severely dented the resources available, but in true *Boy's Own* fashion that team went on to win the Varsity match without them.

I wrote a letter to Brian in the middle of the controversy, setting out what I thought would be a diplomatic way of proceeding. He lost no time in telling me to take my nose out from where it wasn't wanted. I thought this was good advice in the circumstances, and for once I took it.

I played a number of invitation matches during the next season – Hong Kong, Monaco, Paris, Bermuda, La Rochelle and even Belfast. Newspapers paid me to watch and write about the Five Nations matches.

The BBC's *Year in Sport* also asked me to London to appear in their annual review of the sporting year. There were lots of sports people in the studio. Nigel Mansell, Nick Faldo, and a quick thing on rugby. I was asked, "Do you think that the northern hemisphere is starting to close the gap on the southern?"

What can you say? I said, "No, in fact I think the gap's getting wider." It sounded rather arrogant, which I regretted. Perhaps I might have said, "The English team shows great promise, good players abound, and if the English can only get a decent league system established, some greater fitness and athleticism among the players, and a severe restructuring of administration, then the gap wouldn't be widening quite as fast as it is at the moment." I didn't think there was the time for that so they got the condensed version.

About this time I gave a speech to the annual rugby writers' dinner about growing professionalism. I suggested that we had to understand the forces at work and control the flow otherwise the wave would break over us. This speech turned into an article for the *Sunday Times* and the professionalism angle caused a fuss in its own right as I was paid for writing it, and that was against the rules.

The Warden of Rhodes House, Robin Fletcher (Olympic bronze medallist, a DSO, and a man of powerful intellect) asked to see me one day as he'd had a query from Dudley Wood, the secretary of the Rugby Football Union and a keen amateur. "The copyright symbol [on my article in the *Sunday Times*] implies some proprietary interest signifying money," was how he put it. I was seen as a rabid professionaliser of the game from New Zealand.

My position was fairly strong, I thought. I had argued that professionalism was inevitable and that it was better for the ruling bodies to control its coming rather than be swamped by its unruly advent. Indeed, the substance of this argument came to a practical reality back home, later on. The New Zealand Rugby Football Union was nearly overthrown by the World Rugby Corporation – a group of businesspeople which was nearly able to contract enough internationals to hi-jack the game from the traditional administrators and take control of the whole system. I thought then, and still do, that such a move would have been disastrous, and that it would have resulted in money going only to the top of the game and the grassroots would wither for lack of support.

However, the Warden of Rhodes House said, in his peculiar but precise voice, "I couldn't possibly comment on whether it's a good idea or not for rugby to be played on an amateur or a professional basis, I simply haven't the knowledge. I am sure you are in a far better position than I to comment on that. There is this concern of the Rugby Union, however, and I think you should sort it out immediately."

It was resolved by the money being paid to the club and coming back to me through various expenses.

Oxford terms are eight weeks long and packed with academic, social and cultural activity. They go very fast. In October 1988, Troy Coker and I went to play for the French Barbarians against the New Zealand Maoris. It was the first time I'd played against my own country. Wayne Shelford was captain of the Maori team. Other players included Eric Rush, Frano Botica, Zinzan and Robin Brooke, Steve McDowell and Hika Reid. The halfback was Brett Iti. They played like a top New Zealand team (Brett punched me in the first ruck).

It's remarkable how changeable your attitude is when you're looking from a new point of view. When you're on foot you notice how arrogant motorists are; when you're driving it's easy to classify pedestrians as vagrants.

Watching this fine New Zealand team play I thought, "Why can't they relax and enjoy themselves?" When things were going badly they'd hunker down over the ball, never let it go, never take risks. They'd only start to enjoy themselves if they were far enough ahead. They'd never do anything to risk a loss.

Of course, it was exactly how I used to play when I played for New Zealand. That's how we play at any level, at any time. The downside to the English attitude (being carefree and careless of success) is that you lose all the time. New Zealand wins but the downside for us is that we don't enjoy it so much.

The Varsity match is very intense, like an international. You train and prepare for twelve months for nothing else. On the day before the match you travel to London, and stay at the Lensbury Club.

For most of these players it was the match of their lives. That's a very infectious feeling; the atmosphere was a bit like the first Baby Blacks test match. I was very keen to play well and live up to expectations. We had a remarkably strong backline, all of whom (bar two) were internationals, or went on to be internationals (Brian Smith for Australia and Ireland, Dai Evans for Wales, Ian Williams for Australia, Rob Egerton for Australia and me for New Zealand). This year we had beaten Major Stanley's XV for the first time in many years. We were hot; we were hyped up, this was the day.

Most of the team had been accustomed to playing in front of three hundred people, two dogs and their girlfriends. The crowd was intensely partisan, almost tribally so. The match is played in front of an enormous crowd and to the same noise level of any international. The two teams get to choose the referee. We chose Clive Norling for his ability to keep a match moving, for his perm, and for his tight shorts.

Cambridge played well at a hectic pace, both teams ran with the ball in the Varsity tradition. We were reasonably closely matched in the forwards but Troy Coker made a difference. We were superior in the backs and we finished well. We ran well, scoring four tries and keeping our line intact.

Then something happened that I still muse over from time to time. It was late in the game. Rob Wainwright, the current Scottish captain, then playing for Cambridge, cut through and was going for the line when I managed to put him down. Their support was coming in faster than our defence, they were probably going to win the ruck and may have scored. I lay on Rob to prevent the ball coming out. It was a type of professional foul. It wasn't detected. There was no possibility of losing, even if they had scored, but my competitive instincts came to the fore. It was quite unnecessary and also contrary to the tradition of sportsmanship that dominates this age-old fixture, the epitome of amateurism as well. I felt rather guilty about it.

The interesting thing is that had the incident happened in New Zealand, I would have felt quite pleased with myself. The feeling of regret also showed that I had lost the total desire to win.

After the Varsity match both teams have dinner at the Oxford and Cambridge Club on Pall Mall. They go to the separate dining rooms with their wives and partners. The flares outside the club are lit (which only happens twice a year). Then everyone goes on to the Vincent's Ball which starts around 10pm, and those who are still able to stand, dance.

Rugby Round the World

That was the end of club rugby, but there was an interesting tail to my playing career of invitation matches. I was flown out to Bermuda as a ringer for an Irish team; and to a sevens team in Monaco; back to the Hong Kong Sevens with the Penguins; and some games for the French Barbarians and Public School Wanderers.

Jacques Fouroux asked me to play in an international exhibition match in Grenoble. To repay one of the French patrons, Fouroux was taking down the French team to play in the patron's home town. Owing to plane delays at Heathrow I arrived only ten minutes before halftime – the only foreigner in the team.

But you know immediately when you're playing with top players – Serge Blanco was at fullback and Franck Mesnel, Eric Bonneval, Jean-Baptiste Lafond and all those grizzled French forwards were there. Language didn't seem to be a barrier. They were very polite in asking for tactical advice (and that we lost the match didn't seem to interfere with the pleasure they took in the excellent dinner afterwards). The fact that they had five Michelin chefs there to cook a course each, to be served with vintage Krug champagne, also helped. I noticed a conspicuous absence of flying food in the room. We must have been getting older. The evening was a marvellous example of camaraderie, and with a number of ancien players there it turned into a celebration of the '77 team that won the Five Nations. It left me hoping we could recreate this scene in New Zealand ten years after the 1987 World Cup win (we better get the invitations out smartly).

They were very good to me for two reasons (which, now I think about it, were both the same reason).

One was that they were intrigued by a captain winning the World Cup and immediately retiring because he found the All Black ethos too restrictive (and writing about it in their newspaper the Monday following the final). The other was that Jacques Fouroux had become infatuated with All Black rugby and was wanting to sieve out some of the Gallic flair in favour of what he saw as the New Zealand machine.

The French oscillate between wild individualism and repressive authoritarianism. You see that in French history as well, most recently in the Gulf War when they went off on their own on a wild foray deep into Iraq, far from any supporting divisions. Their appetite for la gloire conceals a greater appetite for Napoleonic authority – absolute and demanding. French military, political and philosophical history is a history of these opposing forces from Richelieu through De Gaulle to Le Pen. While they have been amazingly unsuccessful militarily (I don't think they've won a war since 1810) they have long been trying to find some golden mean between authority and freedom. Rousseau declared that the highest aim of government was to ensure that citizens were "forced to be free".

Fouroux was a great admirer of New Zealand rugby and our physically imposing backs. He chose his French team to play rugby the way he thought we played it. You run close at the opposition, make them tackle you, try and burst through, draw in the defence and open out their lines. It was a theory based on power as opposed to elusiveness and wasn't actually the way we played. He hadn't really identified the defining principles of All Black rugby.

All Blacks weren't totally confrontational; we used power to make the break but then we relied on speed and elusiveness and support play. We simply didn't do the relentless power play that Jacques was trying to introduce.

France was going through the same sort of controversy about our national style of play that we went through in New Zealand with the Hart/Mains camps. Fouroux essentially tried to close players down rather than open them up.

The excellent *L'Equipe* newspaper tried to enlist me as an arbiter, later the next year, when I was coaching at the Racing Club de France in Paris for a while. As with much of the press, the interviewer was not happy with Fouroux's approach and I probably gave him some ammunition to attack Jacques with. Jacques took the whole thing rather seriously when I saw him soon after in Grenoble. I made up with him later by letter and he was gracious enough to accept it.

Fouroux's style for France was successful in the short term but unsustainable. If a country wants to win you must look carefully at technique and be able to do the things that rugby requires you to do to win matches. But then you have to use those techniques in a way that builds a coherent style of play – and one that expresses the character of the country, the players' and spectators' perception of themselves and their culture.

That sounds airy-fairy, but it has some very practical applications.

France sees itself as a nation that generates *la gloire*. In the French catalogue of their characteristics, style is very important. *Le style, c'est l'homme.* A try is a try – but a try scored with dash, daring and flashes of originality is worthy of examination by cultural critics.

If they could have a referendum on it, a pushover try would be worth two points. But an interception on your own goal line and a pitch-long run involving seven passes would be worth ten points. In Fouroux's view a pushover try was the best sort of try because it was based on power and discipline. To the extent that he won matches he was right. To the extent that he was fired from the job because the country repudiated his style of play he was wrong.

How do we see ourselves in New Zealand? Traditionally we have seen ourselves as tough, uncompromising, resourceful.

You see these qualities in many areas of New Zealand, not just on the sports fields. Down in Hawke's Bay where Brigit comes from, the farmers are extraordinarily tough. They break their legs on the farm and walk home. One outstanding individual from the Cape rolled his four-wheeler down into a gully; it had crushed him several times on the way down, broken his collarbone, five ribs and punctured his lungs. He only just managed to get the bike upright, and back to the road where he was found unconscious by a neighbour. When they retraced his route they found that he'd come through five gates. Each time, he'd got off the bike, opened the gate, got on the bike, driven through – and got off each time to close the gate behind him. When asked why he'd risked his life to do this he said, quite unaffectedly, "Oh, if you don't, stock wander and someone's got to come and clear up after you." That toughness is part of our character; and now I believe we are using it to better advantage than earlier this century.

These characteristics remain, but we are adding to them. Today, we also see ourselves as innovative, skilful and willing to take risks. We have added a risk-taking ability to our more longstanding courage to take the long march. It is easy to see all these qualities throughout New Zealand society both in our dealings with each other and with the world.

When France toured New Zealand in 1994 I travelled from

Wellington to Masterton to see the team at their match against Wairarapa Bush. Pierre Berbizier, my friend and opponent in four tests, was the coach; several of the players I knew well from my time in the Racing Club in Paris. Pierre invited me to his team talk before the match. It was a fascinating experience. In New Zealand team talks we sit in a very intent semi-circle round the coach. We're all dressed properly – with almost military precision. We sit looking down, silent, intent, concentrating on the match ahead. By contrast, the French players were strewn all over the hotel bar room, leaning on the bar, sitting in groups of two and threes, standing by the doors, in front, or behind the coach, shirts in or out.

But the message was precisely the same, and the team listened with the same intensity. The coach went over what they were trying to achieve, why it was important; he picked on two or three individuals who needed that extra bit of motivation, telling them what was required. He also went over the basics – retain the ball, make the tackles, keep backing up – but all with marvellous Gallic gestures and expressive turns of phrase.

It was fascinating to see the differences, but also the substance of how to win a rugby match was the same. Unsurprisingly, top teams all over the world subscribe to universal truths of how rugby games are won. You've got to do the simple things well; and you've got to do the difficult things well, too. And you've probably got to feel confident enough to have a crack at the impossible things from time to time.

International teams divide into two streams – the Latin temperament and the Anglo Saxon. New Zealand is the only team that benefits from the Anglo Saxon temperament enlivened and enriched by the Polynesian strand.

The big difference between us and the northern hemisphere when I played was athleticism. More northern hemisphere players are looking better in the showers nowadays, but in those days there was a pronounced lack of athleticism and therefore a lack of explosiveness, that combination of power and speed. That's the stuff that decathletes have, long smooth running strides, running upright with their arms pumping. Quite a lot of our new athleticism is to do with our Polynesian players. They say white men can't jump – there's truth in that.

I also see the long childhood seasons of playing outside, diving and running and playing scrag, the hours spent on those long, one-rope swings that reach over the banks above the streams, the outdoor early years of New Zealand.

But out there in the world you can see strong national styles of play. In fact, it's impossible to separate rugby personality and playing style from the social environment. These styles grow out of the culture. New Zealand and South Africa evolved in a specific way when immigrants came to work in a new land and found rugby a way of developing social relationships. But the northern hemisphere has its own social conditions which also strongly influence the way they play.

It's quite a broad-based game in England in that it's played by a lot of people – perhaps the largest number of people in any country, but the game has been very disorganised.

Until recently, England had a reputation for languid administration. For instance, the amateur spirit that informs the game was amusingly expressed by a character called John Scott, a delightful man who wrote to the paper after my "professional article" appeared in the *Sunday Times*. John lambasted me and my attitude, rounding off his piece with the view that it was the very amateur spirit I was so keen on seeing off that had won the two world wars. Because John was an Oxonian I got to know him a little. He is a man of many cultural and sporting interests and, in the amateur spirit, was capped some time in the 1950s for England (John Scott was famous for goal kicking). As the story goes, he got himself to Paris, got out onto the pitch and started playing. When he was tossed the ball to take the first penalty he said, "Oh, I don't think I'm your man for that."

The captain said, "Aren't you John Scott from Rosslyn Park?"

"Harlequins."

"Damn. Have a go anyway."

The structure of the game was equally chaotic. A club would play forty-odd matches a year, quite indiscriminately, most of them low-grade games.

Though the Courage League has been established, it's taken some time for the tradition of playing for an unimportant result to work its way out of the system. The amateurism of their play, historically, is partly the result of the sort of people who play – but all those low-grade games every season haven't helped (nor all that drinking).

The Courage League is establishing the idea that winning is better than losing because if you lose too much you'll get relegated. Now there is a point to winning, a goal to aim for.

As a nation, England has often had skilful, individual backs. They usually have big forwards, too – as you'd expect from a catchment area of sixty million people. Too often the big forwards, some at two metres plus, have been heavy but slow. And their huge forwards are in some way a mental disadvantage for the team and their coaches. Because they've got the biggest forwards they feel they should use them. They are obsessed with power. They've been seduced by the idea that a good big man will beat a good small man. But the whole direction of the game has gone away from that – pace is far more important than it used to be. In New Zealand our good, big men have also been good, big, fast men. Until recently, England has lacked athleticism. They've been less your life guard and more your power-lifter with big waists and thighs. The All Blacks like to think they could get half the team an audition for *Baywatch.* Until recently you wouldn't have wanted to see the English pack in their togs on prime time television. It is just in the last few years that the English forwards have begun to combine handling skill and speed with size. The results have followed.

The English backs have talent but have never really got it together as a team. There's too much individuality to be very successful; the best players have been chosen regardless of their ability to complement each other.

They're too intelligent to believe they're likely to beat the All Blacks and while they are generally quite an arrogant team, I think that deep down they lack confidence before the game starts. The Welsh and the Scots have the ability to suspend their disbelief before the game and can work themselves into a national fervour to win or die. The English have a scepticism they pride themselves on deep in their soul. (One illustration: Oxford University was opening a branch in Kobe. A letter was written to *The Times* – "Now, if only we can get them to take on the Brigade of Guards and London Clubland we could witness the wholesale collapse of the Japanese economy within ten years." It's an amusing letter, an amusing attitude, but represents also an ironic streak in the British soul which can be disabling when it's time for action.)

England is also fragmented – this is most of the reason why they are perennial underachievers. Shaw once said something like, "An Englishman can't open his mouth without making some other Englishman hate or despise him." And that still obtains in some measure over there.

And because they are a large country with strong regional

differences they also lack a national style of play. If the All Blacks adopt a certain style, every club imitates it, right down to schools' first fifteens. In England the North is very different from the South, the Wasps are different from the Harlequins and Bath is different from West Hartlepool.

We have these regional differences, too. Canterbury relies more on an unsophisticated robustness – the shortest way to the goal line is straight ahead. Otago nowadays play a frenetic game of limited contact, always searching for the open spaces. Auckland are cool and pragmatic: pushover tries, midfield set-ups, running fullbacks – whatever works. But these are mutations that contribute to, and are superseded by, the great evolution of the national game.

Professionalism could be a great advantage for England – all the best players will play union, they'll have a big industrial base to draw on for funding. But right now they've made a serious error in the way they've brought in the money system. Wealthy individuals have bought clubs. They now have a system quite like the professional soccer system. The clubs have all the money, and by employing the players they have most of the power. In New Zealand, the central union is the primary employer, and consequently in control. The strength of the national team is assured.

In professional sport, the money makes the rules. The employer needs a return on his investment. Clubs will naturally act in their best interests. Test rugby will come second. That's the way it's been set up.

Right now, the split continues between the professional clubs and The Rugby Union. The game is even further from having a national identity.

As an aside, the All Blacks having ten members of the team from Auckland helps cohesion and purpose enormously. These people play together all the time, that's partly why the front row is such an awesome unit; Fitzpatrick and Brooke in the lineout, Jones, Blowers and Brooke in the loose forwards, the key combinations learn to play together, developing telepathy and mutual support. Only Australia shares this advantage. There, Queensland and New South Wales are the only two serious provincial events (ACT is a recent addition). The Super 12 ought to help Australia as these players will get more time together.

But in England where tradition is stronger than in other countries, they have got into a vicious circle. People are reluctant to admit that winning is important because they don't win enough. New Zealand is quite the opposite: we say it's the only thing because that's what we do. What you do, and what your supporters expect you to do, constitutes a powerful mental habit.

Even when the English get ahead there is a lack of finish that remains inexplicable. Instead of going for the jugular, and putting their opponents away, they allow the match to drift.You see this lack of purpose in other areas of English society. Their car industry was in terminal decline. There was nothing really wrong with the workers, or the finance, or the plant – it was the English way of doing things that was wrong. The Japanese turned up, introduced their management systems (flatter hierarchies, more responsibility for workers) and Britain is once again a net exporter of motorcars.

It's a vision thing. It's about leadership. England would, I think, be a very hard team to captain. You never get the impression they'd die in a ditch for the cause (or the captain). A characteristic comment about almost anyone would be, "Delightful fellow, but . . ."

It should be remembered that England is the home of the clobbering machine we complain about so much in this country. In fact, our press is relatively benign. The UK popular press is the most savage in the world and their malice is enlivened by penetrating wit and knockabout humour (actually, it's an Australian invention, a gift from Rupert Murdoch). The English pride themselves on their sense of humour, but sometimes it might be seen as having a morbid effect on their ability to do themselves justice.

How do you beat the English? You wouldn't want to slug it out with their big ponderous forwards; you ruck, rather than maul, move the ball away from the breakdown and keep the ball alive. The All Blacks showed exactly how not to do it against the Lions in the second test in Wellington in 1993. They showed exactly the right way to do it in the semi-final of the World Cup two years later.

The Struggle for the Soul of New Zealand Rugby

For years, as a player and observer, I watched a great struggle for the soul of New Zealand rugby. The battle had begun while I was still at school and continued after I'd left the All Blacks. It was still going on when I returned to New Zealand after a five-year absence. There were times when progress seemed slow and there were times we seemed to be going backwards, but the new spirit of rugby eventually prevailed. This was the spirit that valued backs as well as forwards, the spirit that embraced style as well as power, the spirit that revelled in the glory of running rugby.

Now more than ever, this spirit is evident on the playing field. I believe there will be another battle for the soul of our rugby and it will be off the field and will be about money and power; we will come to that later in the book, but I can say here that the battle to reward flair on the field has been fought, and that the good guys won.

New Zealand rugby probably troughed twenty-five years ago (interestingly, this coincided with one of the most brutal periods of the game). The All Blacks lost the 1970 test series in South Africa, they lost the 1971 series in New Zealand against the Lions, they lost four non-test matches on their tour of Great Britain and France in 1972-73 (when Keith Murdoch was sent home for punching a security guard). In 1973, the All Blacks were beaten by the Juniors, a President's XV and an English team so weak that it had managed the outstanding feat of losing to every provincial team they played in the lead-up to the test.

In one of the bitter ironies that litter sport, the chief victim was a man who was anything but representative of the problem. Ian Kirkpatrick, with his sublime play and gracious manner was replaced as captain; some of the old guard went with him and the rot was stopped. But we didn't turn the corner until Graham Mourie took over as captain. His leadership put a new emphasis on the intellect as an important element of the game.

The hallmark example of this new era was the second test against France in 1977. Bludgeoned into submission by the French pack in the first test, the All Blacks played hit-and-run rugby in the second. Hopelessly outgunned in a frontal assault, the team mounted a guerilla campaign; short lineouts, quick throw-ins, ruck-and-run. The match was won from a quick throw-in from Mourie to Lawrie Knight, to Mark Donaldson, to Bruce Robertson, to Stu Wilson, who ran a great line to score under the posts.

But as I say, the evolution was of the intellect, not of the spirit (that was to come later). By definition individual, the intellectual approach rested with a few leaders and found expression in tactics, and approaches to training and motivation. Personal accountability was important, as was the quality ethic (as management theory has it).

But there was still a limited sense of freedom in play; there still remained a strong sense of boundaries between what you could and couldn't do, should and shouldn't do.

Graham Mourie's post-match interview after the second test loss to Australia in 1982 implicitly blamed Mark Taylor for trying to run the ball while playing into the wind and conceding a try in the process. We lost, Graham seemed to say, because we took unnecessary risks; we should have understood our boundaries more clearly.

Perhaps it was Graham Mourie's misfortune to lead in an era in which the team did not have the ability to play total rugby. More likely, it was just too early; the time wasn't right. The new freedom of the New Zealand *glasnost* which brought with it so much expansiveness and self-confidence was yet to gain traction.

During this early period there were a few ripples of the new wave. These were the Wellington backs – Dave Henderson, John Dougan, Dan Fouhy, Jamie Salmon, Bernie Fraser, Allan Hewson and Stu Wilson – they played with great style and carefree humour.

I remember the bloodied and battered Canterbury number eight crashing to the ground over the tryline. Stu bent down to kiss him on the top of his head and, striking an effeminate pose, squealed: "Ooooh! You're so *stwong*! So *stwong*!"

But through the first third of the Eighties the All Blacks moved smoothly along without needing the new style to win. However, they could rarely manage sustained, fluent rugby. The third test against Australia in 1982 and the fourth test against the Lions the following year were examples of this. But while there was little dissension inside the ranks of the administration about the future of rugby, the new soul was being born in Auckland, in Canterbury and in the game of sevens.

The new wave hit the All Blacks around the time of the Cavaliers and the Baby Blacks, and transformed the team for the first World Cup. The tide began to go out when Buck Shelford was dropped and the tension began to rise between Alex Wyllie and John Hart, and between Auckland and the rest of the country.

Early in my own All Black career our team spirit was earnest and sincere – phlegmatic even. It was overtaken by a more expansive, creative vision of what we could do if we tried to achieve our potential.

We discovered this was the way to win – and by a lot. By taking risks, by making mistakes but backing ourselves to recover from them, we won. Our thought was that if they scored twenty points it didn't matter, as long as we scored forty. It's all a state of mind. Both teams may be equally good, but if one of them dreams up an expansive vision for themselves and their lives, they will prevail.

In the period following the first World Cup, John Hart missed out on one coaching job after another. He had been a selector for the World Cup but was subsequently beaten to the coaching job by Alex Wyllie. Many thought it was the brash Aucklander losing out to the popular provincial. Hart also said he could only take time off work to be coach and not selector. I think New Zealand saw this as rather presumptuous – and while John did have to back down, he returned after a year and accepted the selector's job then. There began a difficult relationship between Hart and Wyllie as John started to compete for the loyalty of the players and support of the public.

Then Wayne Shelford was dropped, and a Bring Back Buck campaign was aimed at Hart.

The fraught relationship went right through to the 1991 World Cup until Hart was asked to be co-coach with Wyllie – probably the single least plausible option available.

Almost inevitably the wheels came off. The team didn't play well throughout. They beat England, the United States, Italy and Canada – and lost to Australia in the semi-finals. And, despite beating Scotland in the play-off for third place, it was a poor effort all round.

So Hart put his name forward for coach, this time against Laurie Mains.

Laurie had been coaching Otago for nine years; he had done well to bring the team up into the top half of the league, he'd coached them to play to their strengths and to refrain from risk. And in the year of the 1991 World Cup, with fourteen All Blacks absent from the Auckland team, Otago won the national championship and Laurie had the national platform to be considered the best coach in New Zealand.

There was bitter opposition in the provinces to Hart; the way the relationship with Wyllie had failed to work was laid at his door. He was seen as a disloyal, self-serving Aucklander – a true representative of the Auckland spirit. Then there was the block vote from the South Island for the South Islander, and Wellington's anti-Auckland bias. So Mains began three of the least successful years in New Zealand rugby. Amongst the worst performances were a loss to a World XV in 1992 (Mains' first test in charge) and a series loss to France in 1994 – at home!

Hart challenged again in 1994 and was knocked back for the third time.

After the 1995 season, Mains retired. He'd been a poor selector because he didn't have a clear understanding of why he was selecting, he didn't have a vision of the style he wanted to play. He chose the best players he could – but they weren't picked to complement each other and they never gelled as a team. He also tended to be too short-sighted: if a class player lost form he'd be dropped. Laurie didn't seem to realise that form is temporary and class is permanent.

He also tried too hard to programme the team. He didn't make the jump from coaching teams like Otago to coaching the All Blacks. We now had a team of great capability, and the more he schooled them to avoid errors the less responsive they became to the opposition. If the plan was to dominate lineouts and the plan failed, they didn't have the scope to respond in changed tactics.

If selections aren't right and you change – and the selection still isn't right – then every man and his dog has an opinion about who should be picked next. Everyone's uncertain. And in a sport where confidence is crucial, top performance is impossible.

Sean Fitzpatrick took a lot of the heat for that, but it wasn't fair. That laid too much tactical responsibility at his door.

Laurie Mains was technically a very good coach. He could help players, he was diligent, he watched a lot of videos. But he didn't have the vision or the sweep. Had he combined his love of the game, his commitment, his skill in coaching individual techniques with the confidence to trust the creative powers of New Zealand's best players it would have been a very different story. The success of 1995 could have started three years earlier.

There was a good example of this in the 1994 Bledisloe Cup against Australia. New Zealand had lost to France twice already that year, and we were well down against Australia at halftime, it had been a miserable year, and here the team was looking down the barrel of a further, final defeat. They realised they'd have to score at least twice to win, and unless they threw off the shackles they'd never be able to do this.

It was like those old serial stories; in one bound, he was free. The team threw off the limited style that Laurie Mains had drilled them in and gave us the most remarkable comeback the All Blacks had ever experienced. Jeff Wilson dived over the line for what would have been the winning try but George Gregan knocked the ball out of his hands – but the point holds. The team, after three years of playing to a let's-not-lose formula, found they could be much better than they were.

And once the creative force was unleashed it was impossible to put it back in its box, and a fine performance in the 1995 World Cup resulted.

I think, finally, that Laurie wasn't in tune with the sense of freedom and individualism that was taking over the whole of New Zealand society. He tried to manage the team too centrally. He came from a command culture where orders emanated from the centre. He came from an era where matrons had despotic powers over their wards; where army sergeants barked orders and everyone jumped to obey; where teachers stood at the head of the class and the pupils chanted rote learning.

There were advantages to that way of life. There are those who look back on it fondly. But power has been, and is being, decentralised more and more. People are taking more responsibility for themselves and each other without recourse to a central authority.

Times had decisively changed.

The protective embrace of Gerard Wilkinson. Who says Wellingtonians don't care for Aucklanders?

Peter Bush

The intensity of serious rugby is such that you feel at your most alive when playing. You are processing more information per second that in any other experience – it's like being in a car crash. *Ross Setford*

"Here, it's about time you got dirty, John." This was rule number one for me – if in doubt, give the ball to Kirwan. *Ross Setford*

Gloriously unaware of the mayhem in his wake, Michael Jones in full flight. Without doubt the peerless player of my generation. *Rugby News*

Sevens heaven. Above: With Wayne Smith after New Zealand's first championship win at the Hong Kong Sevens in 1986. Below: After completing the third leg of a magnificent 1986 sevens treble (prior to Hong Kong we'd won a New South Wales invitation tournament in Sydney) in the Sports Aid For Africa tournament in Cardiff. Interesting to note the other three players in this photo – John Schuster, Frano Botica and John Kirwan – all went to rugby league. *Rugby News*

Tip-toeing through the Frenchmen during the 1986 Sports Aid For Africa tournament in Cardiff.
Rugby News

Try time against Italy in the 1987 World Cup opener at Eden Park. In support, as always, is John Kirwan.
Photosport

French halfback Pierre Berbizier gets his pass away despite my attentions in the 1987 World Cup final at Eden Park. *Rugby News*

The 1988 Varsity match at Twickenham – a rather balletic pose. *Rugby News*

This is the first time I saw the best players in Wellington in action. I remember thinking, "Uh oh." With me is Graham Williams. *Peter Bush*

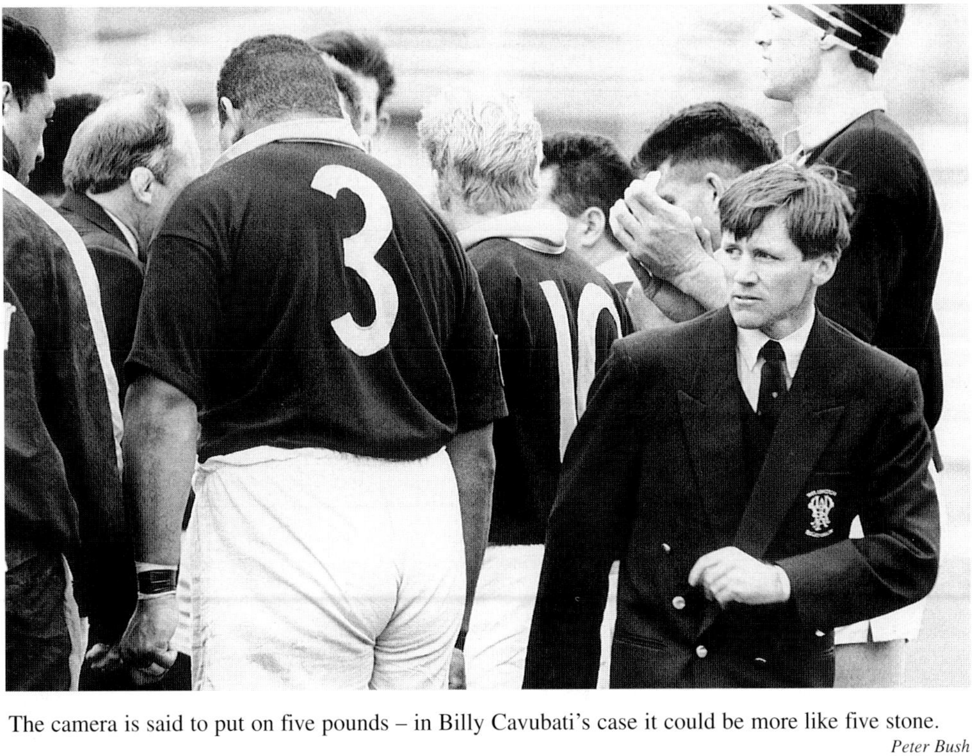

The camera is said to put on five pounds – in Billy Cavubati's case it could be more like five stone. *Peter Bush*

The Prime Minister's decisions were generally made in a more considered way. *Evening Post*

Real Politics and Sport

I came back to New Zealand in 1992 and was asked the following year to coach a provincial side. This was a whole new dimension to the game for me. The more I think about Wellington the stranger it becomes. It was a situation where I had almost nothing to gain and almost everything to lose. I didn't know any of the players, I had little experience of coaching, and I had no political support (that is, a cadre of people who were on my side, promoting me). That is important anywhere but particularly in Wellington. There is nothing more important than a political base when it comes to coaching rugby in Wellington. Everything I had learned about on-field rugby I should have applied off-field. Support play, the vision, the commitment you need from those around you – all these were vital in a larger way than I knew.

Neither did I really have the time to do the work (I had two children under three).

The job I had was flexible in terms of hours but the hours were long and unpredictable.

All in all it was something I should have done later. Much later. If at all. So I took the job.

At the time I didn't perceive it as reckless, but challenging. Men and women are said to evaluate risk/reward ratios with one consistent difference: men invariably underestimate the risks.

I recognised all these problems at the time but went ahead with it. Why would I do something so silly? To be honest, vanity must have played a part. But also, I wanted to show I had something to give; I wanted to put something back into the game. Wellington was traditionally one of the strongest provinces in New Zealand but had fallen on hard times. To have been specifically sought out to bring the team back to glory was flattering. I assumed, for reasons that elude me now, that I could be successful. It was a unique opportunity. The combination of a flexible employer and young enough children would never recur. Very soon after the age of three, children start needing you on Saturday mornings, they want you at home, not out coaching a rugby team.

So I talked myself into it, and more importantly, talked Brigit into acquiescing to it as well.

The seeds of some of my problems were sown right at the beginning. I tried to manage these in order to gain support with the Wellington administrators and coaches of the various clubs. This was the key political group – and it was quite different from Auckland which had progressed beyond this tail wagging the dog deal.

The clubs in Auckland recognised the direction in which influence ought to travel – that is, from the provincial team to the club level. In doing so, they recognised that the clubs ought to be run not for the exclusive benefit of the province, but certainly to support the province. The clubs didn't always like it but they had the insight and the maturity to accept that this was the way it needed to be if the province was to prosper, and actually they themselves were to prosper, too. If the province does well, club membership goes up, that's how it works. It's a lesson Wellington has yet to learn.

Essentially, New Zealand rugby must be run for the benefit of the All Blacks. If this is done, the benefits cascade through the whole country to every level of the game. A strong All Black team is a decisive national benefit; it brings young players through – right from primary school – wanting to emulate their heroes. Public support via the turnstiles helps financial health and sponsorship is easier to find. Getting the top team right gets kids in at the bottom and a whole virtuous circle begins – play improves, administration improves, there is more money to invest in player development.

Now, it is extremely hard work building the game from the bottom up – perhaps it's never happened. Rugby league in this country was a basketcase until the Winfield Cup broadcast this cross between pro wrestling and *Gladiators* on television, made heroes and gave players something to aspire to.

So what do we need to sustain the All Blacks? We must have a good provincial system. That demands good competition at that level to develop and expose the players. At the next level down, the same principle applies – good club rugby is required to develop and expose players for the next level up.

The point is, none of this is a zero-sum game. The province does not succeed at the expense of the clubs. A successful province attracts players and develops a winning ethos. Club rugby becomes stronger, administrators and coaches become proud to be associated with the area; the snowball starts rolling.

However, in Wellington it doesn't quite work like that.

In Auckland, all clubs look towards the Auckland provincial side as their mentor. Clubs in mature provinces don't seek to impose their style on the provincial team. Rather, they adopt the provincial team's style in order to have a greater chance of supplying some of their players.

In Wellington, it's the other way round. It's more of a baronial system and the two big barons are the Petone and Marist St Pats clubs. Both clubs are tight-knit and cohesive.

At Marist, the players come out of Catholic schools to play for a club that represents their background, their families and their interests. At Petone they come from different schools, different backgrounds and working men's rather than religious interests. The collectivism has an economic base rather than anything else. They have been successful, and that has given them self-confidence; they have endured. They have a strong, single-minded view on the world and, as a result, more policy input for Wellington rugby comes from the vestry, or from the bar of the Petone Working Men's Club, than from all the boardrooms in the province.

That is not always a good thing. Clubs like Petone and Marist have a very personal view of rugby. And it could be summarised, "We want our coach, our players in the team, and our style of rugby to be Wellington's style of rugby."

Both Petone and Marist have this same, single-minded view. Marist would always argue for a more powerful pack (because they had a more powerful pack themselves), and Petone, with its larger Polynesian population, would support a more open, running back game.

So, I would be lectured by coaches from Petone or Marist – and sometimes they would be coherent and sometimes not – and would receive very different instructions on how rucks and mauls should be set up. In all this there was no doubt that the coaches were concerned for Wellington rugby. They wanted the province to do well but they couldn't quite see it happening without them in charge.

Both clubs were dominated by former players; both coaches were former hookers of the Wellington team, both famous sons of their clubs, having played a hundred matches for Wellington. Both had finished playing in the late seventies, the generations that started to decline as I was starting to play. Both were huge lovers of the game and had made a real contribution coaching their clubs. And both had wanted the job that had been given to me.

So, while they were both happy to give their frank view about any issue, both were reluctant to offer what you'd call support, or to provide ideas to gain support from the clubs, or to develop a proper provincial strategy. That wasn't a reflection on my abilities in particular – the problem still exists in Wellington. The clubs still stand on the sidelines criticising the way the forwards go in on the ball because it isn't the way their forwards go in on the ball.

The people who did take a larger view were the sponsors (Lion Breweries), former coaches like Bill Freeman, and some business people who provided employment and support for life skills courses for the players. But there was no sense of the province's greater good in the majority of the clubs.

Auckland, by contrast, had been through all this and come out the other side. They had been successful and had used that success to establish coaching, club competitions, club transfer rules, representative programmes and budgets, B-programmes and Colts – all that was needed to set up rugby in the best interests of the province. And Auckland still provided opportunities and involvement for all the clubs and players.

As John Hart and Malcolm Dick realised in Auckland, you have to break the mould of club parochialism before you can build a successful administrative system for rugby. Once you've established the principle, and it has been successful, people will tend to fall in behind.

Wellington hasn't had that success and, therefore, it has become a breeding ground for clamouring voices claiming to be the true Messiah with the one true answer of how to go into a ruck.

Knowing all this, it was Mission Impossible. I had made the right decision in Oxford – where I knew I was a foreigner – but made the wrong decision in Wellington – where my foreignness was less obvious but just as real. You must have an understanding of the region and an association with the team to lead it properly. John Hart's example should have educated me. He grew up in the Auckland environment, he was a successful club player, a successful Auckland club coach, he knew everyone, he'd been through the problem years. He wasn't foisted into the position, he emerged. He fought a tough battle to gain initial selection. Not everyone had a sense of the rightness of it, but he was a local, he had a power base – there was a sense of legitimate authority. And this seems to me to be the essence of leadership (except in times of successful revolution); leadership must proceed from legitimate authority. People must know you and trust you – as you know and trust them.

Interestingly, Jim Bolger rarely leads from the front. It's partly due to his extended intuition, his gut feel is that the numbers will eventually work. But the reformers – Roger Douglas, Ruth Richardson, Simon Upton and Jenny Shipley – are either gone or waiting for their time (or in Richard Prebble's case, both) while Bolger is still there.

Hart isn't a politician by any means. If he was, it wouldn't have taken him so long to coach the All Blacks. But he has an instinctual feel of what to do and who to have on his side before doing what he wants to do. He knows he needs the support of this person in that position, those clubs, these societies, those communities. At times, his self-belief has seen him act without the support he needs, but he has always known the risks he has taken.

I think I was out of tune with a large range of New Zealand society when I returned. The past and the future were out of joint. The gears had crashed in our country through the Eighties; I was quickly given an inkling of how people were feeling about the changes.

The first contact I'd had with New Zealand since leaving was the National Party pre-selection process for the Tamaki seat following the retirement of Sir Robert Muldoon. I put myself up as a prospective candidate for the seat and was, in short, whacked with a wet fish and sent packing.

I believe a lot of New Zealanders, particularly in Tamaki, felt betrayed by people like me – young, academic, management consultant types. They were saying, "We don't like what's happened to our country in the last few years, and we don't like people who represent more of that future." The same sort of scepticism was to be found in Wellington rugby. They were happy for my success and achievement in a general sense, but to take the next step and have such a person influence their local organisation was a different matter altogether.

The Prime Minister, at any rate, took a more benign view, and I went to work for him as a policy advisor and executive assistant in his private office. I performed something of a halfback function, operating between the people developing policy and the politicians.

Perhaps because I remain susceptible to idealism I still have an idea of the majesty of politics. Good government has a very real impact on our lives and prospects. The level of taxes, the quality of education, interest rates, the health system – all these are affected for better or worse by government actions. It takes a lot of courage to do the right thing, and to keep doing it when you are unpopular.

But the life of a politician can be miserable. Separated from family, always in the public eye, poorly paid (compared to professional rugby players) and only the top few have genuinely challenging jobs. And finally, the career path can be something of a dead-end. It is hard to move out of Parliament into another career. I was fascinated to read David Lange saying this year that he believed he should have left Parliament after he resigned as Prime Minister. He said he lacked the confidence to go back to practising law.

I worked for a very different Prime Minister. The first Bolger administration had an enormous policy agenda. Two terms in opposition had stimulated the growth of young, intelligent, ideological, conviction-politicians. They combined to create a slew of economic and social policy changes in health, housing, welfare, Treaty negotiations, education and labour law. This combined with a deficit-busting Finance Minister to produce an active and deeply unpopular government. On top of all this sat Jim Bolger.

If nothing else, his example should have served me as a model for managing the politics of Wellington rugby. A consummate chairman of the board, Jim Bolger would let debate run on until a natural direction began to emerge. Then, knowing his goal, he would begin to marshal the arguments. He would nudge both sides towards his position by taking the most acceptable parts of their argument and redefining them: "So I think what you are saying, at least partly, is that . . . " and then, turning, "And yes, your point, which isn't inconsistent with Bill's about . . . " He would then summarise Bill's point in a way which ensured the circle was closed.

Bolger's political intuition and sometimes inchoate feel for where he should be heading is extraordinary. He gets little credit for this before-the-fact insight because he doesn't come across as a far-seeing visionary. But I noticed several times that he would make an observation about future events, be scoffed at by the commentators –

and be proven quite correct as events turned out months later. However, other columnists and commentators would have already occupied that position and taken the credit for the insight.

His most substantial ability was in committee and in caucus where he demonstrated the art of acknowledging the contribution of everyone involved. He also had the capacity to work halls, clubs, factories – the face-to-face work that is an integral part of building grassroots support.

Let me grasp this nettle of my time in Wellington.

This is the story as I see it.

It was well-recognised among various Wellington administrators – including David Gray, David Smith, Paul McKay and Murray Mexted – that Wellington's administration was not keeping pace with the changing world. The union was dragging behind Auckland, Otago, Canterbury, Hawke's Bay, Waikato and North Harbour. They wanted change, and they wanted a new image for the game in Wellington. That's why Murray called me. In retrospect, they probably should have called someone with a bit more marketability in Wellington, someone who had, first and foremost, the legitimate authority to lead this change in the province.

As I say, I could see the problems but I was over-confident.

I went through the interviews, told them what I'd do, and they appointed me. But we failed even to start on the right foot. Instead of announcing me as a candidate, a possible coach, and taking me through the process of selection in a relatively public way, and having the supporters and players carried along with it all, it was decided to conceal the appointment and give it a fanfare revelation.

So the announcement of the appointment was made at a breakfast press conference where I was called into the room. The convenor said, "And the new coach is . . . come in David." Personally I have no appetite for being promoted as a Messiah. First, because I'm not, and second, it doesn't fit with the New Zealand psyche; we don't like pedestals in this country, or people on them.

The journalists asked some very pertinent questions, like, "Have you ever coached before?" (Only a bit.) And, "What do you know about the Wellington players?" (Not very much.) And, most embarrassingly, "How many times did you watch the team play last year?" (Once, on television.)

Another problem I haven't mentioned was that I was replacing a famous son of Wellington rugby, Andy Leslie, ex-captain of the All

Blacks, a Petone player and a Wellington coach who didn't want to go. And while all the clubs except Petone were happy to see one of their non-members being booted out, he was rightfully a well-regarded man – popular and altogether not the best person to be edging out of his job.

Things started in a pretty ordinary way (this is a New Zealand euphemism for a wee bit unfortunate; you know – disastrous). My main sponsor on the selection committee, the team manager who was on the management committee, and a vital man for building support at the top level, was immediately dumped from the committee by the clubs. Was I being over-sensitive again? It was hard not to see this as his punishment for installing me.

I should – I know I should – have gone round all the club rooms at least once during the season and drunk at the bars and asked people for their ideas and their support.When the club match I was watching was over I should have been there for an hour and a half developing goodwill, being seen. That's an important function of the provincial coach, to give time, to give of himself – and that's as it should be. People should feel they can talk to their representative coach. My young family made this more difficult than I thought.

There is only one way to counter the failing of a weak political base – and that is to win matches. You hang by a thread if you don't win. Success transforms everything. Like in revolution, success turns terrorists into freedom fighters, and traitors into cabinet ministers. But even victory is a poor substitute for that deep, grassroots affection in the bars and club rooms because it is feverish support and burns out very quickly – as soon as the team starts losing.

Anyway, to get down to the job in hand, the most important thing I saw immediately was that the quality of the players was thin, and we needed to build a new team. Players are very loyal to the coach who picks them and not at all loyal to coaches who don't – as we know – and that's quite understandable. But I also felt the existing players should be given the benefit of the doubt and be given the chance to prove they were better than they seemed to be. I maintained the status quo for the first few matches but I knew what I was looking for.

I was looking for more explosiveness, more urgency, more pace and more discipline, an ability to impose a style of play on the opposition.

For this you needed three things.

i) A clear style which fitted the new rugby as it was played, according to the new rules.

ii) Leadership on the field. You can drill it off the field but you still need two or three people on the pitch who can make the key decisions and keep the team's concentration together.

iii) Players who are capable of implementing strategy. For that they'd need the physical capabilities but also the mental capacity to learn. Out of that comes consistency, concentration and accuracy.

You're not looking for blind obedience out there – you don't want cannon fodder; far from it. But that commando-like quality of being a self-governing unit, but also an integral part of a team, requires many things: discipline and technique and a mastery of the mechanics of the key elements of the game – set pieces, ball retention, tackling, body position in the forwards, passing in the backs; all the rational elements. Once these basics are in place you open the team out to the romantic aspects of the game, the sparks of inspiration, the ability to take risks, to counter-attack and to find the true potential of the team. If you can get that balance right – and the rational has to come before the romantic – then the team can succeed.

Unfortunately, we didn't have enough of the vital ingredients – there was no sense of style, and I was too inexperienced to make it clear. We had no cadre capable of on-field leadership, and the mental abilities of the team were limited. This is very interesting, and has wider implications (or I wouldn't mention it).

If you tabulated school results and employment histories – a crude way of measuring intellectual achievement off the field – you would have found an extraordinary contrast with the Auckland team of my time. Look at it this way:

The Auckland team comprised:

John Drake	Investment banker
Iain Abercrombie	Marketing executive and now general manager for Lion Breweries.
Steve McDowell	Gym manager
Andy Haden	Millionaire entrepreneur
Gary Whetton	Product manager for Fisher and Paykel
Glenn Rich	Property developer and construction company owner
Alan Whetton	Owner/driver of a truck (now player/coach in Japan)
Michael Jones	MA student
David Kirk	Medical doctor

Grant Fox	Managing director Harvard Sports Marketing
Kurt Sherlock	Accountant
Joe Stanley	Owner/driver (later player/coach in Japan)
Terry Wright	Accountant
John Kirwan	Entrepreneur
Lindsay Harris	Self-employed trader

Compare this with the Wellington team. Seven were unemployed. Three worked as builders' labourers. Two ran their own businesses. One worked in marketing, one worked in a bank. One was a bar manager and one was in a clerical position.

The point is not to suggest that one group of players were better or worse people – but which group was better equipped to be a successful team. Ambitions, organisational abilities, long-term horizons – all these are fundamental to success in work careers and a rugby career is no different.

It was like the first part of an American film about the underdogs who were going to win the national championships. But alas, we never got to the third reel where we carry home the cup.

Here are some vignettes that give an indication of what we were dealing with. I was rung up early one Sunday morning by one of the players wanting to know whether he should take an evidential breath test or a blood test – he was at the police station and wanted a medical opinion about which was likely to produce the lower result. Another player assaulted a woman after a match in Otago and the situation developed into a wider conflict – a bit like the start of the First World War. I went to wake up another player who was allegedly at the scene because the police were outside wanting to interview him; he was impossible to wake because he wasn't asleep (he had passed out). Another player was sent off in our 1993 Ranfurly Shield match, flagged by a touch judge for over-vigorous rucking. He was put in the sin-bin for five minutes where he contended that the touch judge had got the wrong player. When the official appeared behind the posts to adjudicate a penalty, our man let him have it (verbally only, but quite enough). Up went the flag and off went the player (it's an automatic red card for committing an offence while in the sin-bin – it's quite a rare offence). These are all incidents that players who are All Blacks don't feature in.

Bill Cavubati, the weighty Fijian prop, briefly left and went to

Australia on a big-money offer. One day he simply didn't turn up to a match we had to play. There had been rumours he was going, and because we had an important match coming up I asked him whether he was going to be available for it. He assured me he was, but when the plane came to take us to the game, Billy was nowhere to be found. In Australia he said that he wasn't being helped enough at home, and not being developed as a player. He lasted three weeks over there, didn't turn up to training, and was back in Wellington within twenty-one days, asking for his place in the team again. Which he got. This in itself tells a tale. Why would we re-select such a disloyal player? There was so little depth in the team we had no choice.

There were seven Caucasians in the Wellington team and the rest were Polynesian. There will be those who want to draw racial conclusions from this fact. However, the All Blacks this year have precisely the same racial balance; it's not about race, it's about attitude.

The sad thing about the team was that the ones with the mental capacity didn't have the size or speed. And the bigger ones didn't have the mental capacity to concentrate, to set goals, to develop.

Nevertheless, in that first year we did quite well. That is, we'd do well for part of the game, but time and again we would falter in the latter parts. The pressure always goes on in the last quarter; that's when you find out what's different between the teams. Some teams clock-watch (they're tired), others ignore the clock and want to score tries in extra time. There's no mystery about why teams win in the last ten minutes – that's when the big questions are asked.

Sooner or later someone would miss a vital tackle or make a bad mistake, and that would demoralise everyone; there was no collective capacity for goal-setting ("they will not score in these next ten minutes!") On-field goal-setting is a vital way of keeping your end up in difficult circumstances. There was, in general, the lack of on-field leadership which meant it was impossible to forge a common will. I don't mean an inability of the captain, but a widespread lack of ability to contribute to decision-making and to lead by example. There were not enough players who could draw out the reserves of ambition or personal insight; to demand the answer to the question, "What have I, or you, got to do to contribute to our not losing this match?"

We did improve in this. The quest was to build individual mental capacity. That's where the game starts, building ambition to play better into some kind of structure, with achievable goals to aim for, to manage time, to expand the time horizons, to plan for weeks ahead, not just day-to-day.

A lot of the guys thought they were doing this. They said things which people with positive attitudes say. They'd say, for instance, their ambition was to play for the All Blacks, "We want to be the best!" But it was a vainglorious attitude, an empty desire to be selected to play for their country, because very few ever did the things you have to do to be chosen.

At a very basic level, you needed be on the pitch fifteen minutes before training started, warming up, practising the skills you'd need for a match. But even when the guys did turn up early you'd find a prop attempting drop kicks, or a back jumping in the lineout, or someone else trying to raise some sponsorship on a mobile phone.

Too many couldn't translate their wants into the things they had to do – to get fit, to lose weight, to gain weight, practise their skills, plan and organise their lives to go to bed early; to not drink the night before a game, to keep off the dope.

It was finally pitiable to see them claim to want to be the best team in the world and expect to make it without the sweat and tears. Much better players than they had done everything possible to make it into the All Blacks and had failed.

I say there are too many players round the country like this. They think they can get there without the work. It has always been very, very hard to get to the top in sports, and it's harder now than in my day as things have got more professional.

It's important to make these generalisations, even though an important minority of the players in Wellington set goals and worked very hard for success. Wellington is not alone. I only pick on Wellington because that is where my experience lay. There is a disturbing trend in New Zealand for players to put their hand out before they put their hand up. The correct order is – performance first, reward later. And I say this with a genuine hope that it will help players not to miss their chance.

Every successful player needs an achievement plan for three years ahead. You calculate which games in the coming season you'll be peaking in. You'll see that in such a game you'll be playing against a current All Black and that's the chance – perhaps the only chance you'll ever get – to outplay the guy and get noticed. That match will be a test. You say, "If I can get all my passes away while the scrum's going backwards I'll have passed the test." It's by passing a series of such tests that you know you're a better player at the end of the season than at the beginning.

As a coach you build this in the only way you know how – by drilling individual skills and team patterns, and by telling the players what it takes to succeed.

In the absence of any raw talent for goal setting you provide a team structure they can fall back on.

Players have got to look inside themselves and ask basic questions. Props have to ask, how can I scrummage better and block in the lineout and get from scrums to mauls quicker than the opposition? And when we are down, can I find a moment to recommit myself to the game?

Not everyone can ask these questions, others can't answer them personally. So you drill the team so they do it automatically. These are the things that are done hundreds of times in training. That's what the coach builds; consistent performance of each person's tasks.

For instance, playing for the All Blacks, and for Auckland, at any scrum wherever it was on the field, every time the opposition put the ball in I'd say to Alan Whetton, "First man, AJ", meaning he had to tackle the first man if they went blind. I would have said it to him two or three hundred times a season.

Wellington's first game of the 1993 NPC was against Taranaki, in May. We then had a break until August before resuming the campaign against King Country. This was a lucky ballot, as both teams were amongst the weakest in the competition. We beat Taranaki in New Plymouth and looked longingly towards our first home game against King Country. As it was, there were 100km-an-hour winds which suited the opposition. They may have been uninspiring but they had the ballast to withstand high winds. However, I was pleased they were our second match because they were a "weak" team in the competition and a second win would give us heart. We could feel like winners, even if it was only Taranaki and King Country we had beaten.

There was a flaw in this plan I didn't anticipate: we lost. We went down to the worst team in the first division – that's very bad for morale, and anyone who had faith in my ability had that faith tested then. It was a rotten loss. We had to finish in the top four to get into the semi-finals and it turned out that King Country was the match that cost us our place. Most of the problem was bad selection, and that was down to me.

The Prime Minister had turned up at Athletic Park to watch his electorate do battle with his policy advisor's team. The politics for him demanded a King Country win. We didn't let him down.

There was another controversy I got embroiled in (why was everything so difficult suddenly?) Our Western Samoan players were hardly ever available for the province. I said in an interview that it would be more difficult for me to select them if they continually chose Western Samoa over Wellington. So someone complained to the Race Relations Office. I wanted players who were committed to the team and they wanted me to meet with the person who was complaining in a sort of family conference where they could present the case. I didn't have the time or the inclination to listen to this twaddle.

As it happened, I selected quite a lot of of Pacific Islanders and was well-supported by their community. One of them didn't have a visa and was nervous of admitting he wasn't a New Zealand citizen – which would have scotched his chances with the All Blacks (which he is now). You have to be in your country of origin to make the application, so I paid for his flight back to Western Samoa where he could sort the matter out. This didn't get reported to the Race Relations Office.

Also, I saw it as my job to mentor the players off the field and build their confidence. I put a life skills course together to develop their capacity outside the game. This sort of training is more important than it sounds. "What's the point in teaching a lock how to read a balance sheet?" some people might ask. But a) that's a rather scornful view of locks, and b) players need a life outside the game. Playing careers don't last forever, or even for long, usually.

My plan didn't work. I arranged lecturers to donate their time, a curriculum, and premises. If any of the guys had turned up we would have had a proper course going, but they all dropped out except two, and then they dropped out. This was like trying to build rugby from the ground up; it was too difficult.

Not that surprisingly, the second year was worse. We were making progress but we were still slipping down that Ngauruhoe shale. We won twelve out of eighteen matches – but when the crunch came against the top provincial teams we faltered, threw away our chance, and thereby proved we were a middle-pack team.

Teams like Counties, who have much less to draw on but have more leaders and character, have shown what it takes to be successful.

I thought very hard about standing for the third year. I was ambivalent. While I felt that leaving would be to leave the job half done, yet it wasn't a good reason to hang on. The only reason for coaching a province is a burning passion to build the players you have into a better team.

In the end I did put my name forward and, in the Wellington way, the committee that the chairman had carefully chosen in order to re-appoint me, dumped me. It was a lucky escape for all of us, I suspect. The news came through while I was in Jakarta at an APEC meeting with the Prime Minister. The airspace row with Paul Keating was running hot, and we were meeting the Chinese leader, but the headline news, for a brief moment, was that the coach of the Wellington rugby team had been dropped.

I put a lot of work into Wellington rugby during these two years, as did my co-coaches Graham Williams and Wayne Guppy and managers Paul McKay and David Smith. Murray Mexted, as a selector, invested his inimitable enthusiasm and style. We all nudged the province forward, and that process has continued – but much remains to be done.

Coaching is peculiar. I got more nervous as a coach than as a player – and more frustrated. The idea of my playing as well as coaching was even considered by me, to fill that on-field leader gap. But then that would have been a coaching failure and would have tended to turn the team into robots.

Mind you, at times, that might have been an improvement.

Let's Do the Wild Thing

One of the first things to understand about rugby is that it is a violent game. Sometimes it is extremely violent. While violence isn't the point (as it is in boxing or, say, hurling) it is integral to the game. You can't play well without suffering it, or being prepared to administer it.

I'd go so far as to say that the team who can control their violence and apply it most effectively is the team that is likely to win.

Control is a function of time and place; you don't apply violence because you're angry – or not just because you're angry – but because you know that physical dominance is required. This tackle, that ruck is a physical contest, a test of strength. The winner of the physical contest becomes the winner of the mental contest and ultimately the winner of the game.

There is a codeword for violence in modern times which is used to hide the fact of violence, and to euphemise it. The word is aggression.

I remember a New Zealand commentator using the word well on a French tour. The French play (filthy, at the time) was drawing pained disappointment from the commentator, "Ohhhh, there's no need for that kind of thing," he'd say. But then Lawrie Knight, I think it was, stood up, pulled his opposite number upright out of the scrum, and smashed him in the face with his enormous fist, Bam! and then did it again, Bam! and the commentary really ignited, "Well! There goes Lawrie Knight! He's really learned how to make use of his aggression on this tour!"

Aggression is what polite people say instead of violence. It means physically imposing your will, style, tactics on the opposition – and there is no question that New Zealand and South Africa have been the most successful rugby playing countries in the world because they are the most violent.

Clearly, I don't mean the dirtiest teams. South Africa mixes controlled violence with behaviour you could sue for; the Welsh (particularly in their club play) can appear to believe the stoush in the pub car-park has started early. And the French can be extremely creative vis-a-vis brutality. In New Zealand, our violence has been within the rules and constructive. Kiwi violence is designer violence. It is known to be disciplined, focused, practical and effective in the larger enterprise of winning the match. It is one of the particular strengths we share with South Africa. That may be why we, as a country, are so touchy about our relationship.

Why is this?

You have to look at the evolution of our respective societies. Both South Africa and New Zealand were immigrant countries broken in by backbreaking toil. Women were imported to provide helpmates, workmates, bedmates (or wives as they were known at the time). And the females tended not to be the fragrant, Home Counties blondes, but the strapping lasses from the Scottish Highlands, the Dutch lowlands and the Irish peat who came to work and breed. (James Michener is very good on all this.) And they bred strapping, strong, tough people whose experience was of labouring and working with their hands. To this day, that remains the bedrock of the South African experience.

Their rugby culture during its years in the wilderness suffered some regrettable distortions. Drugs are rare in rugby. New Zealanders have really only been known to experiment with No-Doz. South Africa on the other hand had rampant steroid abuse (after all, you had to be big to get into the Springboks).

Some of their more unpleasant play in domestic matches, and soon after they returned to world rugby, probably came from Steroid Rage Syndrome. Uncontrollable rage is a side-effect (like acne). Because they weren't playing in world competitions, but in their own little backwater, some hillbilly characteristics came into play. It must have become part of their subculture because, when they came back into international competition and had to submit to steroid tests, they went down one after the other. They've cleaned up their game somewhat, but just this year at least four players have tested positive for anabolic steroids.

But the fact remains we have more in common with South Africa than many New Zealanders may like to think. For instance, we had the same experience of immigration – big, strong, mentally tough, taciturn people. But having said that, our Highland strain was less sizeable and less broad in the beam than Dutch matrons. Add to our style a Polynesian wildness and exhilaration and there you have another element you don't find in the relentless Boer method.

The Polynesian strand in our national psyche lifts us – the more elusive running, the side-step, the joie de vivre. You see it in Maori sportspeople, the cavalier attitude to failure, a devil-may-care certainty that fortune favours the bold.

They also brought in a different physique – shorter, squatter and with great power in the legs, backside and lower back. These are our peculiar physical strengths and it is these we have developed into a competitive advantage.

In England, there is a public school reticence to knock someone to the ground – even if it meant you'd get the ball. We don't suffer from that inhibition.

Likewise, Australia's rugby is based on university and private schools and has less of the working man's communication through physical means (in working men's pubs there are fights).

In the way that these things happen, our strengths come through as uncalculated ways of winning matches. Because they were successful, the methods became received wisdom and became a tradition. We became famous for our forward strength and ruggedness. It hasn't always been so. The speed and versatility of New Zealand's early years, the years when we were known for our dash and daring, gave way to the great, crushing forward-power theory from the Thirties on.

That's why South Africa has been the herculean task – because it's a battle between like-minded countries on the same mental and physical turf. Both know that the winner will be the one that dominates the other physically. So this contest draws on the deepest part of our psyche. We dominated the country by this physical means (clearing bush) and that flowed into the way we saw ourselves, that's what made us pioneers; it became one of our life forces. So when we play South Africa, both of us with the same approach, it's like the irresistible force meeting the immovable object.

Hence the phenomenon of Kevin Skinner in the Fifties. He'd been heavyweight boxing champion and was widely acknowledged to be the most powerful prop we'd ever had. We were struggling in the forwards (two young props had been seen off by the Springbok hardmen) so they brought back Skinner. Folklore tells how he whacked the first Springbok prop and then switched to the other side of the scrum to whack the other one.

No other teams except the Springboks have set out to physically intimidate New Zealand. The French have been able to occasionally, and the Australians try, but all other teams tacitly admit physical defeat before the match starts. They are not tough enough, and not violent enough.

The attitude is breaking down now as the rules change, and speed and elusiveness become more important. It's not the man who can lift the biggest boulder any more, it's the speed the biggest boulder-carrier can run at that counts. The saying in rugby that a good big man will always beat a good little man is still true but it is changing in important ways. Locks are becoming slimmer, while wingers are becoming much bigger.

The French – the only other real contenders for physical dominance – can be thoroughly violent in their approach to the game, and that is partly because of the way the game is set up. It's based on competition between villages – it's very parochial. Frano Botica, who played club rugby there, said his team mates on certain away games would go into the changing room, open up their kitbags and remove something that looked very like a baton. "What's that?" Frano asked. "Eet ees a baton," they said.

It was used for protecting themselves against the local supporters and was taken to every away match. The coach insisted on it. He also insisted there was no point in trying too hard on away games (they used to drink wine with their large lunch before the match) because it was not only very rare to win an away match, it was actually dangerous as well. There is a rule in French rugby that the captain of the home team has to escort the referee off the field, for instance. Home villagers have also been known to block the bus from leaving in order to attack the players.

I read recently of a match between Dax and Grenoble where Dax, the away team, scored a last-minute try to win the game. Two hundred people invaded the pitch and the referee was attacked and assaulted. He shouldn't have forgotten his baton.

The English have a deceptive attitude to violence. Their style of speech sounds so effete that you don't always take note of the underlying ruthlessness in their national character. These are the people, after all, who invented concentration camps, the indiscriminate bombing of civilians in World War Two and bodyline bowling. They also have the most impressive football hooligans in Europe.

But the ability of the British Lions in the Seventies to absorb and apply violence probably germinated in New Zealand. On the 1971 tour, the only British team to have beaten the All Blacks in New Zealand, two British players were beaten up – like in a fight, a pub brawl – during a match. It was as if two medieval villages had decided to put on jerseys and settle the rivalry once and for all in front of forty-thousand other villagers. Sandy Carmichael and Ray McLoughlin were the Lions props on the end of it. One went home with fractured cheek bones, the other didn't play again that tour.

That Canterbury match was the nadir of violence in rugby. It was different from anything before or since. That was a straight brawl, and not a natural part of New Zealand culture. New Zealanders – particularly men at that time – were painfully polite, overly couth in polite society (or mixed company, as it was called).

The Lions adopted as their motto after this – particularly on their tour to South Africa three years later – "Get your retaliation in first". And their code for this was "Ninety-nine". When the captain called out, "Ninety-nine!" everyone had to punch the man nearest them. The theory of violence behind this was that the entire team couldn't be sent off (not that anyone ever gets sent off in South Africa for punching).

During this time the Lions took in some of that Welsh roughness; the Welsh supremacy in the game was at its height in the northern hemisphere. Players like JPR Williams were known to be impervious to pain, almost like the All Blacks. The Welsh have a proletarian base in their rugby, they come out of the mines; they're mentally rougher, they have an uncouthness which was an important asset in old guard rugby.

That's why a lot of criticism has been aimed at rugby in New Zealand by urban liberals. They often find distasteful the building site/fishing boat/shearing shed strain in the national character. And despite much change, the origins of rugby remain rural, male, working class.

So New Zealand began with a reputation for applied violence and developed it into a strategy for winning – and then it became a tradition. The idea that our scrum could be pushed backwards was an assault on our national virility. When the British pack in 1977 was so much bigger and more technically proficient than ours that we couldn't hold them, we put up a three-man scrum (to get the ball out more quickly). It was an effective tactic but it sat uncomfortably with

New Zealand because it made a nonsense of the physical confrontation. However, we did it. I couldn't see South Africa ever putting a three-man scrum down to ensure victory – they wouldn't be able to admit they had that weakness. It is an interesting observation on New Zealand style that even our most deeply-engrained psychological traits are subject to pragmatism and innovation to ensure victory.

So, apart from brief periods in South Africa, and apart from the 1977 Lions and the Nantes test in 1986, New Zealand has enjoyed physical domination. At root, though, it's been a mental thing.

There is little fear in international players' minds of getting hurt. Most players have left behind a sensible concern for their well-being. Jean-Pierre Rives (who is now a modern sculptor) once played with a dislocated shoulder strapped to his body (and attempted to make tackles).

Nevertheless, our opponents have often admitted physical defeat before the match starts. They say to themselves, "I'm not able to apply my technique and all my training because the All Black forward pack is always closer together, and quicker, and in greater numbers than we are. Two of us are around the ball and here come four or five of them, and they've got their arms round each other and they're going to blow us away." And when that happens a few times, and the opposition experiences the lack of concern about where the All Black boots end up, they become resigned to defeat. As experience grows, this resignation establishes itself even before the game begins.

New Zealand rugby was revolutionised in the south of the country when Vic Cavanagh in the 1940s made a discovery that applied violence, legally, to great effect. It was a way of clearing the ball away from a tackle quickly, legally, and demoralising and hurting the opposition at the same time. You hurt your own players too, but you didn't demoralise them.

The technique was called rucking. Your pack binds and drives past the ball, at the same time using your feet to scoop out the ball, their players, your players. It's worth repeating that it wasn't, and isn't, illegal. The key distinction is the direction of the boot. If your foot's going forward it's a kick, if it's going back it's a ruck. You're not on top, stomping, you're driving forward like a combine harvester, spinning the players round and out. The technique leaves its mark on you. Loose forwards, veterans of the bottoms of dozens of rucks, came off with hundreds of sprig marks on the back and shoulders.

The distinction between rucking and the practice of stomping, hacking, and otherwise savaging the opposition illegally was lost on the British then, and ever since. Fleet Street saw their fairy-footed English players being rucked and set up such a wail – foul! unfair! not the game! – that it wasn't worth the candle and we stopped doing it over there.

But to this day, New Zealand retains its reputation of a very physical, very aggressive approach to the game. We never went out to hurt the opposition for its own sake, but we were indifferent to the pain and damage we were able to inflict. And it must be said that the convenient injury that stopped Australian Steve Cutler winning all the ball – it wasn't entirely a coincidence.

I have to admit that I was as physically aggressive as anyone. While I didn't have the capacity to go round punching people myself, it's part of the halfback's function to deploy the strength and aggression (I'm glad of the euphemism now) of the forwards. You drive them as hard as you can into rucks and mauls to blow other people away; you chase high kicks and smash the catcher to the ground. It's not enough to contain him and allow him to turn and hold the ball and wait for support. You have to smash him to the ground and grab the ball.

In scrummaging it's very important to hit first and to make contact a bit below the point of leverage; if the others are back on their haunches a bit then you have the advantage – when you're the hitter you have your power further forward.

The approach to violence in rugby started to change at the top level when I started playing in the early Eighties. A lot of the pressure came from mothers who were watching close-up what was happening on television. The same thing happened in America during the Vietnam War (though to a rather greater effect). Women started to have an unpubliciscd influence on the game – in rule changes and in the interpretation of the rules.

Before this time, the New Zealand Rugby Football Union had no centralised disciplinary procedure. The local union might stand a player down for a match to show they didn't condone punching or biting or any other indiscretions players might have a weakness for. But the local unions were under pressure not to stand the guy down for too long – that wasn't in the interests of the province.

The national union came to see what a bad advertisement for the game it was, especially when television was broadcasting matches live to the mothers of the nation. In Britain, with its much stronger ethos of "playing the game" a much tougher stand was being taken. If you were sent off in Britain you were automatically banned for six months – the rest of the season. Over a period of time the national union began to take a tougher line on violence. They instructed referees to dish out harsher penalties and supported them when they did. There was a time when a sending-off was sufficient punishment; now further stand-down periods were added.

It was quite a change for us because, remember, in that 1971 match between Canterbury and the Lions, no-one was sent off. In that match, people were climbing over each other to get a punch in on an opponent's face, people were chasing their opposite numbers in order to punch them; play would suddenly be interrupted by a fist fight – and as I say, no-one was sent off.

The authorities also introduced a new convention – touch judges could flag for a foul, a punch or a high tackle. It's hard to imagine the outcry this caused. Nearly everyone was against it. "Bloody touch judge!" they said. "What's it to do with him?" They were held in lower esteem than traffic officers. And part of the skill in administering violence, people felt, was in avoiding being seen by the ref, and if you managed that, good luck to you. But having a touch judge with authority, suddenly you've tipped the balance in favour of authority (like speed cameras). Spectators and players alike hated it. "Interfering in the game!" was the phrase, like having Patricia Bartlett suddenly blowing her whistle for swearing.

Let us recall that early North-South match where we were much the weaker team but had our tough, grizzled, gnarled South Island forwards who liked to play Auckland, "Because they're soft!" That was the motivation – and, as it turned out that day, they were right. We didn't have the skills but we had motivation and aggression, and we won. I doubt whether it would play that way today. As steam replaced sail, and as transistors replaced valves, as Gameboys have replaced video ping-pong, so speed has replaced weight as a criterion of success.

But Canterbury always felt they could beat Auckland because country boys were tougher than city slickers.

Now that's changed completely. In a sophisticated way, Auckland is the most violent team in New Zealand. It's so well applied – and not always legally (blocking people off the ball, obstructing them, driving over a collapsed scrum, accidentally connecting with an elbow) – that they are effectively unbeatable.

But it would also be wrong to emphasise that as Auckland's modus operandi. From 1983 on, rule changes have meant the game is played so fast that there is much less time for these sorts of fouls. Because the game relies on explosive power, the grunting and straining was replaced with short bursts of focused aggression, making contact and unloading the ball, going into a tackle and leaving the ball in place to be taken on by your support. And the longer the ball stayed in play the less inclined were players to get into fist fights or brawls (fighting is so much more tiring than playing).

Rule changes also stipulated that if you didn't release the ball you were penalised; thus rucks kept moving and there came to be fewer dark nooks and crannies for working out personal grievances.

The pace also meant that if you were detained punching someone, you were left out of the game, you were doing nothing to help your team win.

So a combination of coaching, law changes and administrative concerns have seen overt violence decline – but physical domination is an integral part of the game. It's still central.

The result is an inevitable level of injury. I've almost never left the field because of injury, but here's my tally. Cuts and scar tissue around the eyes (the bony ridge splits early). I've had stitches in both eyebrows and both ears (I missed John Kirwan in a club match once and he trod on my head as he went past). I've been knocked out three times, cracked teeth, and had three broken noses (most rugby players break their noses at least once – well, look at us). My nose was straightened out in the changing room by team mates, twice, and once behind the grandstand at the Palmerston North Showgrounds (it makes a graunching sound – which is nothing to do with the fact that your mates have no qualifications to straighten noses). I've dislocated both little fingers (put them back in myself on-field). I've had sprained ligaments, a sprained wrist, a sprained shoulder AC joint, left knee partially torn ligaments (twice), an almost fully torn chest muscle, sundry sprained ankles. It's quite common to get broken thumbs (Peter Wheeler broke his thumb on Hika Reid's head, punching it; but Peter didn't mention it so he could play for England three weeks later). There were also countless haematomas and muscle tears to count. But I mean it quite seriously when I say that I am remarkably free from the physical side-effects of a rugby career.

Most rugby players have a catalogue of injuries that only workers in the most dangerous industries suffer.

Black and Blue

The number eights often suffer from cauliflower ears. This is caused by rubbing on the ear that scrum caps won't prevent. It's an inflammation that causes fluid to rush into the soft tissue of the ear. Ultimately the whole ear becomes one solid slab of flesh (it's difficult to hear through the contusion). You can treat it by putting a needle in when the wound is fresh, to release the fluid. If you leave it until the area has cooled down the fluid turns to scar tissue and you've got it forever – like luggage. Unfortunately the treatment is painful, and forwards, who are impervious to pain on the pitch, writhe and squirm in the changing rooms as the doctor and his needle do their awful work.

The finest examples of these sideways afflictions can be found on Gary Knight and Alan Whetton, and they also account for part of Andy Haden's characteristic appearance. Players used to be negligent about their ears until sometime around the mid-Eighties when women became more unforgiving about the way men looked.

Arthritis for older players is a real problem. Props are vulnerable; the compression of their vertebrae in the neck and back stores up problems in later life. Osteo-arthritis is the rugby player's most bitter enemy, it particularly affects players' hips and, later, knees. Bryan Williams suffered very badly, Jock Hobbs had a hip operation at thirty-seven. When the glory days have gone you can be left with the pain of a permanent condition that affects many parts of your life – even the ability to play with your children. That's a sombre thought. But for many, international rugby is the peak, and whatever's on the other side of the hill can wait.

Hurry up Please, it's Time

Time rushes on when you're a professional sports person. You're usually out of it by your early thirties. Golf players and professional darts people can go on longer (in darts the only real strength you need is to lift the beer). But in rugby, soccer, tennis – sports which require a lot of physical fitness and strength – the upper age is about thirty.

So, for thoughtful players there is a melancholy aspect to test matches, each one is a step closer to the end of your career. And there is always the thought that each test could easily be your last.

For me, it was important to be reconciled to the end of my career. I wanted to leave on my own terms. Other people are happy to play till they drop (or are dropped). In fact, most players don't make a judgment about whether or when they've passed their peak – perhaps that decision isn't theirs to make. As the raw physical power of their youth passes they do acquire experience. I've mentioned that the saying, "Age and experience will always beat youth and enthusiasm" is not true in rugby, but there is a cross-over period where age and experience can help youth and enthusiasm to win. This is true for the second half of all rugby careers.

Older players also have to fight a sense of staleness and a decreasing appetite for training – just at a time when you have to train harder.

Oddly enough, All Black players can hang on in the team quite a long time past their best. It's a thing about a team sport like this that the output is the result of a number of people doing a number of things: all the three-quarters combine to put the wing in for a try. That's why players can be well past their peak before the decline is obvious. It's easy for players and coaches to get caught up in the general delusion that a long-serving incumbent player is the best there is. And it's the toughest decision a coach has to make, ending the career of a very good player.

Only when the team loses do coaches look seriously at making changes. That's why losses can be new beginnings and are as important to the game as winter is to the cycle of natural growth.

So, when the new player comes in full of fire and passion, we are startled by how much the team has been lifted. It's also true that ex-All Blacks can decline very quickly into quite ordinary provincial players.

The process of pensioning off players has not traditionally been handled well in New Zealand (players usually learn they've lost their place, along with the rest of the country, from the media). As the sport gets more professional this process will get more traumatic because the selectors will be taking away self esteem, kudos, status – and also income.

The transition to life after professional sport is difficult. Many young men at twenty-three will have been earning four times what they'll be earning at thirty-three. Top young All Blacks are now making about $200,000 a year – but have limited ability to learn anything to help them earn anything like that after they finish playing.

It's a total reorganisation of a working life – saving, growing, building your capabilities, facing increasing responsibilities and possibilities – and the opposite of most people's financial career. At the youngest age you're earning the managing director's salary and enjoying the social status that goes with it, and then suddenly, ten years later, you're earning the post boy's wage. It's almost like you've been made bankrupt.

Peaking early (while it's better than not peaking at all) has its dangers.

One school of thought says it's graceful to go early, on your own terms. But there is tragic grandeur about playing on year after year, daring the selectors not to select you.

The most tragic career terminator is injury. David Halligan's, career ended before it began. A marvellous player (we were in the Otago University team together), he was selected to play for the All Blacks for a test against Scotland in Dunedin in 1981; he pulled a muscle in the second training run when practising a kick-off, was replaced by Allan Hewson and the window of opportunity closed in David Halligan's face.

Jock Hobbs, Robbie Deans, Andy Dalton, Bruce Hemara, Gordon

Macpherson all had their All Black careers finished by injury.

Nicky Allen burst on the scene, a real free spirit as a player and a person. He played fabulously well for the briefest of careers. Against Wales in the 1980 Centenary Test, he was a maestro. He stayed on to play club rugby, injured his knee in a tackle and later, when just past the height of his powers, died tragically on the field, from a brain haemorrhage in a tackle. But serious injury is astonishingly rare. Players at the top are technically very good; they know how to scrummage, how to drive into rucks and mauls and are also physically well-developed – strong neck muscles protect vertebrae, and strong leg muscles protect knees against catastrophic injury.

The group of people whose careers seem to have been most tragically affected by injury are referees. They all appear to have had a marvellous playing career blighted by a mysterious knee injury just before they made their names that forced them to take up the whistle.

There is also the other side to the hill of well-structured competitive progression. There are president's grades, golden oldies and reunion matches. But All Black golden oldies matches prove to be anything but fun. They have a reputation for being the least likely to be played in the spirit of enjoying a frolic in the sun in Bermuda (they take this as a compliment). They always win – for the same reason they won when they were playing for their country. They may be in their forties playing American twenty-eight-year-olds but they will not be beaten.

In some sense you are conditioned to accept the end of your career because it's an ever-present reality. Every season you're up for selection, and even if you're playing well and in the team, there's a chance you'll be injured, someone else will get your place, someone else will join the club, or province; the coach will change and a new style of play will become the vogue.

I was conditioned by all these experiences myself. I was dropped as All Black captain, in Otago I wasn't picked at all: and then there's always an arbitrary element in selection.

So there is a constant insecurity and a knowledge that the end could come more quickly than in most careers.

That's why, I think, it is important to manage your playing career as a finite part of your life, beginning when you've left school and finishing when you're finally dropped. In the beginning you've left school, you've joined a club, you're headed towards the club A team with your sights on the provincial team. That's the breakthrough, the first of five or six stages.

The next stage is being picked for your province and then getting a trial. In my day it was the North-South match, or an All Black trial. Today, it's a Super 12 squad. Once you make that you are playing at All Black level. If and when you get selected for the All Blacks you've made your major goal and your sights immediately change to becoming a memorable All Black, staying in the team and becoming a good international performer (which isn't automatic by any means). And that's the middle part of your career, consolidating your reputation.

Then there is the final phase, holding your peak as long as you can – three to four years at most, usually. Then you go quickly to the denouement. Do you retire at the top? Or do you go into a longer decline? I quit early, at my peak at twenty-six. At the same age that Dave Loveridge started his career I bailed out.

Seeing your career in these segments allows you to plan – you see your career as finite. You think about your other career and what you are going to do when you finish. I've found it surprising how many players are bitter about the career they never had because they were chopped short (usually by one year, in reality). The way I propose it, players have something to go out to – they're not out of a job, they retain their social contact – and they've got something to do on Saturdays.

The All Blacks can stuff people's lives up as well as make them. Peter Fatialofa, before he became part of the Auckland team, was a self-confessed hood on his way to prison. Jonah Lomu made similar comments about his prospects. The discipline, the organisation, the structure, the coaching, the goals set for him and the motivation he summoned to meet them sent him off in a new direction. He found confidence, self esteem – and a new society because being a member of the team does open doors for you.

There is a flip side to that story. You might be a man in a comfortable job in a small town with a small town girlfriend and a sedate, relatively predictable life. You get into the All Blacks and are swept up into a world of international tours, you are suddenly the object of fascination, admiration, imitation. Suddenly, going back to the small town and your long-time sweetheart isn't so appealing.

All Black life has made players but also destroyed some unfortunate others. It's destroyed marriages and careers. And in the professional game the casualties will get more spectacular. Players will play as long as they possibly can, and the years of their professional life will be spent not developing contacts and skills for the future, but on a pitch where their usefulness is harder to maintain as time goes on.

Part of a successful transition is to keep your individuality in the group. I felt I had to be not an All Black, specifically, but David Kirk, the All Black. I felt you had to have your own interests, be yourself, not try to become the archetype the All Blacks had evolved into.

So what of life after the game? Are the qualities you develop playing rugby any use elsewhere?

I work now in the oil and gas industry, heading up part of Fletcher Challenge's New Zealand operation. It's a young industry and has traditionally attracted the high rollers and big risk takers. It costs $15 million to drill one well offshore – still a lot of money to spend in a month. But the results are proportionately spectacular if you find oil or gas. It is an industry in which Triumph and Disaster (the "two imposters" Kipling talked about) loom larger than in, say, being a doctor. That is doubtless why I was more captured by the challenges of rugby than of medical study – and indeed, why I'm in oil and gas rather than rugby now.

Doctors have a certain temperament; some say medicine is an hereditary disease and that theory may be borne out in my case. My father is a doctor. He didn't inherit the disorder because his father was a schoolteacher, but I think my mother's side has something to answer for. My mother's father was a doctor, my mother's brother is a doctor and I have a doctor cousin (he's the son of the doctor who is my mother's brother).

I got out of medicine by degrees. I enjoyed the training, I had a great time at Dunedin, and some of the behavioural studies work was especially useful in dealing with difficult forwards.

But while medical training is a great training for life, it didn't have the gripping power of a career where you could build teams, achieve goals, feel the rush of large, public successes.

And it's usually true that the achievement of sportspeople is good for your career in whatever field you choose. In amateur days – when who you knew was so important, rugby was one of the important networks. And actually, it's still the case that one of the important c.v. entries in Britain is a Blue.

Why? Perhaps because people assume that it requires hard work and perseverance. That's true, and there is inferred a respect for high standards, and that's true, too. Increasingly it implies the ability to work in teams. Most good players recognise that they succeed only if others around them succeed.

They also recognise the format of modern teams and other fluid working environments – that is, loose teams as opposed to hierarchies.

It implies resilience, the ability to put up with disappointment, to learn from failure, to have a growth attitude, so that when you find you've crested one hill only to have another peak revealed, you start climbing again.

Sports leaders also know that leadership is not about telling people what to do, and making sure they do it. Team leadership is far more about boiling down options, sharing the decision-making and building commitment to the achievement of the chosen goals.

You're huddled up deep in the second half and you're ten points down. Someone's got to discover whether the team should be going down the middle or going wide, running set pieces or dropping goals. Someone's got to find the theme to play to, and be able to describe it so that the team isn't ordered to play a certain way, but is inspired to; it becomes a shared vision.

People listen to others who know how to win. Maybe it's their reputation, or their total commitment to winning, or that undefinable charisma.

But in the end, what do you have when you're finished? A collection of memories, of friendships, a character that has been partly formed by this powerful culture . . . but the most vivid moments on the field are the tries. Those are the moments – when you break through, when you run round behind the posts, the moments you hear a surge from the crowd; it's a roar, it's like a noise, but it's more than noise, it's the audible manifestation of collective triumph.

These are the bright memories. Sneaking round the side of the childish melee with that ball the size of a pumpkin to fall over with it for a six-year-old's first try on a rugby field; weaving and spinning to score in the corner to win the quadrangular tournament for the school; doubling round JK for the deadlock-breaking try in the first-ever Auckland-North Harbour match; taking Michael Jones' pass on the inside, bursting for the line, diving for glory, coming up grinning, World Champions at last. From six years old to twenty-six, from first to last; such bright moments, such bright memories.

The Perils of Professionalism

When I came back to Auckland after a summer holiday with my family, I discovered the polo club I belong to had split. A second club had started in Auckland and suddenly a rush of players had decided to leave and many of the good players had gone.

The reasons behind this are interesting. Polo in New Zealand is much less expensive to play than in other parts of the world. You can run a small string of polo ponies and play a season for about $5000. In country areas, where the game has always been played, you get a broad cross-section playing it – farmers, saddlers, farriers – and it can cost even less.

However, in less well-favoured countries than ours it is an expensive sport, and one that probably wouldn't survive without the interest and money of wealthy patrons – Kerry Packer and the Sultan of Brunei are probably the two biggest such. The patrons build professional teams of international players – and reserve a place in the team for themselves. Thus, in a thirty-goal tournament you might get a team consisting of one ten-goal player (that's the highest handicap for the best players), two nine-goal players and a two-goal player (the patron).

The patrons own the teams and have all their players on contracts. And because the horse does nearly all the work, the game quite suits middle-aged, rather overweight, rich men. These patrons want to play with the best players possible – even though some self-deception is necessary. If the game were played on merit the patrons would neither see the ball, nor stay on their horses. The professionals on the other team are likewise reluctant to play to their limit when it would mean humiliating the opposing patron (they might be wanting to work for him next season).

Far from being exposed to the full rigour of play, patrons are also knocked easy balls as near the goal mouth as doesn't look too obvious (the pros know a happy patron is one who scores).

It doesn't stop there. Hard-driving business people who become patrons usually want victory and they will go to the extent of hiring lawyers to find loopholes through which they might pinch a win. One such lawyer scrutinised the rule book and found the words: "The winning team shall be the one that scores the most goals." On this basis, his patron – or client as he's called in legal circles – challenged his recent one-goal defeat.

He did so on the basis that polo is played on the handicap system – the scoreline before the match has started might read two-nil in favour of the weaker team. But these are handicap goals and, as the lawyer argued, they are awarded not scored. Therefore, the patron, losing the match by a single goal claimed his team had scored more goals than the opposition and should be awarded the victory.

In my view, this is unattractive behaviour. Yet, it's how the game survives – and there would not be a hundred and fifty high-goal polo professionals touring the world with horses waiting for them at each venue if it weren't for these patrons.

But it is equally necessary for patrons to exercise some self-control, some perspective, some sense that there are other values in the game – some sense of sportsmanship, as we used to call it. To play for reasons other than their own need to appear successful.

Sport is something which demands you strive physically and mentally to develop, where you frequently get what you deserve. It is a stern examiner of character and gives an opportunity of real self-revelation. It is able to teach you what you are capable of, and when you've found that out you can realise your limitations.

Once a year, all the polo clubs in New Zealand select their teams for the Savile Cup tournament, and they do so on merit. This ruled out some of the wealthier club players so they – as I say – left the club forthwith and took the better half of the players with them.

This cuts across the unwritten rules of advancement in sport, the rules by which character is built, skills are developed. Put yourself in the place of a twenty-three-year-old, three-goal player who has slogged his way through to be selected – only to find his place isn't there because a one-goal player has taken it.

But there we are: the Auckland club has to deal with high costs – down in Wanstead in Hawke's Bay the annual subscription is $180, up in Auckland it's $1500. In Auckland you have to pay for things that are done voluntarily in the country. So Auckland needs to grow the club, to provide facilities, and a suitable club rooms to attract members. And these members aren't going to be the saddlers and farriers of the area, they're going to be advertising agents, computer salesmen, property developers – people who have different expectations of a club than country boys.

It's all perfectly understandable, but I still don't particularly like it.

And it's not confined to polo, of course. You see the same thing happening to young, talented players in amateur rugby. At certain prestigious Auckland schools (which have an annual need to beat certain other prestigious Auckland schools) there are sixth form sporting scholarships that give big Polynesian boys a place in the first XV. I am happy to see big Polynesian boys given the benefit of a prestigious education – but then, what lessons are being taught to the boys who've played their way up the school teams? The boys who played prop for the junior colts, the colts, the second XV, the boys who suddenly find themselves with no chance of the ultimate school position because their place has been taken by a ring-in?

I'm sorry to see this working in polo, and I'm sorrier to see it at school – one place where the amateur ethic can still thrive. And, in addition, I believe it makes incredible any lessons the school might otherwise give about the value of loyalty, camaraderie, sportsmanship. Winning is more important than any of these virtues. Welcome to the world, boys, it's all coming at you faster than it ever has before.

And yet, the overpowering desire to win is not a universal in professional sport. Michael Long, for instance, was putting in the final of the Johnny Walker Classic. Four to play, he was one up and if he held the lead would receive $280,000. He addressed the ball, looked to the hole and, when he looked back, the number on the ball had disappeared. The ball had rolled back a few millimetres. No-one had seen, but the player went to his partner to tell him (once you've addressed the ball, any movement counts as a shot). It cost him $140,000 by the end of the day.

But sportsmanship wasn't always unusual. I can remember batsmen used to walk; fieldsmen would signal when they'd caught the ball but it hadn't carried the distance.

These actions are based on values that are beyond winning the game and I believe it's important to preserve them.

Professional fouls (and it's no accident that professional fouls are more common in professional sports) are now more common in rugby. The most frequent is a purposeful but feignedly-unintentional obstruction. You turn your back and walk in front of active players; you can kill the ball near your own line (like I did in the Oxford and Cambridge game). You can feign injury.

But as values decay you have to bring in rules and penalties which make professional fouls, on balance, not worth committing. It ceases to be a moral thing and becomes a cost/benefit calculation. It's not a foul against the spirit of the game but it's become a question of whether the action is profitable or not. The game's not being played for fun, or self-expression, or to push the boundaries of what we thought was possible.

That's why the administration has encouraged the awarding of penalty tries and sending off (which used to be very rare). In soccer, a calculated professional foul is an automatic send-off.

There used to be shame attached to being sent off or for causing a penalty try to be awarded but not any more. The reaction is that it's a tough game, these things happen and the disciplinary procedure will punish him. Precious little shame attaches to punching, stomping or high tackles. These are considered nothing more than regrettable. However, shame still attaches in some measure to gouging, biting and kicking in the head. But maybe not for much longer.

The reason that shame attaches itself is because these actions are still seen as a breach of self-control. There are endless opportunities to damage people on the pitch and the game is only able to be played because people do exercise self-control. Not to do so strikes at the very foundations of the game – but that's not the way people think of punching any more. None of us have heard those words "You ruddy sod!" for many years now.

I would make a plea for the sustenance of the values that nourished the amateur game – notwithstanding the money that is there for professionalism.

All the business activity that surrounds rugby should not conceal the fact that it is still a sport. And what makes sport ethically different from a business? In the end, it's not what it creates outside the individual, it's what it allows individuals to create within themselves. It is for those moments when players are at their most alive, neither preparing for something else nor reliving it at leisure later, but improvising at speed in a fast, fraught situation where character is often deeply revealed.

We are social animals. We only achieve our potential in association with each other. Individuals are inspired to achieve more than they would by themselves. Sport is a great vehicle for this, and spectators can, by association, live some of that magic.

But if the game becomes so professional, so devoid of ethical values that it loses its heart, there will be nothing in the transaction between players and spectators except entertainment.

Whether or not professionalism will be good or bad for the game, it is inevitable. The key is to try and manage it to our best end. How do we manage to capture as much of the good as we can?

The first point is that mass participation is essential to the game. We must encourage that. If only a few can succeed, fewer people will play. We have good structures for coaching and playing. We must keep them. There is nothing more demoralising for enthusiastic amateurs than disorganisation – turning up for training and finding no coach, or no team, or the pitch occupied by a hockey training session because it hasn't been booked.

We have to make sure that those people who care, and who are prepared to give their time, are encouraged to do so by getting something back. The important thing here is to give. In an amateur game people give their time and themselves; in a professional game they sell their time and themselves. There is nothing morally wrong with a fair commercial transaction but there is usually little which builds what needs to be known again as virtue. It sounds old-fashioned to talk about moral example, but courage, selflessness, duty and perseverance are important qualities in sport as in life.

In a professional context these examples need not count. What counts is fair transaction. We must have better administrators, managers, medical officers. If they don't perform by the objective yardsticks that are only too public come match-day, they go. Under professionalism everything is accountable – this is great for quality. The game improves as a spectacle and for most of those involved. The risk is not that the game will decline, but that it will be successfully empty.

Money becomes a quantification of the players' value. They can't afford to commit crimes of violence on the field – they can't afford to be sent off. They used to argue that professionalism would make winning so much more important that individuals would be encouraged to commit acts of violence. The tendency is in the opposite direction.

He who pays the piper calls the tune – and in this case the piper-payer is the body of consumers, or spectators as they used to be called. And what consumers of rugby want is entertainment. If the spectators aren't entertained the rugby union won't prevail – that thought makes the union very receptive to new ideas.

The rules have changed more in the last fifteen years than in the hundred preceding them. And that's improved the game rapidly. The trend has been to keep the ball in play longer. So now you can't kick the ball dead – that provokes a scrum back. You aren't allowed to retreat behind your twenty-two or pass behind the twenty-two to kick for touch. The advantage is played, lifting in the lineout is legal (which helps clean ball rather than a melee developing). The number eight is required to stay bound in the scrum rather than detach – thus freeing up space. We now have a use-it-or-lose-it rule – if you go into a maul and are held you have to move the ball.

But one of the biggest perils comes from the biggest plus: the money. Now, let's not be pious about money, it's a good thing for players to be able to better their situation and help their families. But it needs handling. Players' earning curves are the opposite of a conventional career – they're completely front-end loaded. It will probably never be this good again.

My view is we ought to help players among all the excitement of their playing careers with the less enjoyable aspects of their lives: putting money aside, building other skills, training, getting further education. And this helps players develop a good attitude towards the game as well. They can tour the world, get status and even at the top, even at your finest hour, they can face the inevitable end because they've got a future after the game.

This isn't always the easiest thing for some players who may not have taken their schooling seriously – and to some extent, this is inevitable. They were great athletes. We probably have to accept that they will put most of their energies into sport. But we must help them build a life outside sport.

A playing career is so transient – eight years is not a long time and it may be over at your next training run. You're a former All Black for a very long time, and even the top players don't last long in reputation. Who now celebrates the tries and tackles of Mike Clamp, Victor Simpson, Arthur Stone, Bruce Smith, Brian McGrattan, Hika Reid, Geoff Old.

When I was coaching Wellington, my very first act was to bring along some ex-players to talk to the guys. I suppose it was a bit of a downner for them. Bernie Fraser told them about the unsuccessful transition he believed he'd made from being an All Black – he'd never settled, never learned much and felt he hadn't achieved what he should have done. Allan Hewson told them that he'd never cared particularly for anything other than rugby and cricket when he was playing – not even money; but when he finished he went back to Petone to open a stationery store and sell insurance. He found it hard but he stuck at it and made it work. Brendan Gard'ner told how he hadn't been interested in building his skills but he'd been lucky enough to get a job with a trucking company and he also had knuckled down, worked hard, and eventually been rewarded with a partnership.

As the drive towards professionalism increases there may be significantly more stories like Bernie's.

Top All Blacks are paid about a quarter of a million a year. There was a year or two of windfalls during the transition when there was a premium being paid to many players by the organisations trying to control the game.

The more normal pattern occurs in America where someone like Michael Jordan – the outstanding team member – is paid $20 million a year; the next most able is paid $11 million; the next five get between $2 million and $3 million and then there's a scattering of half a million to a million. The top man gets more than all the others put together.

Professionalism has ethical conflicts and other perils that we are only just getting to grips with.

The New Zealand Rugby Football Union survived the first, and probably most dangerous, challenge in 1995 when all the players bar two signed up with an Australian organisation, the World Rugby Corporation. The Aussies who were attempting to put it together never had the money, in spite of the signatures. They signed the players up so they could go to television companies to sell them the rights to professional rugby. Then the players would be leased back to the New Zealand Rugby Football Union – or anyone else who would pay.

Details remain murky, but some time after the WRC challenge was repulsed, a document arrived in the hands of the New Zealand Rugby Union implicating Laurie Mains. He was then the All Black coach. It appeared that he, a key agent of the NZRFU, was, with other senior players, involved in some way in a new organisation in which they would be major financial beneficiaries. All the leading players showed precious little loyalty to the organisation which had given them so much.

Right at the start of professional rugby the WRC affair showed how awful the unfettered drive for money could be. There were accusations of intimidation of players, and people pulling out of contracts and threats of law suits.

It's not money that is the root of evil; it is, as the proverb tells us, the love of money that's the problem.

The World Rugby Corporation was hard put to sign up all the All Blacks but they would have had to do far more than that. They would have needed to get about seventy players signed up. Twenty-five or thirty players are replaceable – as the Cavaliers showed. Even if the top fifty absconded it wouldn't permanently damage the All Blacks; they are replaceable.

Ironically, it was the country most awash with players that put a stop to it. The South African union started throwing very large sums of money at their captain and the house of cards quickly folded.

The New Zealand authorities handled the aftermath in a very characteristic way: they ignored it. The game had survived and they hadn't the stomach for further upheaval. Some of their own officers were seemingly involved. The thought of a general inquisition was too much for the Council. They did everything they could to keep it off the agenda, but even when they were forced to consider it, they parked it, to avoid any unpleasantness.

My feeling was that the team had showed serious lack of judgment and had acted against the best interests of themselves and New Zealand rugby. If the players had ended up in a WRC contract they would have been mixed and matched, put into a pool of players who would have been balloted to play for Brisbane or Melbourne or whatever. They would have been fifteen guys in hooped shirts called the Kiwi Cavaliers, or something, and they wouldn't have felt they owed their supporters anything, and the feeling would have been reciprocated.

Children who still look at the All Blacks as national symbols would have seen their heroes trooping off en masse to play for money, and they would have imbibed the lesson that there is no higher value than playing for money.

Performance at the top level is going to become remote in other ways.

Rugby is an unusual sport in that it is very accepting of a wide range of physical types. At school, there is a place for fat boys, for slow boys, even for relatively unco-ordinated boys. Most boys can play rugby if they want to, there's a position they can make their own, there are so many teams there's a place for anyone who's keen. And parents can follow their son's career in a way that would be impossible in soccer or basketball.

But the way the sport's going, the physical characteristics will become so extreme that height and weight requirements will mean there's no place for the vast majority of players. If, at eighteen, you're just 85kg and 1.80m, even though you have the skills, there's no place for you – and you'll know it. Unfortunately these trends will continue anyway in the forwards – professionalism will bring them on sooner.

There will be those who play socially and who watch the professional game on television – and there'll be fewer and fewer people in the middle playing competitive club rugby.

But it's just as important for All Blacks to play club rugby, to involve themselves with players at the middle level of the game. Why? The fact is, it provides example and inspiration for club players. I'll never forget the warmth with which the opposition would shake my hand at the end of a game, literally thanking me for playing against them. It was clear that they felt a real connection to the black jersey and to the team they saw on television. And they could boast to their mates on Saturday as they watched the test, "I played against him last month. He's not that good. I caught him twice round the scrum, I charged a kick of his down and he didn't score!"

With professional rugby, it's unlikely our top players will play club rugby at all.

In any event, the game has so far survived this first rush to money and we've made the transition relatively smoothly. But I couldn't help reflecting on my speech to the rugby writers' dinner in London eight years earlier when I had warned of the risks of the national union not managing the transfer to professionalism. My prediction had been that the pressure for change would be irresistible and that if they didn't ride the wave they'd be swamped by it. To some extent that's come true in England. Rich individuals and rich clubs have battled with the national union for power over the game. Now, players' first loyalty is to their club, not to their country. And English rugby will never fulfil its potential while this is the case.

It will be a whole new ball game now, with contracts. Already the lawyers are into it, the specialists – employment lawyers, contract lawyers, competition lawyers, maybe there'll even be consumer guarantees. Players are even now in the process of bringing court action against the union's player transfer rules as being a restraint of trade.

They are also finding clashes of sponsorship. An individual player has a sponsor paying him to wear Nike boots; he becomes an All Black and finds the team is obliged to wear Mizuno boots.

The fight with the WRC cost New Zealand rugby dearly. The result in financial terms was a $6 million loss for the NZRFU last year. In effect, the union had to buy the players' loyalty and it wasn't cheap. Too many players were paid too much. Players who had no intention of playing the following year were given a couple of hundred thousand dollars. Junior rugby, small provinces and ultimately ticket purchasers foot the bill.

The demand for entertainment is limitless; watching the recent Super 12 games we are watching games that almost routinely include passages of play that would have astonished and ravished spectators when I was growing up – play such as the Barbarians could only have attempted in their wilder, more carefree, moments.

The real spirit of rugby is to be found in there not being any overt transaction. No-one is totting up who owes what to whom. This only happens in family and friendship when some stronger bond, some stronger feeling of obligation and responsibility, makes quantifying the relationship irrelevant and actually diminishing.

It is one of the curious paradoxes of friendship that it should be at once so strong and so fragile. Both parties in a friendship owe each other a great deal of loyalty and support. But neither can ever call in the debt. For the very existence of the debt is dependent on both understanding that only friendship freely given is friendship at all. If one friend says they are owed because they have given of themself any debt is immediately extinguished.

The essence of sport is based on it not being a quantified transaction. Bound only by what I alone know I owe others, I am free to give but not to take. The world of written contracts could not be further from this. It introduces the ultimately quantified transaction: the sale of services for money.

I believe we somehow have to rebuild the ethical heart of sport in the cold structures of professionalism. And if we can do it with sport we may be able to do the same for other institutions and activities in our heavily commercialised civilisation.

There You Have It

Rugby still plays a large part in the lives of many young men in this country. Memories we share go back generations. The trip back after the match, for instance, will be familiar to tens of thousands of New Zealanders: the lights from the cars on the roof of the bus, the glow from the sprig marks down our backs, the six pack of beer and the prospect, in my case, of a deep fried muttonbird at the pie cart in Gore. Some of us will never be as happy in our lives again, and that has a sadness of its own.

Why do we play? What, apart from this happy glow we have in the bus, do we play for? Maybe team sport is a race memory of our hunter lives. Thirty thousand years ago the men with the bows would go one way and the men with the nets would go the other; today the flankers break left and the backs break right – but we all have the same look in our eye, and the adrenaline is surging in the same way. Maybe we love it for the exhilaration of feeling our strength in action, of deploying our skill and using our gifts, grateful for our endowments which are concentrated in this common endeavour, the game.

I don't hunt; few of us do. But I'm not a professional sportsman either; quite the opposite. It's actually essential for me to escape the world of work and routine into a more real world. Playing highly disciplined sport is an opportunity to be free. You can seize the moment in play and make it yours. You may be playing a pattern in a style you have rehearsed a hundred times – but there are always opportunities for a brilliant moment doing something you never dreamed you were capable of. Those are the moments you remember forever, some of the most memorable moments of your life, moments of special intensity, of deep intuitive contact that you don't get anywhere else.

For psychological good health you need to be strong and to belong.

Sport gives you this in an intense way. The team is small enough for each person to play a crucial role. And everyone recognises you for what you do. This gives you many things, but here are some: to be part of a combination that executes a set move perfectly, to see everyone running the correct angles and leaving the opposition bewildered and disarrayed. And it's more than that, it's knowing you have the ability to improvise from broken play and by reading body language to anticipate which way your man's going and which way the opposition thinks he's going – in those moments you can have a sense of being carried along by a larger force.

Everything's happening at full pace so there is little time to think, you react by instinct, you share with your team a sense of heightened awareness. Because your reactions connect you to everyone in the team, you are part of a chain reaction of people linked together, a huge complex calculation of angles, speeds, times, positions in a group mind.

When Campo was running down the touchline in the 1991 World Cup semi-final he threw the ball blindly over his shoulder and his team mate was there – right there – to take it.

Moments like that have a magic about them that have the power to move us; it's a form of telepathy. Even though his centre might be yelling, "*I'm here, I'm right here!*", all Campo knew was that he wasn't alone, there was someone there within two or three metres, certainly no more than four metres – but it's not easy, or even likely, to make an ordered pattern out of the evidence. It's all happening at ten metres a second, he doesn't know whether the guy is accelerating or moving at an angle, or whether he's assuming Campo is going to take the tackle and flip the ball up or what foot he's on, or whether he's concentrating or where anyone is going precisely to be in the next second and a half when the ball goes up. And without looking, Campo delivered it precisely into Tim Horan's waiting hands – who went on to score.

These moments are full; anything can happen in them, that's what makes you so alive. And it's not just what happens around the ball. I'm thinking of a moment from an otherwise forgotten game. I'm well away from the action but not running to the ruck, curiously, because I can see AJ detaching himself and moving round to take my place behind the locks – and because he hasn't seen JK running a left line (he'd follow him if he had seen it), I reckon he's going to swing it right and wide, so I'm going to insert myself into the line by coming fast through inside Joe – and here's the ball, suddenly, mysteriously delivered at speed but softly into my hands.

There You Have It

As I've said, when you play the game to its limit, winning is a by-product, it's not the point. The All Black team is always capable of rising into this new dimension where they are playing against the game itself, pushing back the boundaries of rugby – to play so fast, with such precision, without errors, with a sense of fluency and creative interaction between all the players so that people can watch a match and know they've never seen rugby played like it.

Many people have talked about the importance of winning. That English soccer coach is always quoted as saying winning wasn't a matter of life and death, it was much more important than that. But teams whose sole objective is winning a match will never be successful in the long run. The sole objective should be to play the game as well as it can be played – winning is the by-product of this aim, and if you succeed in this strategy you'll find the wins come by enormous margins.

In this state you can throw passes from absurd positions and pick them up in a way that is only possible because the moments are supercharged. And everyone feels it. The centre who ran a line across the field for a scissors pass that never happened – he was an integral part of the try on the other side of the field that came at the end of the move.

This working together so intensely is utterly individual and yet totally co-operative. The randomness of the world, the maelstrom, falls into a perfectly fitting jigsaw. Everything the opposition tries to do fails to interrupt you or your relationship with the game you are creating.

And it's all happening in real time. Perhaps actors and other performers have the same experience of drawing up unknown resources but I feel sport's harder, and faster, more demanding. If you forget your lines the audience might not notice. You can't drop the ball without the game going into reverse. The drama on-field is intense, it's personal, it's a public spectacle with a narrative, and a climax that reveals character in action. And it tests its players to the limit.

Sport gives you the opportunity to live in the moment in a way that few other things do. After a pint of beer or a glass of wine it's surprising how much more interesting the world around you gets. That's because past and present have dropped away and you concentrate on what is actually happening immediately around you. It's like that on the rugby field most of the time, for the hour and a half of play. And it's the series of moments that you play for – being with friends, with colleagues, with people you like and don't like, people with whom you have nothing in common except the game and living together at the highest intensity, absolutely present.

And in those games there are moments you remember of perfect co-ordination, they have a halo round them. Moments of perfection in life are rare and so you remember them vividly, and all the processes that go along with them.

For instance: on one day, you remember the ball is flying overhead, going backwards and you are running for it. The question you are considering is whether you can catch it or not; it'll depend, probably, on what foot you're on, so you are timing the arc of the ball with the fall of your feet. It's like a swimmer at the end of a lap – do you put in the extra stroke before the tumble-turn? You are considering the importance and the risk of taking the ball on the full; if there isn't the time for the extra step you will require an extra stretch, a lunge, a lurch even, to push forward to get your fingertips there, and keep your balance if that turns out to be possible. But then, how much will the lunge slow you down, and does that matter? And how important is it? And do you feel lucky, because if you do, that can really help.

So the following things might happen. You might be able to take it on the full and as a result run a line which electrifies fifty thousand people in the stadium. You might miss it and fall over. You might catch it and fall over. You might, more prudently, steady your stride, hang back, let the ball bounce, give it enough room for it to do its unpredictable thing, you could probably gather it and set up a ruck. There's a flanker on your right coming in, there are three of the wrong coloured jerseys coming in behind you, and the arc of the ball has subtly changed, as a gust of wind has lifted it, and the autumn leaves are flame-coloured in the trees, winter's on the way, and you now have two-tenths of a second instead of three-tenths of a second to decide what to do . . .

The best of sport is the sense of life being taken on the wing. I have been at my most alert, most concentrated, most alive playing intense rugby. This is what I remember about it and why I value it as a rich experience.

If all you care about is winning, if you aren't enjoying the play – if the relief of not-losing is the biggest emotional gain – then the best of it is lost.

I have heard a story of a man dying in his thirties and he complains to St Peter that he didn't have time during his shortened span on earth to do what was necessary to get into heaven. But recorded in the big ledger is the amount of time he was actually alive: six minutes and twelve seconds. The rest was somnambulism. Sport is a great way of rising out of ordinary life and living in the present. It happens in love and in meditation. It is not given to all of us to be great lovers or mystics.

The All Black tradition is also an expression of our culture, of our identity, of our ability to excel, to achieve great things. The team exists in the abstract. It's more than its players. We come and go through the team like ghosts, for our seasons. Some of us are remembered, none of us are really missed. The play is always for today and for tomorrow. The team is always pre-eminent. It makes its players, it creates us.

We have the world famous, world beating champion team – not merely a team of champions. The All Blacks can lose all its players and still play international rugby against the rest of the world.

It's a very physical entity but it's also a body of shared belief; a history of triumph and occasional disaster. But above those, it is a fine expression of ourselves as New Zealanders.

And though the All Blacks change as the players change, although different moods and styles ebb and flow, its purpose is always the same: to play this curious, convoluted game to the limit of human ability.